Cinematherapy

The Girl's Guide to Movies for Every Mood

Also by Nancy R. Peske and Beverly West:

Frankly Scarlett, I *Do* Give a Damn!

Classic Romances Retold

And under the pseudonym Lee Ward Shore:

How to Satisfy a Woman Every Time on Five Dollars a Day

Meditations for Men Who Do Next to Nothing (and Would Like to Do Even Less)

Cinematherapy

The Girl's Guide to Movies for Every Mood

NANCY K. PESKE AND BEVERLY WEST

A DELL TRADE PAPERBACK

A Dell Trade Paperback

Published by Dell Publishing
a division of Random House, Inc.
1540 Broadway New York, New York 10036

Library of Congress Cataloging in Publication Data
Peske, Nancy K., 1962–
Cinematherapy : the girl's guide to movies for every mood / Nancy K. Peske and Beverly West.
p. cm.
Includes index.
ISBN 0-440-50850-9
1. Motion pictures for women—Catalogs. 2. Video recordings—Catalogs.
I. West, Beverly, 1961– . II. Title.
PN1995.9.W6P48 1999 98-45674
016.79143′57′082—dc21 CIP

Printed in the United States of America

Published simultaneously in Canada

Book design by Virginia Norey
Original Art by Daniel Lynch

March 1999

1 3 5 7 9 10 8 6 4 2

RRD

This book is dedicated to our grandmother,
LaVerne Anderson Peske,
and Bev's mom and Nancy's aunt, Marilyn Knox,
who introduced us to the beauty of rainy-day matinees,
and the exhilaration of remaining in charge of
our own remote controls.

Thanks to Sally Powell, Nancy Carr, Hellie Neumann, Carol Peske, Barry Neville, Pam Conway Eisermann, the staffs at Video Express, both Couch Potatoes on First Avenue and International Video in New York City. Special thanks to our editor, Kathleen Jayes, for her insight and keen sense of humor, Nancy H. Landau, and to our agent, Neeti Madan, one of the brightest new stars in our personal chick flick.

And finally, very special thanks to George Darrow, Nancy's husband, and the only man we know who will willingly sit through All This and Heaven Too.

Contents

Introduction

As we women know, movies are more than entertainment: they're self-medication. A good flick is like a soothing tonic that, if administered properly, in combination with total inertia and something obscenely high in fat grams, can cure everything from an identity crisis to a bad hair day to the I-hate-my-job blues.

Of course, medicine is a precise science. You have to match the movie to the mood or the treatment won't work. Watching *Terms of Endearment* when you're struggling with mother issues and want validation that it really *is* her, not you, can be very therapeutic. Watching *Terms of Endearment* when you're wallowing in self-pity, helplessness, and total despair because you have to go for a physical in the morning and you're phobic about doctors may not have the same healing effect.

All of this can make choosing a movie a bit complicated, can't it? Men, of course, don't have this problem because they have only two moods: on and off. But we women have a tangle of spiritual resonance, emotional history, and psychological nuance to unravel while browsing through the shelves at our local video store. It's enough to make your head spin. So what's a gal to do?

Cinematherapy is designed to help you out in these moments of crisis. No longer do you have to spend hours in the video store, scrutinizing the description of the woman's film you've managed to pry out from in between *Terminator 467* and *Rambo XIX*, when all you really want to do is rush home, rip open the bag of chips, pop in the right movie, and curl up in a fetal position. Now all you have to do is look up the chapter that corresponds to your mood and pick a movie from the list of films we've prescribed. It's that easy.

You say that just like the old song goes, nobody likes you, everybody hates you and you're gonna eat some worms? Choose a movie from our chapter called "I'm Gonna Eat

Some Worms: Martyr Syndrome Movies" and revel in the masochism. Boyfriend behaving like a subhuman again? Turn to our chapter called "Yeah, Okay, So He's a Jerk, But He's Sooooo Cute: Dysfunctional Romances," and remind yourself that you're not the only woman in the world to fall for a guy with smoldering eyes, good hair, and a patent on lame excuses. If it's that time of the month and you're experiencing extreme mood swings, turn to "Vacillating Between Copious Weeping and Homicidal Rage" for a list of our favorite PMS Ragers and Weepers.

If you're not sure what mood you're in—do I wallow in despair or rediscover my inner Scarlett?—try flipping around and reading a few reviews at random, or consult the index, where you'll be able to look up films by titles, actors, and actresses. Bring the guide with you to your video store, or use it to check out the latest pay-per-view, premium channel, or movie channel offerings. (We strongly advise against watching movies on regular channels that pile on the commercials. How can a gal sustain a mood with all those interruptions? As we've all tried to explain to our significant others at one time or another, there is something to be said for momentum.)

We'll also steer you away from those flicks that are ostensibly women's movies but are actually just faking it (and you know how unsatisfying *that* is): movies like *Crossing Delancey* (forget your taste in men; only your grandmother's can be trusted), *How to Make an American Quilt* (stuff those qualms about your fiancé and marry him because it makes a charming story for the quilting bee), and *My Best Friend's Wedding* (be a good person—let your pig of an ex ruin a nice young woman's life).

As you read the reviews you may ask, how could they leave out my favorite movie, or what about that one that everyone was talking about? Well, there are three possibilities. One is that the picture in question may have been marketed as a gal's film (a romantic comedy, for example), but on closer inspection it was too focused on men's experience—a man's movie in disguise. Also, we had to limit the number of reviews in this book, and sometimes we felt it was better to use the space to recommend an overlooked gem than to remind readers of a much publicized and talked-about movie. And then again, maybe we just hated the damn thing. Hey, it happens.

It basically comes down to the fact that some folks like beef and others like cheese. Variety is the spice of life. But we were fortunate in that the two of us are on opposite ends of the spectrum in terms of our cinematic palates. Nancy has a thing for Alan Rickman's sirloin stoicism, and Beverly is drawn to Gary Oldman's ripe Camembert excess. So while it's cost each of us a lot of money in video rental fees trying to prove the other wrong, we have managed to come up with a pretty good cross-section of the women's videos currently available.

If you'd like to point out to us an amazing women's movie that we've overlooked, or rail against our choices, or send us Alan Rickman's home address (or Gary Oldman's), please feel free to contact us by e-mail at: Nakape@aol.com or via snail mail c/o Dell Books, 1540 Broadway, New York, NY 10036.

We wish you many hours of therapeutic viewing pleasure with the movies in this guide. And remember, sitting alone snuggled up in a comforter and watching a movie that helps you to understand your feelings is taking care of yourself. You should feel good about that. So the next time you climb into your fuzzy slippers and indulge in a favorite flick, take a moment before you hit the play button, and think about how nice it is to be in charge of your own remote control.

Chapter 1

Vacillating Between Copious Weeping and Homicidal Rage: PMS Movies

It's that time of the month and you're feeling bloated and unloved, aren't you? We know. It's difficult to approach life positively when you're retaining enough water to irrigate a small desert. And how can you be expected to face the world with a smile on your face when the dermatological equivalent of Mount Vesuvius is erupting in the middle of your forehead? But he doesn't understand, does he? He never understands. And do you know why? Because he's a *man*!

If your mood is one characterized by copious weeping punctuated by sudden and inexplicable bouts of homicidal rage, grab yourself a box of Puffs, an industrial-size batch of some artery-clogging, waist-expanding delectable and watch one of our favorite PMS movies guaranteed to nurture the inner bitch.

Prescription:

Step 1: Assess Your Mood

Assess your mood right now. How do you feel? Are you sad or angry? Here's a test. If a commercial about the look and the feel of cotton came on right now, would you:

(A) Get misty about the fabric of your life?

(B) Slap the first man you see upside his thick head?

Step 2: Choose Your Poison

If your answer was (A), then you're feeling sad. Select a movie from the Weepers list and prepare to spend the next couple of hours blubbering into your Cherry Garcia.

If your answer was (B), then select a movie from the Ragers list, lock up the breakables, and let the vicarious angst fly, because you are good and *pissed*!

Of course, there's no guarantee that how you feel at this moment will bear any relationship whatsoever to how you feel five minutes from now. So it might be wise, given the mercurial mood you're in, to line up a double feature with a film from each list . . . just in case.

Step 3: Take Your Medicine

Mood movies can be powerful medicine, so, as with all medications, administer with care. Do not exceed the recommended dosage and don't forget to read the warning labels!

Weepers

▪ ***Born Free*** *(1966)*
Stars: Virginia McKenna, Bill Travers
Director: James Hill
Writers: Joy Adamson and Gerald L.C. Copley

Joy Adamson wrestles with her maternal and moral instincts as she contemplates returning Elsa, the lion she's raised from an orphaned cub, to expanses of the African savannah. Does she keep Elsa as a pet and protect her from the harsh realities of the wild, or does she return Elsa to her path, no matter the personal cost, so that she can live just as she was Born . . . Free? (*Strings swell*)

This allegorical weeper about the anguish of letting go is guaranteed to turn anyone into a human soaker hose, which is not only cathartic but helpful in reducing water-retention levels. In fact, during the scene in which Elsa visits Joy for the last time with little cubs of her own, your boyfriend, provided you haven't banished him from the room yet, may even break down and shed an uncharacteristic tear or two. Or at least he would if he wasn't so wrapped up in his repressed Western, linear, masculinist emotional constipation. Men!

> ⚠ Warning Label: *It may be advisable to take a salt supplement to prevent dangerous dehydration.*

■ ***To Gillian on Her 37th Birthday*** *(1996)*
Stars: Peter Gallagher, Michelle Pfeiffer, Claire Danes
Director: Michael Pressman
Writers: Michael Brady and David E. Kelley

True love cut short by a sailing accident off the shores of Nantucket is tragic enough, but the weepiness factor is maximized in this shameless tearjerker because we get to relive that painful loss again and again as each night widower David Lewis (Peter Gallagher) bids yet another final good-night to his beloved Gillian (Michelle Pfeiffer) after a moonlight frolic on the beach. Oh yeah, we know she's dead, and he knows she's dead, and God knows she knows she's dead (having fallen slo-mo from a sailboat mast two years ago on her thirty-fifth birthday). But it's such sweet agony to be reminded over and over that life without Gillian and her life-affirming/grim reaper–tempting stunts is not worth living. Adding to the distress is the fact that David's inability to move on is threatening his relationship with his adolescent daughter (played by teen angst queen Claire Danes), whose face crumples in pain and eyes begin reddening each time she is reminded that Mom isn't coming back and Dad may be stuck in a permanent state of altered reality.

Yeah, there's just something about that love-transcending-death thing that really turns on the plumbing. This reminder of the anguish of letting go and the beauty of carrying on is pure emotional Drāno.

> ⚠ Warning Label: *Keep a bailing bucket handy.*

▪ ***Love Story*** *(1970)*
Stars: Ali McGraw, Ryan O'Neal
Director: Arthur Hiller
Writer: Erich Segal

What can you say about a girl who dies? A girl who loved Mozart, Bach, the Beatles, and Ryan O'Neal in the halcyon days, before his cherubic cheeks went to bloat? What can you say about a girl who came from the wrong side of the tracks, but managed through pluck, intelligence, and really good bone structure to land a scholarship to Radcliffe? What can you say about a girl who looks great in knee socks, who wins the heart of the cutest guy on campus and gives up her chance to study in Paris to teach the kids' choir at Camp Tuckahoe in order to put her husband through law school? And then, just when she's about to produce an heir with her sensitive scion, who can make angels in the snow and pursue a partnership track with equal fervor—just when he's about to reconcile with his father, secure his inheritance to the better portion of the Boston Common, and move on up to the East Side, she contracts an unnamed but imminently lethal disease that fells her in just twenty-three minutes of screen time, before she even gets to open an account at Bergdorf's.

What can you say? Only two words: *boo hoo.* Next time you're feeling like a tangled puppet in the hands of fate, pop in this weeper and rain sorrow on the bosom of the earth.

⚠ Warning Label: *It might be best to ask your significant other, who does not make angels in the snow or stand to inherit the better portion of the Boston Common, to make other plans for the evening. At times like this, love doesn't necessarily mean never having to say you're sorry.*

▪ ***Butterflies Are Free*** *(1972)*
Stars: Goldie Hawn, Edward Albert, Paul Michael Glaser
Director: Milton Katselas
Writer: Leonard Gershe

What could be more tragic than a love story starring Goldie Hawn as a sixties sylph who interpretive dances her way through this *Love American Style* morality play in an unzipped peasant blouse and a halo of blond bedroom curls before the unflinching gaze of Donny, a blind man whom she mistakes for a Peeping Tom? Donny, played by Edward Albert, is a sightless visionary who mouths transcendental epithets like "there are none so blind as those who will not see," and looks an awful lot like a period Brad Pitt with a Peter Maxx print shirt and a white cane.

Donny provides a spiritual foil for Jill, the tousled waif next door, who eats like a horse and still weighs two pounds, and confuses a fear of intimacy with a thirst for freedom. When Jill dumps Donny for Ralph Santori (played by a pre-*Starsky* Paul Michael Glaser), the studly Italian director of the avant-garde performance garage down the street, Donny is plunged into an emotional darkness that reduces this saintly seer to a lost, frightened little blind boy, only with a really good haircut and bedroom eyes. Guaranteed to turn on the maternal instinct plumbing full force.

▪ ***Marvin's Room*** *(1996)*
Stars: Diane Keaton, Meryl Streep, Leonardo DiCaprio
Director: Jerry Zaks
Writer: Scott McPherson

Diane Keaton stars as the sweet-faced Bessie, a virtual saint who has dedicated her life to caring for her barely lucid but beatific father and her batty but lovable aunt, whose hearing aid shares a disturbing cross-connection with the electric garage-door opener. Always giving and never receiving, this modern-day Florence Nightingale is forced to confront her inability to accept love when she is diagnosed with leukemia and must turn to her emotionally withholding sister, Lee (Meryl Streep), and Lee's angst-ridden, pyromaniacal teenage son, Hank (Leonardo DiCaprio), to donate bone marrow and save her life.

This is a movie about loving and being loved, about giving and receiving, about sacrifice and reward, living and dying, maturing and regressing . . . and about that searing image of a petulant but angelic Leonardo DiCaprio tied to a bed with leather straps.

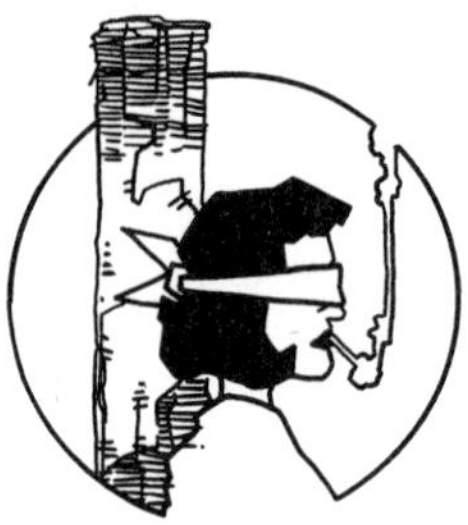

Famous Last Words

We are the luckiest sons of bitches in the world, you know that?

★ Leonardo DiCaprio as Jack Dawson in *Titanic*

▪ ***The Way We Were*** *(1973)*
Stars: Robert Redford, Barbra Streisand
Director: Sydney Pollack
Writer: Arthur Laurents

Katie (Barbra Streisand) and Hubbell (Robert Redford) are like chalk and cheese. He's rich, she's poor. He's an athlete, she's a brain. He's a soldier, she's an agitator. He's true-blue, she's flaming red. Despite the irresistible pull of opposites attracting, these star-crossed lovers never do find common ground, although they do drool over each other for the better part of a half century.

This is a movie about time going by, about missed opportunities, about the inability to ever go home again. Watching this movie is rather like driving on a Los Angeles freeway at rush hour. You miss your exit because the signage stinks, and while you're searching for a way to backtrack, you miss the next exit. Next thing you know, it's three decades later and you still haven't made it to the mall. It'll drive you to tears!

> ⚠ Warning Label: *This movie rates high on the frustration scale. If you suffer from hypertension or high blood pressure, exercise caution. And don't forget to signal your lane changes!*

▪ ***Beaches*** *(1988)*
Stars: Bette Midler, Barbara Hershey, John Heard
Director: Garry Marshall
Writers: Iris Rainer Dart and Mary Agnes Donoghue

A New York child star, C.C. (played by the irrepressible Bette Midler), and a poor little rich girl, Hillary (played by the repressible Barbara Hershey), meet on the boardwalk in Atlantic City. These two little girls from different worlds form an instant bond by the bucolic seashore, and a lifelong friendship is born. Cut to thirty years later. C.C. has become a star and a femme fatale. Hillary has become a lawyer and a mom.

This dichotomy makes for obvious difficulties, since all lawyers want to be stars and femme fatales, and all stars want to be lawyers and moms. Their difficulties almost drive them apart, until tragedy strikes and these two women come together once again, this time for another magical summer at the sea. There they rediscover their love for each other, and realize that they aren't rivals, but the wind beneath each other's wings. You won't just cry a river, you'll weep an ocean with this one!

> ⚠ Warning Label: *Be sure to check your long distance carrier to make sure you have a good rate, because you're bound to end up in a cross-country confessional sobfest to your long-lost best friend for several hours.*

▪ ***Paradise Road*** (1997)

Stars: Glenn Close, Pauline Collins, Francis McDormand, Jennifer Ehle, Julianna Margulies, Cate Blanchett

Director: Bruce Beresford

Writer: Bruce Beresford, based on a story by David Giles and Martin Meader, based on accounts by survivors of the Belalau prison camp

It's one thing to draw up an agreement; it's another thing to make sure you get an executed copy for your files. Case in point: the Geneva Convention. Japan. Little oversight there, fellas. Not good. As a result, Sumatra was just not the place to be during the war years, particularly if a gal had a hankering for food, water, shelter, medicine, freedom, and a shred of respect for humanity.

Based on real-life reminiscences, *Paradise Road* is the story of hundreds of women and children who tried to escape Singapore in 1942 and ended up spending the entire war in a Japanese prison camp, miles from civilization, forced to eat insect-ridden gruel, beaten mercilessly for minor offenses, and tortured for hours in the burning sun. And those were the good old days, before the food and medicine ran out entirely. To maintain their sanity and unity against their cruel and barbaric captors and the equally morale-destroying behavior of catty, paranoid, and xenophobic fellow prisoners, two of the women (Glenn Close and Pauline Collins) decide to start a vocal orchestra. Using mere scraps of paper to scribble their scores on, the women practice until they can lift their voices in one harmonious vibration that moves their guards to drop their guns and the prison director to remember his own humanity for just a moment and fill the tiny clearing in the jungle with his own plaintive folk song.

This one has so many tearjerking elements—torture, death, dying kids, foolish old ladies learning the true meaning of life before they succumb to malaria, death, executions of the innocent, death, haunting Beethoven melodies, death. Brace yourself for the brutality before the uplift. This one will leave you spent.

Words to Live By

When you're in love with a married man you shouldn't wear mascara.

★ Shirley MacLaine as Fran Kubelik in *The Apartment*

■ ***The English Patient*** *(1996)*
Stars: Ralph Fiennes, Kristin Scott Thomas, Juliette Binoche
Director: Anthony Minghella
Writer: Anthony Minghella, based on the novel by Michael Ondaatje

A man goes to heroic lengths to keep his promise to his beloved, only to arrive late because he was detained by a group of stubborn, paranoid, jingoistic men who can't make an exception just this once for God's sake and give him a jeep without his presenting identity papers. The unlucky pilot (Fiennes) haltingly tells his story to an equally unlucky nurse (Binoche), who is just beginning to understand that love means grand passion and loss, transcendent joy and the deepest of suffering. This is a lesson she'd better internalize quickly if her new boyfriend insists on keeping his job as a mine defuser.

With sweeping, sensual vistas, tales of forbidden passion, and men whose honor and commitment to the same woman can be destroyed only by death, *The English Patient* will enthrall you right up until the moment when you must experience the inevitable despair of having to let go of all that you love. Exquisitely painful.

> Warning Label: *Send him out for the evening, because at 2 hours, 40 minutes, it's going to be one long night for anyone with XY chromosomes.*

Words To Live By

A woman should never learn to sew, and if she does know how, she shouldn't admit to it.

★ Kristin Scott Thomas as Katharine Clifton in *The English Patient*

▪ ***Dying Young*** *(1991)*
Stars: Julia Roberts, Campbell Scott
Director: Joel Schumacher
Writer: Richard Friedenberg, based on the novel by Marti Leimbach

The first time that gorgeous blue-eyed Campbell Scott gets the dry heaves for hours and passes out in his exquisite modern bathroom, our Julia realizes there's a reason home health care workers earn more than burger flippers. Yes, he's wonderful, straight, gorgeous, rich, and single—but he's dying of leukemia. And he throws up a lot. Talk about poor romantic prospects! Of course, he claims his chemo's over with, and Julia is too busy furiously tidying up after him, tossing out his collection of junk food and *Playboys*, purchasing plenty of leafy, green, beta carotene–rich vegetables, and sailing down the river of denial to face the inevitable.

If the anguished looks and furious railings about deception don't make you burst out in tears at the unfairness of it all, the golden sunsets and life-affirming nude dashes out onto the meadow will wrench 'em out of you.

▪ ***Love Affair*** (1939)
Stars: Irene Dunne, Charles Boyer
Director: Leo McCarey
Writers: Delmer Daves, Donald Ogden Stewart, and Leo McCarey, from a story by Mildred Cram

Dunne portrays a spunky, ukelele-playing gal who bonds far too well with Boyer's aging Italian mama for the dreamy European playboy to let her get away. After a whirlwind romance aboard a luxury liner, each agrees to dispose of their betrothed and meet up in six months at the top of the Empire State Building to get hitched. No explanations needed for no-shows, they readily agree. Uh, is this a setup for disaster or what?

Of course, the best-laid plans are thwarted by impetuous jaywalking (they should've listened to Mayor Giuliani). The heroine's pride prevents her from inflicting her imperfections on the man she deeply loves and she insists on keeping Boyer in the dark about her motives, despite the heartache she will cause him.

The 1957 Cary Grant/Deborah Kerr version (*An Affair to Remember,* also directed by McCarey) is just as weepy as the original and Grant is equally debonair as the pained lover, but Kerr just can't match Dunne's sparkle. Still, Kerr gets to don some scrumptious gowns—and in Technicolor to boot. Which to choose? Hell, rent one, and rent the other in six months (just look both ways before you cross the street).

Lethal Liz Line

I swear, if you existed, I'd divorce you.

★ Elizabeth Taylor as Martha in *Who's Afraid of Virginia Woolf?*

▪ ***The Joy Luck Club*** (1993)
Stars: Tsai Chin, Kieu Chinh, Ming-Na Wen, Tamlyn Tomita
Director: Wayne Wang
Writer: Ronald Bass, based on the novel by Amy Tan

Four mothers, four daughters, eight stories, and countless sobs as dysfunctional young women discover that life in China for their mothers was just one gut-wrenching tragedy after another. Funny, isn't it, that even in China men are the common catalyst for agony, madness, and suicide? Guess some things are cross-cultural.

Hearing their mothers' stories inspires these young women to find their inner Scarletts and refuse to be pushed around any longer. And just when you've cleared your nose and begun to wipe away your smeared mascara, there's that ending. Loss, acceptance, sisterhood, mother–daughter relations—just name a hot-button emotional issue and it's there in this dazzling crescendo of tears, which melts into quiet credits, over which you will provide a soundtrack of sobs. Watch it with Mom for an extra emotional wallop.

Destructive Inner Dialogue

I'm going to the fourth world. It's sort of like heaven; only better, because there aren't any Christians.

★ Kate Winslet as Juliet Hulme in *Heavenly Creatures*

■ ***Ghost*** *(1990)*
Stars: Patrick Swayze, Demi Moore, Whoopi Goldberg
Director: Jerry Zucker
Writer: Bruce Joel Rubin

As viscous fresh clay slips through Demi Moore's fingers in the classic pottery wheel love scene, so too does the perfect relationship as Patrick Swayze's blood slowly drains from his body when he is senselessly, brutally murdered. (*Ladies, start your tear ducts.*)

Swayze and Moore play two lovers who, up until Swayze turns into the ghost of the title, had everything going for them (except for his inability to say "I love you," a character flaw that apparently only death can cure).

A despondent Demi gets misty when going through the detritus from her late husband Sam's pockets, but when an ornery psychic (Goldberg) shows up with a message—Sam is right here and he can move pennies through the air!—rivers emanate from Demi's brown eyes. Can she catch Sam's murderer? Will Sam have to leave her to Go Towards the Light? And will Demi's eyes be loaned to Africa to ease the Ethiopian drought?

■ *Truly Madly Deeply* (1991)

Stars: Juliet Stevenson, Alan Rickman
Director and Writer: Anthony Minghella

He was the love of her life, her everything—her best friend, her adoring husband, a man as passionate in his lovemaking as in his cello playing, a man so protective that she can still hear his whispered words of caution that so stir her soul: "Don't forget to lock the back door." (Hey, if your dead husband had the drowsy drawl of Alan Rickman, your soul would be stirred by his nagging too!)

Astonishingly, our heroine's abject despair over her loss becomes terrifying exhilaration when her beloved comes back to her, especially since he's developed the astonishing ability to scare off rodents infesting her dreary North London flat. But true love means letting go—a truth that is much easier to accept when one has broken free of the magnetic pull of earthly desires. Fortunately, as it turns out, unconditional love and spiritual transcendence are not only nourishing for the soul, but unbelievably sexy when you throw Alan Rickman into the equation.

Sit back and let the bittersweet reality of the tides of true love, ever ebbing and flowing, engulf you.

> ⚠ Warning Label: *Boyfriend/husband intimidation factor here is high and may inspire pouting about women's unrealistic expectations. Watch it alone and remember, it's only a movie.*

Faking It: Gal Films That Are Really Guy Films and Totally Piss Us Off

Jerry Maguire *(1996)*
Stars: Tom Cruise, Renée Zellweger
Director and Writer: Cameron Crowe

Ostensibly a romance about a man who learns to appreciate a long-mistreated woman, *Jerry Maguire* is a maddening tale of a sweet-natured doormat who puts up with a self-centered man (Tom Cruise) whose best quality is his Hollywood smile. So what if he isn't actually in love with his wife? He's good to her kid—what more could a single mom hope for? Well, passion for one, and maybe a shred of interest in who she is as an individual. She won't find it in a movie directed by Cameron "Hey, I never said I was good with female characters" Crowe. Instead, Dorothy settles for Jerry's pathetic declaration (in front of a chorus of pitiful divorcee harpies) that she "completes" him, happily accepting her role as yet another extension of her husband's all-star male ego. Woman, get thee to an empowerment seminar. Codependency is, like, so 1980.

Ragers

- ***I Shot Andy Warhol*** *(1996)*
  Stars: Lili Taylor, Stephen Dorff
  Director: Mary Harron
  Writers: Mary Harron and Daniel Minahan, additional material by Jeremiah Newton

A disaffected iconoclast (played by the disaffected, iconoclastic Lili Taylor) earns a living as a prostitute in order to remain in New York and spread her message of radical female separatism. In between tricks, she pens passionate laundry lists detailing the inhumanity and brutish carnality of the male species. When her fate brings her into contact with Andy Warhol, she demands that he give her fifteen minutes of fame. When Andy fails to make good on his offer (largely because he's a *man*!) she shoots him in the gut.

This quirky bio-pic is the cinematic equivalent of full frontal assault. It has the vicarious effect of beating a man repeatedly about the head and shoulders. At this time of the month, who could ask for anything more?

⚠ Warning Label: *Don't expect a plot. This is pure blunt force.*

Classic Bette Byte

Oh Harry, you're an angel. If your mother hadn't been such a bitch, we might have shared something important.

★ Bette Midler as C.C. in *Beaches*

■ ***Heavenly Creatures*** *(1994)*
Stars: Kate Winslet, Melanie Lynskey
Director: Peter Jackson
Writers: Peter Jackson and Frances Walsh

Nothing like a stroll down adolescent alley to get in touch with the ax-murdering parricidal maniac within. Two New Zealand schoolgirls, Juliet and Pauline, ramble through a fantasy world of presexual passion, which they have superimposed, with rapturous precision, over the stark and isolated provinces of grim reality. When they are threatened with separation from each other and exile from their magic kingdom, the power of their emerging sexuality sets upon the world with Freudian fury, smashing everything that comes within arm's reach. Based on a true story of two women who are, indeed, walking the streets today (one is mystery writer Anne Perry).

> ⚠ Warning Label: *If you have mother issues, don't watch this movie with your mother in the room. Especially if there are any large rocks in the vicinity.*

▪ ***Play Misty for Me*** *(1971)*
Stars: Clint Eastwood, Jessica Walter, Donna Mills
Director: Clint Eastwood
Writers: Joe Heims and Dean Riesner

Clint Eastwood is a laid-back, hypermodulated, FM-style DJ in the Bay Area circa 1970. You know the type: double-knit, bell-bottom trousers, wide belt, ruddy, well-sculpted face, piercing eyes, frog in his throat. And he loves jazz . . . of course he does . . . and a positively shimmering girl named Tobie (Donna Mills, who else?), who has a frosted blond shag, frosted lips, *and* frosted eye shadow that perfectly matches her loose-fitting, breathable-fiber ensembles.

Our lovers are overcoming his brief affair with another, and she's trying to forgive him, so they hang out on weekends, go to jazz festivals, and stroll through the woods backdropped by the surging tide and a drowsy Roberta Flack ballad. Clint's trying to be good, but that nice, girl-next-door fan of his (Jessica Walter) is just a bit pushy in her own sweet way, probably because she's more of a matte-palletted type who has got to work to make up for her lack of sparkle. But before long it becomes clear that commitment or no, Clint won't be soon forgetting that plain Jane with a penchant for Poe's poetry and a temper that results in frosted blond locks flying everywhere—and that isn't just a trim.

Faking It: Phony Gal Films That Really Piss Us Off

Fatal Attraction (1987)
Stars: Glenn Close, Michael Douglas, Anne Archer
Director: Adrian Lyne
Writers: James Dearden and Nicholas Meyer

We've all been there, so furious we're ready to spend all our free time wreaking havoc on some jerk who done us wrong, who treated us like just another disposable American consumer product, and worse yet, had the nerve not to return our phone calls. But it's hard to identify with a gal who takes it out on a cute little bunny rabbit and sits in her room switching a lamp on and off because she's incapable of creating her own original pathetic scenario (this character-defining scene is stolen straight from *Lenny*). Glenn Close plays a nasty career woman who sleeps around and is so desperate for male attention that she can be stopped only by a righteous, forgiving, and chaste suburban housewife, and even then she rises Rasputin-like to launch one last battle against suburban hypocrisy and audience credibility.

For a much better portrayal of the fury of a woman passed over one too many times—and a much more frightening movie—try *Play Misty for Me.*

- ***Sister My Sister*** (1994)
  Stars: Joely Richardson, Jodhi May, Julie Walters, Sophie Thursfield
  Director: Nancy Meckler
  Writer: Wendy Kesselman, based on her play

Two sisters, serving as maids in an affluent turn-of-the century French household, weather the thankless drudgery of their subservient social station, the unconscious brutality of men, and the traumatic legacy of a homicidal mother by turning to each other. The forbidden passion between them grows desperate, and when the world threatens their sanctuary, they snap, brutally murdering their employer, herself a homicidal mother who in many ways mirrors their own. This female revenge tragedy is a great outlet for all that unexpressed rage you've been building up against just about everybody for just about everything, for just about as long you can remember. Everybody gets what's coming to them in this movie: mothers, sisters, an unsympathetic, misogynist society, and even the metaphorical male who conveniently absents himself just when he might actually have had something useful to contribute. Typical!

▪ ***The Last Seduction*** *(1994)*
Stars: Linda Fiorentino, Peter Berg
Director: John Dahl
Writer: Steve Barancik

If you're in the mood to tamp out your morning cigarette in your last night's trick's granny-baked cherry pie before sashaying into the chaste morning light with your underwear in your purse, then this is the movie for you. Catlike Bridget Gregory (Linda Fiorentino) shows her claws when she convinces her doctor husband to sell medicinal cocaine illegally and then takes off with the money before her husband can pay off his loan sharks.

In fear for his life and his kneecaps, Clay, who is a bumbling strategist at best, hires a hit man to go after his wife and his money. Bridget, who is a regular Machiavelli in fishnets, manipulates a gullible small-town boy, turning him into a weapon aimed straight at the male species. Nothing like contract killings and the objectification of men to take the edge off, don't you think?

▪ ***Sisters*** *(1973)*
Stars: Margot Kidder, Jennifer Salt, Charles Durning
Director: Brian De Palma
Writers: Louisa Rose and Brian De Palma, based on a story by Brian De Palma

Sisters can be sooooo selfish and inconsiderate! She borrows your clothes without asking, she always has to have her own way, and when you bring home a fella, she gets all huffy, plants a twelve-inch cake knife in his back, and leaves him on the bedroom floor. And, of course, she expects *you* to clean up the mess.

Talk about separation issues—these dysfunctional sisters are practically joined at the hip! Brian De Palma directs this creepfest made all the more unsettling by the casting of gal-next-door Margot Kidder as the good sister and her evil twin, both of which you'll identify with depending on your hormonal fluctuations. And that birthday cake looks really yummy about this time, doesn't it? Now if you could just find a clean knife . . .

> ⚠ Warning Label: *Remove all sharp objects before viewing.*

Lethal Liz Lines

I hope that was an empty bottle, George! You can't afford to waste good liquor, not on your salary!

★ Elizabeth Taylor as Martha in *Who's Afraid of Virginia Woolf?*

■ *Who's Afraid of Virginia Woolf?* (1966)

Stars: Elizabeth Taylor, Richard Burton, Sandy Dennis, George Segal
Director: Mike Nichols
Writer: Edward Albee

Set on the bucolic campus of Smith College, this film adaptation of Edward Albee's stage play documents a night in the life of a marriage from hell. Martha, a blowzy, foul-mouthed, gin-soaked professor's daughter (played by a very post–*National Velvet* Elizabeth Taylor in a push-up bra and spandex cocktail pants), systematically, methodically, and brilliantly emasculates her husband, George, a disappointed history professor (played by a post–Mark Antony Richard Burton), who has reached the end of his rope. When a new and promising professor and his squeamish, brandy-swilling mouse of a wife pop by for a nightcap, they all wind up shipwrecked in the North Atlantic of this couple's malice.

This relationship is an emotional *Titanic,* without the lavish period architecture and the band playing on. If it's that time of the month and you're walking the fine line between love and hatred in your own relationship, or would just like a refresher course on how to publicly humiliate your spouse, then this is the movie for you.

Chapter 2

Yeah, Okay, So He's a Jerk, But He's Sooooo Cute!: Dysfunctional Romances

You did it again, didn't you? You found yourself a guy with good hair, a sly, slow smile, bottomless eyes, and no visible means of support. We know, it's hard to establish boundaries with a wet, naked Latin lover awaiting you in a warehouse, smoldering, his mahogany eyes simmering with dangerous and unexpressed passion. . . . Okay, so he ends up being the sort of a guy who would mutilate your cat . . . but for God's sake, look at him. He's Antonio Banderas! And he's wet. And naked. In a *warehouse*!

When you've got the codependent blues, curl up with one of our favorite dysfunctional romances, like *Never Talk to Strangers,* and indulge in the forbidden pleasures of enmeshment without having to pick up the emotional check.

Classic Codependent Quote

That's nice talk, Ben—keep drinking. Between the 101-proof breath and the occasional bits of drool, some interesting words come out.

★ Elizabeth Shue as Sera in *Leaving Las Vegas*

■ ***Sid and Nancy*** *(1986)*
Stars: Gary Oldman, Chloe Webb
Director: Alex Cox
Writers: Alex Cox and Abbe Wool

The sinewy, dangerously sexy Gary Oldman plays Sid Vicious, the doomed bassist for the seminal British punk band the Sex Pistols. Vicious, who elevates the expulsion of bodily fluids to a form of artistic expression, manages to be absolutely adorable, despite his being a smack-addicted, tone-deaf musician with no future prospects and chronic postnasal drip.

The Sex Pistols, who splattered onto the scene on the cusp of the anti-love eighties, dried up after their first album, leaving the hapless but lovable Sid, who had probably spent the better portion of his adolescence circling the rim, to finally slide down the drain and out of sight. Of course, before he goes, he stages a star-crossed love affair with his soul mate, Nancy Spungen (Chloe Webb), a celebrity-obsessed American dominatrix who has about as much hope as Sid does of ever seeing the other side of thirty, but loves him despite his leaky plumbing. They fall into punk love. Big surprise—they don't live happily ever after.

■ ***No Man of Her Own*** *(1932)*
Stars: Clark Gable, Carole Lombard
Director: Wesley Ruggles
Writers: Milton H. Gropper and Maurine Watkins, based on a story by Edmund Goulding and Benjamin Glazer

She's just a small-town librarian, so desperate for a little action that she's threatening to run away with the next Fuller Brush man who shows up. But since Connie Randall (Carole Lombard) is a platinum blonde with a brain, a bod, and a self-possessed attitude to match, she immediately attracts the most likely prospect to blow into Glendale in a long time: Babe Stewart (Clark Gable), who, despite being without his trademark mustache, manages to smirk his way into her heart. Oh, he's fresh all right, walking her up against walls and looking up her skirt, all the while grinning like a Cheshire cat and working those eyebrows but good. Don't worry, she can handle him—after all, she's a woman who can wear silk lounging pajamas while staying in a rustic cabin by the lake without looking positively silly.

Of course, Stewart's got to be hiding something, since he's far too sexy to be a respectable gentleman, and reputable fellows who work in brokerage offices don't have art deco bachelor pads with eighteenth-century pianofortes and a budget that allows for Lombard's endless array of high-fashion silk, satin, and sequined gowns. But before things can get too ugly, the purity of Connie's love and her carefully measured patience cause him to give up his gambling ways and get a nice cushy day job.

Moral of the Story: Women who can carry off silk lounging pajamas can call the shots in any relationship.

World-Class Wrecks

You'd be lovely to have around just to sprinkle the flowers with your personality.

★Carole Lombard to Clark Gable in *No Man of Her Own*

■ ***Emily Brontë's Wuthering Heights*** *(1992)*
Stars: Juliette Binoche, Ralph Fiennes
Director: Peter Kosminsky
Writer: Anne Devlin, based on the novel by Emily Brontë

Not only is this the most stunning version of Emily Brontë's immortal classic* but Ralph Fiennes's Heathcliff has got that latently homicidal *je ne sais quoi* that makes him irresistible to all of us codependent romantics. He's absolutely gorgeous as he stalks the embittered halls of his purloined family seat, deep in the throes of all that delicious inner angst. You could just eat him up.

Okay, so he's completely destroyed the lives of two generations of kinsmen in his blind obsession with his lost love, Cathy (played by the earthy yet ethereal Juliette Binoche). Okay, so he starves baby lapwings in their nest, marries his rival's sister for her fortune, and then drives her to an early grave. But he talks to trees, his Gypsy tendrils wild in the wind soughing across the moors. And his dark eyes smolder as he clutches the dying Cathy to his tormented, leanly muscled breast, his brow furrowing, first with rage then with despair, as he bids a final farewell to the other half of himself.

And then there is that pair of supple, impossibly tight leather riding breeches . . . throw in a riding crop, and you'd give him your firstborn for just one moment in the saddle.

■ ***Ethan Frome*** *(1993)*
Stars: Liam Neeson, Patricia Arquette, Joan Allen
Director: John Madden
Writer: Richard Nelson, based on the novella by Edith Wharton

Edith Wharton's ode to the repetition compulsion (a psychological term for the compulsive need to repeat the same dysfunctional relationship no matter how many times you fall flat on your face) is given new life and dimension with Liam Neeson's teddy-bearish portrayal of the ill-fated farmer Ethan Frome.

None of the tragedy that unfolds is Ethan's fault. He's just a mild-mannered innocent with big, soulful eyes and the most remarkable lips. How could he help it if he was born the only son of an invalid mother, and forced by circumstance to give up his dreams of adventure in the big city to care for her in her ailing dotage?

*We admit Timothy Dalton wasn't bad in the 1970s version, but he was much better in sister Charlotte's *Jane Eyre*, and though Laurence Olivier was unmistakably hot in the 1939 version, the movie wraps up about halfway through the book—no fun.

It wasn't his fault that the all-enduring servant girl he marries turns into the very same whey-faced convalescent he just planted in the cold New England earth. And he couldn't help but fall in love with the vibrant and bright-eyed Mattie Silver, with whom he takes one last chance at love before the final catharsis that turns his bright and shining girl into . . . well, we don't want to spoil the surprise ending! This one is so deeply affecting, you'll want to watch it again, and again, and again, and again. . . .

■ ***Leaving Las Vegas*** *(1995)*
Stars: Nicolas Cage, Elizabeth Shue
Director: Mike Figgis
Writer: Mike Figgis, based on the novel by John O'Brien

Don't say you don't understand because you know that you do. We've all done it. There we all were, at one time or another, minding our own business, just another night walking the Strip in a pair of fishnets and a spandex mini, just leisurely trolling for the first john of the evening. . . .

And there he was, in a slick sports car and a urine-stained suit, with a trunkful of rotgut and a belly full of broken dreams. And we were helpless, weren't we? We couldn't resist those liverish, bloodshot eyes, those ravaged, unshaven cheeks, that irresistible death wish. And what did we do? We did what any other self-destructive, codependent, masochistic enabler would do: We asked him to move in and tried to talk him out of drinking himself to death!

Pop this movie in, admit defeat, and guzzle the Cuervo Gold of Denial.

> ⚠ Warning Label: *For God's sake, this time don't eat the worm!*

■ ***Legends of the Fall*** *(1994)*
Stars: Brad Pitt, Anthony Hopkins, Aidan Quinn, Julia Ormond
Director: Edward Zwick
Writers: Jim Harrison, Susan Shilliday, and Bill Wittliff

This sweeping epic is really just an homage to Brad Pitt's golden mane. Tristan Ludlow is a gorgeous iconoclast in chaps. And despite his being the apotheosis of masculine perfection in the classic Greek sense, he's out of step with the world around him. He scoffs at war, makes friends with Indians, grows an unkempt beard, and punches an occasional bartender. But he doesn't mean it. He's really just a lost, motherless little boy—sweet, sad, sunny-headed, but with a broken heart, crying out for the power of Susannah's love to heal him.

Unfortunately for Susannah (Julia Ormond), Tristan's health regimen includes ten-year-long hunting expeditions into untrammeled woods, extended voyages along uncharted seas, and many a musky evening spent entangled in the tropical embraces of various Tahitian teenagers.

But he's so beautiful. Practically mythic. And the way he rides up over the crest of that hill (which he does several times in the course of an hour and a half), his sunny locks blowing in the hot gusts of summer, his head high, his gaze steady as the herd thunders blindly forward, guided only by his sure, gentle hand. The Montana sun crowns him like a laurel. And those thundering hooves. His seat in that saddle. That petulant hollow at the small of his back, undulating effortlessly, completely in tune with the bursts and swells of his horse's furious gate.

You get the idea. Tristan Ludlow is a codependent's caviar. Pass the beluga, baby!

Pearl of Native American Wisdom

It was those that loved him most who died young. He was the stone they broke themselves against.

★ Gordon Tootoosis as One Stab in *Legends of the Fall*

■ ***The Shining*** *(1980)*
Stars: Jack Nicholson, Shelley Duvall, Danny Lloyd, Scatman Crothers
Director: Stanley Kubrick
Writers: Stanley Kubrick and Diane Johnson, based on the novel by Stephen King

Finally, Wendy Torrance thinks, a chance to start anew. Jack can write that book, get away from those memories of the past—his drinking days, and that awful night when he accidentally rearranged little Danny's rotator cuff. Yes, all that's behind them now, and what better place to get away from it all than an isolated mountain resort in Colorado, unreachable by car until the spring. Good thinkin', Wendy!

And little Danny will love it. All those long hallways perfectly suited for the Big Wheel, enough industrial-size cans of peaches to stave off scurvy in a small underdeveloped nation for at least half a decade, and the ghosts of several slaughtered children to play with. We'll say it one more time . . . Good thinkin', Wendy.

Wendy leaves her husband undisturbed so that he can write that novel he's always been talking about, but as usually happens when we attempt to choreograph our dysfunctional mate's psychosis, things start to seep in through the walls. For one thing, if Jack's demons are being exorcised on the page, why are they starting to stalk the hallways, commingling with the tortured spirit of a former innkeeper/ax murderer with a clipped British accent and firm opinions about patriarchal obeisance? And what's with that naked old lady in the bathtub?

At last it dawns on Wendy that maybe things aren't going to work out as she had hoped. But breaking up is hard to do when the shortwave radio's on the fritz, the phone lines are down, there are several feet of snow on the roads, and the only available vehicle is a twelve-ton Sno-Cat without power steering.

Think about Wendy next time you decide that all your hubby needs is a little R&R to get in touch with himself. And bring along the cellular, just in case.

■ ***A Streetcar Named Desire*** *(1951)*
Stars: Marlon Brando, Vivien Leigh, Kim Hunter, Karl Malden
Director: Elia Kazan
Writers: Oscar Saul and Tennessee Williams, based on the play by Tennessee Williams

Best Bodice-Ripping Lines in Mood Movie History

❍ "That ain't tactics, honey. It's just the beast in me."
—The sleek, grinding Elvis in *Jailhouse Rock*

❍ "Haunt me, torment me, but do not leave me alone in this void where I cannot find you."
—Laurence Olivier as the earthy Heathcliff in *Wuthering Heights*
(This line is so good, it could pick up a corpse . . . and does!)

❍ "How 'bout making me vice president in charge of cheering you up?"—Bad boy Cary Grant to Audrey Hepburn in *Charade*

❍ "Say jyesssssss."
—Stranger Antonio Banderas to a reluctant Rebecca De Mornay in *Never Talk to Strangers*

❍ "Nobody puts Baby in a corner!"
—The indignant Patrick Swayze in *Dirty Dancing*

❍ "It's no use. I've struggled in vain. I must tell you how much I admire and love you. Miss Elizabeth, my life and happiness are in your hands."
—Laurence Olivier as the ever chivalrous Mr. Darcy in *Pride and Prejudice*

❍ "Don't move—because this is a moment so filled with understanding that I can't bear to see it come to an end."
—Charles Boyer while gazing adoringly at Bette Davis in *All This and Heaven Too*

❍ "No, I don't think I will kiss you. Although you need kissing, badly. That's what's wrong with you. You should be kissed, and often, and by someone who knows how."
—Clark Gable as a teasing Rhett Butler in *Gone With the Wind*

❍ "How can I write, with the taste of you in my mouth?"
—A distracted Ralph Fiennes to Kristin Scott Thomas in *The English Patient* ■

When Marlon Brando's Stanley Kowalski staggers to the base of that New Orleans tenement staircase—his biceps straining against the gauzy tenuousness of that impossibly flimsy T-shirt, bellowing for his mate like a wounded panther in the thick of the fray—he not only stuck a firecracker in the eardrum of the American theater, but provided perennial male adolescents the world over with a good excuse for behaving badly. This is the ur-text for the American bad boy—the urban tough guy in the T-shirt's most perfect apotheosis. . . . And the writing ain't too shabby either.

■ ***Never Talk to Strangers*** *(1995)*
Stars: Antonio Banderas, Rebecca De Mornay
Director: Peter Hall
Writers: Nicky Frei, Lewis A. Green, Peter Hall, and Jordan Rush

Mama always said never talk to strangers, but when the stranger is a ponytailed, motorcycled, leather-jacketed Latin lover played by Antonio Banderas, who can inspire orgasms just by pouring a glass of cabernet at the right angle . . . Well, what can you do but "just say . . . jyesssss"?

Rebecca De Mornay may be a brilliant psychiatrist, but when disturbing events coincide with the arrival of her new beau, her hormones displace common sense faster than Antonio can roll his *r*'s. She's realizes that Antonio Banderas, wet and naked in a warehouse with a well-placed chain-link fence, is worth a few sacrifices—like, say, the life of your beloved kitty. A psychopath? Hey, I can work with that.

The movie's marred by silly writing, a dopey ending, and appallingly bad acting by De Mornay, but you won't care because it will push all your bad-boy buttons.

> ⚠ Warning Label: *Don't rent this if you're trying to quit smoking—you'll need one after the butt-munching scene.*

■ ***Suspicion*** *(1941)*
Stars: Joan Fontaine, Cary Grant
Director: Alfred Hitchcock
Writers: Samson Raphaelson, Joan Harrison, and Alma Reville, based on the novel Before the Fact *by Francis Iles*

Plain Jane Fontaine is far too good-natured to fuss when, after a whirlwind romance, she discovers her new hubby is a tad immature and irresponsible. Don't you just hate when that happens? I mean, you haven't even unpacked from the honeymoon yet and already you've got to admit that you've just hitched yourself for better or worse to a lying, leeching s.o.b. who thinks nothing of pawning your family heirloom chairs so that he can play the ponies. But he's Cary Grant for God's sake, so what's a girl to do?

And he really can be quite sweet . . . and thoughtful . . . truly, and even though your imagination runs away with you sometimes and, oh it's silly, really. There couldn't possibly be any connection between his reckless driving on mountain roads, with you in the death seat, and that hefty insurance policy he recently took out on you. . . . *Joan, hon, get a clue!!! You're an apologetic blonde in a Hitchcock movie!*

The ending doesn't make any sense, but then again, neither do dysfunctional relationships and that never stopped us before, did it?

■ ***Love Serenade*** *(1996)*
Stars: Miranda Otto, Rebecca Frith, George Shevtsov
Director and Writer: Shirley Barrett

Remember that summer he blew into town like a gust of funky disco polyester sweat, and you fell like so much stardust beneath his dance boot? And in that ugly little town underneath that endless sky, those Barry White moves and Al Green "mmms" made your blood rise and no one, not even your own sister, could stand in the way of your destiny as his woman. His one woman. But, of course, he has so much love to share, how can he contain his passion for the female form in all its wondrous configurations?

If you feel a slight wave of revulsion rippling through you as you watch this story of a slimy 1970s-obsessed DJ hitting on two painfully sex-starved, naive sisters, remember, it's not that self-centered, calculating, lying bucket of pond scum with all the ethics of a trout that's rocking your intestines. It's the memory of your own personal lying bucket of pond scum rising up from the depths of your subconscious to haunt you. Honey, we've all been there. Shudder and move on.

■ ***Charade*** *(1963)*
Stars: Cary Grant, Audrey Hepburn, Walter Matthau
Director: Stanley Donen
Writers: Peter Stone and Marc Behm

Givenchy-clad Audrey Hepburn is despondent over her marriage (though we wish we all looked so fantastic when we were miserable—"It is infuriating that your unhappiness does not turn to fat!" complains her friend Sylvie, and we've got to agree). But she won't have to suffer a messy divorce from her wealthy husband now that he's turned up dead on a railway embankment—a convenient turn of events, since she's just met the suave, silver-haired Cary Grant. As more and more bodies turn up, he keeps spinning new stories about who he is and what he's after. Certainly she ought to call in the police, or have a detective check out this elusive character, but then again a little murder and intrigue can spice up a romance quite handily, *n'est-ce pas?*

Plenty of ever so charming lying, cheating, and flirting by Grant, and quicksilver dialogue and plot turns will whisk you away and have you believing that the next handsome lying stranger you meet will turn out to be a good guy (and unmarried to boot!).

Classic Codependent Quotes

Women make the best psychoanalysts—until they fall in love. After that, they make the best patients.

★ Words of wisdom from a wizened mentor to psychoanalyst Ingrid Bergman in *Spellbound*

▪ ***American Gigolo*** *(1980)*
Stars: Richard Gere, Lauren Hutton
Director and Writer: Paul Schrader

Julian (played by a pre-Tibetan Richard Gere) is a true man of the eighties: well chiseled, evenly tanned, impeccably dressed, ambiguously heterosexual, and available for a price. Despite the fact that no depth charges of any kind disturb the rippleless confluences of his shallow emotional pool, he looks great in Armani, speaks five different languages all in the same musky, postcoital drawl, and has devoted himself wholeheartedly to the cultivation of a woman's pleasure. No wonder he steals the heart of a neglected senator's wife, who recognizes the value of a man who thinks more about her orgasm than his own.

True, he is a dangerously dissociated male prostitute who is implicated in the psychosexual slaying of a naked woman in handcuffs, but he understands that the G in G-spot stands for Generosity, and for that I think we'd all overlook a mountain of incriminating evidence. Not to mention which, the man can really fill out a pair of gravity boots.

▪ ***Desperado*** *(1995)*
Stars: Antonio Banderas, Salma Hayek, Steve Buscemi
Director and Writer: Robert Rodriguez

Orange explosions and slow motion do wonders to accentuate Antonio Banderas's long black hair, which prances and teases in a manner reminiscent of Brad Pitt's golden mane in *Legends of the Fall.* The cartoonish violence may bother you, but Quentin Tarantino's gratuitous cameo and the sight of a Mexican toilet will certainly make you upchuck. Still, this silly guy-movie is chock-full of well-lit shots of the wounded Antonio. It's not just the bullets, it's the agony of being unable to express himself as a musician, as a lover—a bittersweet agony that manifests in a series of deep sniffs, hissing, and whispered demands for some fellow named Bucho. Salma Hayek plays a fiery Mexican gal whose bookstore is accidentally blown up by her new lover. (Hey, at least he didn't kill her cat.) Can she soothe the tempestuous heart of her troubled desperado before he torches all of Mexico?

■ ***Spellbound*** *(1945)*
Stars: Ingrid Bergman, Gregory Peck, Michael Chekhov
Director: Alfred Hitchcock
Writer: Ben Hecht, based on the novel by Francis Beeding, adapted by Angus MacPhail

Dr. Constance Petersen (Bergman) suspects that something's up with that handsome new psychoanalyst at the office (Peck) when the mere sight of striped upholstery sends him into Theramin-scored freakouts. A quick handwriting analysis reveals he is not, after all, Dr. Anthony Edwardes, but an imposter with a long-term-memory deficit as a consequence of a deep-rooted childhood trauma. Nothing like seeing your brother impaled on a fence to retard your psychological development.

Dr. Petersen is convinced that her patient couldn't have murdered the real Edwardes, because, well, nobody that cute is a killer. "I couldn't feel this way toward a man who was bad," she insists. So despite the words of warning from her mentor (Chekhov) about the gullibility of women in love, despite having the cops hot on their trail, despite her beau's wandering about late at night with an open straight razor in his hand, she's wholly convinced of his innocence—now all she has to do is convince the rest of the world and cure her patient/fiancé of his psychotic delusions—and convince the medical board that it wasn't unethical to sleep with him.

Stupid Guy Quotes

Never had to comb any gal out of my hair.

★ Clark Gable as Babe Stewart in *No Man of Her Own*

Wars are sordid, ugly things. There's no need for them to bother you.

★ Sir William Hamilton to Lady Hamilton (Vivien Leigh) in *That Hamilton Woman*

Stupid Guy Quotes

Well, actually, there's nothing I'd rather do than drop napalm for a living.

★ Nick Stahl as Norstadt in *The Man Without a Face*

There's no point to any of this. It's all just a . . . a random lottery of meaningless tragedy and a series of near escapes. So I take pleasure in the details. You know . . . a quarter-pounder with cheese, those are good, the sky about ten minutes before it starts to rain, the moment where your laughter becomes a cackle . . . and I, I sit back and I smoke my Camel Straights and I ride my own melt.

★ Ethan Hawke as Troy Dyer in *Reality Bites*

▪ ***Immortal Beloved*** *(1994)*
Stars: Gary Oldman, Isabella Rossellini, Jeroen Krabbé, Johanna Ter Steege, Valeria Golino
Director and Writer: Bernard Rose

Who could she possibly be, this woman to whom Beethoven would have left all he had, his immortal beloved? Who could have been the muse to this passionate composer of the ages? Who could've put up with such a nasty, abusive, vindictive, and arrogant louse who drives his dear nephew to a suicide attempt, beats his consumptive brother, and regularly refers to his sister-in-law as "that slut"?

You'll be shocked at the answer to this fictional mystery—an elaborate conceit that draws upon the real Beethoven's mercurial nature—unless, of course, you've ever dated a musician, in which case you'll guess it right off the bat. Be sure to watch for that particularly moving Gary Oldman moment when he lays his head on the piano so that he may at least feel the vibrations of his exquisite *Moonlight* before exploding into a violent but sexy tantrum.

- ***Gaslight*** *(1944)*
  Stars: Ingrid Bergman, Charles Boyer, Angela Lansbury
  Director: George Cukor
  Writers: John Van Druten, Walter Reisch, and John L. Balderston, based on the play by Patrick Hamilton

She saw him do it—he put it in her purse, made a point of it even—and now it's not there. And that painting, where did it go? And just now, that gaslight—it dimmed, she knows it, and yet that snooty servant with the turned up-nose and the pout (Lansbury) insists that she's just imagined it.

If you've ever thought you're losing your mind because you can't remember the little things, this movie will convince you that it's not a sign that you need a vacation, or that you're developing Alzheimer's, or that you're going mad. No, it's him. That's right, *him*. He's

---

Stupid Guy Quotes

It takes a woman all powdered and pink to joyously clean out the drain in the sink!

★ Walter Matthau as Horace Vandergelder in *Hello, Dolly*

Let the name of Moses be stricken from every book and tablet. Stricken from every pylon and obelisk of Egypt. Let the name of Moses be unheard and unspoken, erased from the memory of man, for all time.

★ Cedric Hardwicke as Sethi in *The Ten Commandments*

---

deliberately trying to drive you insane. Oh, he feigns concern, then reminds you how nuts your mother is, but you know it's really that he's just trying to find the jewels your aunt hid somewhere in the attic. Look, he may have all the sophistication and sensuality of Charles Boyer, but in the end he's just another guy lying about where he put your stuff, isn't he?

Stupid Guy Quotes

Well, I don't really think that the end can be assessed as of itself as being the end because what does the end feel like? It's like saying when you try to extrapolate the end of the universe, you say, if the universe is indeed infinite, then how—what does that mean? How far is all the way, and then if it stops, what's stopping it, and what's behind what's stopping it? So, what's the end, you know, is my question to you.

★ Michael McKean as David St. Hubbins in *This Is Spinal Tap*

The Handy Hunk Chart Key

Hunk Ratings:

All-American Boy

Knight in Shining Armor

ASD = *Aristocratic, Suave, and Debonair* BE = *Bedroom Eyes* DMCA = *Devil-May-Care Attitude* EMT = *Eyes Moist With Tears* FSG = *Feckless Schoolboy Grin* LVV = *Liquid Velvet Voice* PBE = *Piercing Blue Eyes* RGH = *Really Good Hair* RUM = *Raw Unpredictable Masculinity* TWL = *That Wounded Look*

The Handy Hunk Chart

Brad Pitt

EMT, FSG, PBE, RGH, TWL

Top Drool Pics: *Thelma & Louise, Legends of the Fall, A River Runs Through It*

We remember Brad best in *Legends of the Fall,* in the summer of the red grass, his honey hair shining in the maiden frontier sun as he mounted the crest of the hill, again, and again, and again, accompanied by a sweeping, epic string motif, and a burnt umber back light that crowned him like a flaming laurel as he found his way home at last to his beloved Susannah. And then, of course, Brad got a haircut, and it just hasn't been the same since. What's with the crew cuts, Brad? Crew cuts cannot sway lyrically in the honeysuckle winds of midsummer. Crew cuts cannot cascade like liquid gold across an antique lace pillowcase, nor can they be shorn in grief and then miraculously replenished in the delicate light of a new spiritual morning. If you ask us, Brad should leave the close-cropped look to Harrison Ford and stick to roles that elevate long hair to a religious experience. ■

Denzel Washington

ASD, BE, LVV

Top Drool Pics: *Courage Under Fire, Cry Freedom, Devil in a Blue Dress, Mississippi Masala, Mo' Better Blues, Much Ado About Nothing, The Pelican Brief, The Preacher's Wife*

It's his carriage, that regal bearing, and the perfectly sculpted muscles that press gently but firmly against that undershirt, shining brilliantly by the blue light of the streets, or the golden bursts from explosions. Yes, this is a man who would look like a Greek god in the fluorescent light of a

. . . continued

dressing room in a discount department store. And that buttery voice that melts the marrow of any woman within earshot, if his dazzling smile hasn't already turned her into a puddle on the floor. Denzel is our tower of masculine perfection, a visual, auditory, and sensory delight, cruelly trapped in the two dimensions of our movie screen. We can only hope to live to see the invention of *Star Trek*'s holodeck, 'cause we'd run the Denzel program till the computer chips sizzled. ▪

Mel Gibson

DMCA, FSG, PBE, RGH, RUM

Top Drool Pics: *Braveheart, Hamlet, Lethal Weapon 1–4, Mad Max, Ransom, Tequila Sunrise, The Year of Living Dangerously*

While it's true that Mel Gibson in fact grew up in Australia, rather than America, no one better personifies the All-American blue-eyed boy next door than he. Just what is it about Mel? The searing sexuality, like the hot unforgiving sun over the wasted landscape of a postnuclear-winter no-man's-land. The sparkly eyed boyish mischievousness that delights in practical jokes and makes us want to scoop him up and ruffle his hair. The manly daring that results in really big explosions that shake the earth and leave only a trembling and helpless pile of rubble. Somebody get us a cigarette. And who could overlook the seductive sight of Mel as a kilted Scot on the Highlands at sunset bidding us to kiss him farewell before he slices and dices every Brit that dares threaten our beloved homeland? And, of course, the secrets beneath that kilt, revealed, unfortunately, only at a distance and then in a long shot. If only our VCR had a zoom function! ▪

▪ ***Funny Girl*** *(1968)*

Stars: Omar Sharif, Barbra Streisand, Kay Medford, Walter Pidgeon
Director: William Wyler
Writer: Isobel Lennart, based on her play

Thrown out of a chorus line because she's got skinny legs and a nose with deviation (hardly a crime against the nation, as Mama sings to her in one of the film's many classic musical numbers), Fanny Brice (Streisand) is determined to be the greatest star (as she sings in another classic musical number) and earn a spot in the Ziegfeld Follies. Luckily, her ceiling-raising declaration of self-esteem (another classic musical number) catches the ear of the director, who casts her in a roller-skate number (you guessed it—classic musical number). When her klutziness draws roars and an impromptu solo (okay, you get the point . . .) draws cheers, Fanny's path becomes clear—comedy, with plenty of, yes, classic musical numbers to feature her dazzling voice. Of course, Fanny does a bit of tinkering with her costumes and stage directions for entertainment value, but her instincts are dead-on. Except, of course, when it comes to men (sound familiar?). Enter Nicky Arnstein

---

Stupid Guy Quotes

First of all Rat, you never let on how much you like a girl. "Oh, Debbie. Hi." Two, you always call the shots. "Kiss me. You won't regret it." Now three, act like wherever you are, that's the place to be. "Isn't this great?" Four, when ordering food, you find out what she wants, then order for the both of you. It's a classy move. "Now, the lady will have the linguini and white clam sauce, and a Coke with no ice." And five, now this is the most important, Rat. When it comes down to making out, whenever possible, put on side one of Led Zeppelin IV.

★ Robert Romanus as Mike Damone in *Fast Times at Ridgemont High*

I love the sea, so beautiful, so mysterious . . . so full of fish.

★ Kevin Kline as Luc in *French Kiss*

Stupid Guy Quotes

A lady with no children is the very best preserver of furniture in the world.

★ David Collings as Mr. Shepherd in *Persuasion*

The world is collapsing outside. And I have an erection.

★ Daniel Day-Lewis as Fergus O'Connell in *Eversmile, New Jersey*

(Sharif), a brown-eyed, wealthy, and handsome gentleman who couldn't possibly be interested in her, could he?

With his ruffled shirt, suave mustache, seductive demeanor, and no perceptible fear of commitment, Nick seems too good to be true. And of course, he is: He's a professional high-stakes gambler with a cloud of doom hanging over him. Damn—couldn't he just handle her appointments and fan mail? Try maintaining a healthy relationship dynamic with a fella who owes everyone all over town while you're pulling down the big bucks. Poor Barbra. Well, at least she can pour her heart out . . . in a classic musical number.

World-Class Wrecks

Of course, you won't be able to lie on your back for a while, but then you can lie from any position, can't you?

★ Audrey Hepburn as Regina Lampert in *Charade*

■ ***The Postman Always Rings Twice*** *(1981)*
Stars: Jack Nicholson, Jessica Lange
Director: Bob Rafelson
Writer: David Mamet, based on the novel by James M. Cain

Frank (Jack Nicholson), an itinerant drifter with the obligatory five o'clock shadow and crumpled fedora full of broken dreams, is picked up hitchhiking by a dyspeptic motorist in search of a digestive. They pull over at a shabby roadhouse for a Bromo-Fizz and a blue plate special, but Frank finds more served up with his eggs than a side of toast. The moment he sets his bloodshot eyes on the beautiful but unfulfilled Cora (Jessica Lange) hovering over a grill full of corned beef hash and unrealized sexual potential, Frank realizes his drifting days are over.

You know, of course, what happens next, don't you? After all, who could resist a noir Nicholson, sating his inner hunger with a meal he can't afford to pay for? Sure enough, Cora, who has spent the better part of her youth married to a elderly Athenian with a passion for the balalaika and neon signage, recognizes that beneath all that road dust and flop sweat is her very own Prince Charming come to preach the gospel of multiple orgasms and rescue her from her short-order life. But first, they've got to do something about Cora's husband.

This movie sheds new light on a host of age-old adages like "look what the cat dragged in," "what goes around comes around," "it's not the meat it's the motion," and "beware of Greeks bearing gifts."

Chapter 3

I Hate My Life and I'm Moving to Bora Bora: Seeking Greener Pastures Movies

It's hell, isn't it? The kids, the job, *him*, the lines at the grocery store, the meaningless streets lined with monotonous bungalows containing a thousand million banal, anonymous lives just like yours. Maybe you're suffocating in a small town, or descending into a downward spiral of misanthropic angst while you wander lost in a big city. Sometimes a gal can't help but think that the grass is greener anywhere but here. But do you really need to throw it all away and start over from scratch?

Take our advice. Put down that packing tape before someone gets hurt and try some cinematherapy before doing anything drastic. In our "Armchair Traveling" films, unlike in real life, you can enjoy thrilling escapes that don't threaten your real-life status quo.

Now, if these don't work for you, you may need something stronger to stop planning a fantasy escape and start dealing with your reality. If you're still pining to move somewhere over the rainbow, check out our "There's No Place Like Home" section. If that doesn't work, bump yourself up to our prescription-only "In Case of Emergency" films, which offer some far less drastic solutions to your dilemma than major relocations and career changes.

Armchair Traveling

Much as you'd like to move to Bora Bora and become a turtle farmer, deep down you know that a vicarious two-hour thrill is a better bet and won't use up so many frequent flyer miles (Bora Bora is, after all, on the other side of the international dateline). Here are some films that offer an excellent armchair-traveling experience. Send us a postcard!

- ***Out of Africa*** *(1985)*
  Stars: Robert Redford, Meryl Streep
  Director: Sydney Pollack
  Writer: Kurt Luedtke, based on the memoir by Isak Dinesen

Karen Blixen (played by Meryl Streep sporting yet another meticulously rendered foreign accent) eschews the restrictive life of a Victorian Danish spinster, and buys a dairy farm in Africa with Bror, her new huband and unfaithful lover's brother. As if this preposterous configuration is not enough, when she arrives at the foot of the Ngong Hills, she discovers that Bror has no intention of raising cattle at all, but intends to plant coffee. Then, when the monotony of the long African rainy season sets in, Bror opts out in favor of an extended safari in the remotest corners of darkest Africa, without sowing a single bean.

Exit Bror, enter Denys (Robert Redford), a fair-haired, azure-eyed Alexander with the appetite of an adventurer, the soul of a mystic, and the heart of a true friend. This combination, not surprisingly, sets Karen's stoic Danish heart aflutter. Unfortunately, Denys is also in love with prolonged stays in remote locations, miles from the nearest phone. He disappears for months in the company of his inscrutable Kikuyu guide without so much as a by-your-leave. And then he just miraculously rematerializes on the verandah one day, without any advance warning, expecting not only dinner but a good story over brandy and cigars!

We know—the sweeping Ngong rain forests on the other side of the fence can look mighty green, particularly when you are watching them in Technicolor. And, yes, Robert Redford does look like a young god as he makes his way over the hilltop, the savannah sun crowning his golden curls. But at least when your significant other is late for dinner, you don't have to journey two hundred miles on the back of an oxcart to find out why.

▪ ***Witness*** *(1985)*
Stars: Harrison Ford, Kelly McGillis, Lukas Haas
Director: Peter Weir
Writers: William Kelley, Earl Wallace, and Pamela Wallace

Samuel Lapp, a young Amish boy, witnesses a murder while on a rare trip to the big city with his mother Rachel (Kelly McGillis). John Book (Harrison Ford), a soulful cop with a big-city lifestyle and a small-town heart, must go undercover in the heart of Pennsylvania Dutch country to protect Rachel and her son from a band of vicious killers bent on silencing young Samuel forever. And, of course, yet another reconstructed Romeo and Juliet scenario ensues, as John Book learns how to speak "plain" and Rachel learns the words to "What a Wonderful World This Would Be," much to the consternation of her disapproving father.

The next time you feel like trading in your suburban lifestyle for a stint in the country, watch this film and remind yourself that while the simple life may sound poetic, getting back to basics means dealing with long hours in front of a hot stove for no pay, a whole lot of cow manure, and a damned slim selection of reading materials. After watching this film, the parking lot at the A&P will look like paradise on earth.

Pithy Provincial Proverbs

She batted them pretty little eyes at you, and you fell for it like an egg from a tall chicken!

★ James Coburn as Tex Panthollow in *Charade*

Jersey Jokes

Go back to Jersey. This is the City of Angels and you haven't got any wings.

★ James Cromwell as Dudley Smith in *L.A. Confidential*

Easy, Sport. I got myself out of Beirut once. I think I can get out of New Jersey.

★ Geena Davis as Charly in *The Long Kiss Goodnight*

CIGARETTE GIRL: ***Susan! My God, we thought you were dead.***

SUSAN: ***No, just in New Jersey.***

★ from *Desperately Seeking Susan*

■ ***Belle de Jour*** *(1967)*

Stars: Catherine Deneuve, Pierre Clementi

Director: Luis Buñuel

Writer: Jean-Claude Carrière, based on the book by Joseph Kessel

Catherine Deneuve, in a fog of classic French ennui, flies the lush confines of her bourgeois milieu to investigate life as a high priced call girl. By day she dabbles in the unspeakable appetites of the debauched French aristocracy. By night she hosts fastidious dinner parties for her unsuspecting husband.

In a typical Luis Buñuel head-on collision between the grotesque and the sublime, the real and the imagined, her worlds ultimately slam into each other, turning Deneuve's canvas, and yours, into a Dalíesque wet dream. Despite the fact that it's virtually impossible to follow the plot line of this free-associative homage to the underbelly, it'll give you at least three more good reasons to despise the French, and ought to nip right in the bud that second-honeymoon-to-Paris scheme you've been secretly cherishing. After watching this movie, you'll be thrilled with a fishing weekend in Wisconsin.

▪ ***Roman Holiday*** *(1953)*
Stars: Audrey Hepburn, Gregory Peck
Director: William Wyler
Writers: Ian McLellan Hunter (front for Dalton Trombo) and John Dighton

Oh, it's all so tiresome, really: standing in those endless reception lines, donning those heavy jewel-encrusted tiaras, waltzing away night after night with minor European nobility and diplomats. The princess (Hepburn) has just *got* to get away, and though she passes out on the streets somewhere near the Coliseum, pickpockets and thugs are nowhere to be found. Instead, she is rescued by a dashing prince—well, okay, he's a reporter (Peck), but in the presence of the princess he's compelled to go above and beyond the call of a mere gentleman, taking her on a wildly exhilarating ride through the cacophonous Roman streets on the back of a motor scooter.

Hey, how come *we* never had dates like this? And how come our impetuous, I've-just-got-to-have-a-change haircuts from an unknown hairdresser off some side street never looked like this? And how come we never have occasion to wear jewel-encrusted tiaras?

Squelch your superego, immerse your id, and pretend that you are Audrey Hepburn for a day. In tiara or out, she's having a lot more fun than you are.

▪ ***The Big Easy*** *(1987)*
Stars: Dennis Quaid, Ellen Barkin
Director: Jim McBride
Writer: Daniel Petrie, Jr.

Oh, no, *cher.* No, no. Don't be shy. Let Remy guide you to the Big Easy. Then he can show you New Orleans. Let Remy show you how to bite the head and suck the tips, so you'll be just like one of the locals. And he'll show you how to eat crawfish too.

Cop Remy McSwain (Dennis Quaid) may be on the take in this atmospheric thriller, but it's easy to forgive a man who's named after a fine, aged cognac, whose six-pack stomach fairly glows in the New Orleans lamplight, and who can emerge from the bayou in a perfectly fitting, bone-dry jeans and sweatshirt combo (hey, we don't sweat continuity down here, *cher*). Ellen Barkin plays the uptight New York internal affairs investigator whose internal affairs Remy begins investigating. Can you spell G-spot?

If you can't swing a trip to New Orleans, try out one of those Prudhomme recipes on a hot summer night, don an oversized men's shirt, and slow it down, *cher*—nice and easy.

Classic Party Repartee

"So listen, Fred baby—"
"Uh, it's* Paul *baby."
"Oh, is it? I thought it was 'Fred baby.'"

★ from *Breakfast at Tiffany's*

▪ ***Beyond Rangoon*** *(1995)*
Stars: Patricia Arquette, U Aung Ko, Frances McDormand
Director: John Boorman
Writers: Alex Lasker and Bill Rubenstein

Your husband has just died, your life's fallen apart, and the last thing you need is a trip to Burma, but your sister's been in your face about getting out and rediscovering life, so you figure, okay, okay, God only knows where the hell Burma is, but maybe I'll die of some tropical disease and be put out of my abject misery. A little night breeze, the magical influence of exotic nature, the stirring sight of a local political march, and suddenly you've gotten separated from the tour group and you're swept up in a revolution, dodging bullets with a sensitive and handsome university professor and running for the Thai border.

After watching a little of this, your problems back home won't seem quite so overwhelming. Why not whip up some coconut shrimp and watch from a safe distance?

Are You Moving Anytime Soon? Cinema Apartments We Covet

As you sit in your cramped little apartment, focused in on that tiny TV screen, what better way to enjoy a fabulous home without a rent increase than to vicariously enjoy these groovy movie pads?

Single White Female

Refinished wood floors, a fabulous view, original woodwork, an affordable rent—all on Manhattan's Upper West Side. Definitely worth killing your roommate over.

Holiday

Kate Hepburn is desperate to escape the stultifying life in her family's Park Avenue apartment, but if she's willing to give up the Greek statuary in the hallway, the elevator to the upper floors (upper floors! in your own apartment!), the art deco interiors, and that wonderfully inviting music room, we'll take it any day.

Pillow Talk

Interior designer Doris Day wants to get back at Rock Hudson for his sleazy bachelor-on-the-make ways, and she does it by turning his apartment into a garish funhouse complete with purple carpeting, orange paint, animal print throws, hanging drapery cords that are apparently attached to nothing, a moosehead, beaded curtains, and a mauve player piano. Okay, it's the pinnacle of bad taste, but wouldn't it be fun for parties? Think of the cool people your bohemian quarters would attract.

. . . continued

How to Marry a Millionaire

Three gals sublease a Park Avenue apartment with huge wooden doors and a terrace with a breathtaking view of Manhattan. Of course, to pay the rent they've got to hock every stick of furniture in the place, but isn't that a small price to play for this incredible space? After all, they're all going to marry millionaires—until then, they can deal with folding chairs and card tables.

Female

A pipe organ mounted on the wall in the foyer, an art deco swimming pool regularly frequented by Adonis-like underlings, a series of buzzers to summon a servant with a tray of vodka, bearskin rugs and satin pillows for after-dinner parties for two, and a nice big round bed. We like the kind of entertaining a working gal could do in a place like this.

Splitting Heirs

Forgettable movie, unforgettable apartment. We're talking about the one that belongs to Eric Idle's lover. Clean lines, a white bed on top of a white step-up platform as the focal piece, and behind the plate-glass wall behind the bed? A one-lane swimming pool, so she can do a few laps as soon as she wakes up in the morning. No more fighting for a lane at Vic Tanney! ■

■ ***Breakfast at Tiffany's*** *(1961)*
Stars: Audrey Hepburn, George Peppard, Buddy Ebsen, Patricia Neal
Director: Blake Edwards
Writer: George Axelrod, based on the novel by Truman Capote

New York handed her a magic wand and with a wave of her hand the backwoods and barefoot Lulamae became the mesmerizing, sophisticated, wild-thing-with-an-upsweep Holly Golightly, who can carry off twelve-inch cigarette holders and looks equally scrumptious in a simple black dress or a cakelike pink confection with matching shoes and tiara (well, she *is* Audrey Hepburn, after all). Like her cat, which she doesn't actually own (who *does* own a cat?), Holly cherishes her freedom and independence, but she is nevertheless determined to marry a wealthy man and secure her future, even if she has to learn to conjugate Portuguese verbs to nab him.

One day, the aspiring writer/gigolo next door (Peppard) joins Holly in her regular indulgence: morning window-shopping on Fifth Avenue (a ritual that keeps her spirits up). The battle lines are drawn: the cynicism of age versus the optimism of youth. Damnation to the ¾-sleeve-suited, stiff-haired patron (Neal) and the yearning ghost of the limited-options past (Ebsen), for New York is the transforming fountain of youth. Throw a zebra-skin rug on the floor and pump that rhumba music, then spread your wings and fly.

> ⚠ Warning Label: *You'll have to set your stomach for Mickey Rooney's cartoonishly racist portrayal of Holly's bucktoothed Chinese neighbor.*

There's No Place Like Home

So you've talked yourself into it, have you? You're convinced that if you leave it all behind you, everything and everybody that's driving you nuts, you can overcome your repetition compulsion and start your life over with a clean slate. Our advice is watch one of our "There's No Place Like Home" movies, put down your one-way ticket, and think again.

■ ***The Stepford Wives*** (1975)
Stars: Katharine Ross, Paula Prentiss, Peter Masterson
Director: Bryan Forbes
Writer: William Goldman, based on the novel by Ira Levin

Much as *Poltergeist* elevated New England architecture to the level of the demonic, this movie forever immortalizes the high-collared, prairie-inspired maxidresses as an archetype of Satanic conformity.

Think you're ready to give up the fast-paced urban lifestyle for a nice, quiet home in the suburbs? Watch this before dialing that real estate agent.

In this creepy flick, Ross humors her husband (mistake #1) and leaves NYC for suburban Connecticut (mistake #2). She tries to maintain her budding photography career while she lets hubby go off to some mysterious men's club (mistake #3). Finally, she does something right and befriends one of the few women in town who has spirit, intellect, and an adult female sexuality. At first she and her friend laugh at these wind-up-doll suburbanites obsessing over furniture polish, but as more and more of the neighbors begin donning the above-mentioned fashion archetype, they realize something truly evil is going on.

A terrifying horror film which proves that blood and mutilation have nothing on the suburban American lifestyle.

▪ ***Peyton Place*** *(1957)*

Stars: Lana Turner, Hope Lange, Arthur Kennedy, Lloyd Nolan
Director: Mark Robson
Writer: John Michael Hayes, based on the novel by Grace Metalious

It's a charming little New England town, with those brilliant colors on the trees in the fall and the quaint steepled church. But underneath it festers an oozing sore of hypocrisy. Tawdry affairs amongst the most prominent of citizens. Cruel gossip spread by churchgoing busybodies. And worst of all, the young people—our young people! They're necking in cars, pouring rum into the party punch, and associating with youngsters from undesirable families, like that tramp in the red dress who everyone just knows has gone all the way. Oh, the horror of it all!

Just when Lana Turner's frigidity and the bubblegum dilemmas of this film start seeming a little too histrionic, the real scandal breaks. You can practically see the shocking B-movie headlines flash across the screen—incest! rape! abortion! murder! Too bad the writers left out those herbal jazz cigarettes because these folks could really use a little lightening up. By the time the good old family doctor makes his solemn soapbox speech exhorting the townspeople to raise themselves up from their sordid little activities, you'll be glad that whatever your particular hell, at least you live in the age of irony.

Guy Films That Are Actually Gal Films

They say women hate movies with chase scenes, explosions, or cowboys with six-guns blasting away. Well, maybe for the most part that is true, but certainly there are a few exceptions to the rule, such as:

True Lies *(1994)*
Stars: Arnold Schwarzenegger, Jamie Lee Curtis, Tom Arnold, Tia Carrere
Director: James Cameron
Writers: Didier Kaminka, Simon Michaël, Claude Zidi, and James Cameron

He's just never home, is he? He's never on time. And he's practically a stranger to his own child. Maybe he's having an affair? Or plagued by feelings of incompetence and trying to compensate by working harder rather than emotionally connecting with the woman who is supposed to be his life partner, thereby reducing their marriage to a shell of the passion that once brought you together?

And then again, maybe he's not.

Maybe he's really an elegant man of the world—a glamorous secret agent who's just trying to protect the gals he loves and the greatest country in the world. In which case, the only solution to his wife's unhappiness is to let her have a little fun escaping the clutches of international terrorists and foiling their plans to blow up something for no particular reason.

As much a spoof of action movies as a screwball love story, and Curtis is hilarious as the mousy wife turned Bond Girl. Sure to inspire some fun horseplay with your own secret agent man.

The Long Kiss Goodnight *(1996)*
Stars: Geena Davis, Samuel L. Jackson
Director: Renny Harlin
Writer: Shane Black

. . . continued

Cookie-baking suburban Jersey housewife gets hit on the head and discovers new talents, like cracking the neck of a full-rack buck, throwing knives like James Coburn (see *The Magnificent Seven*), and chopping vegetables like a sushi chef. Before she can apply for a job at Benihana's, the rest of it all comes back (with the help of some hit men who are chasing her): The personality she left behind eight years ago during another head injury is Charly Baltimore, Cold War operative and trained assassin. Clearly, it's time for a short and sassy bleached-blond look, pelvis-bumping with her cut-rate PI sidekick (Jackson), and a cigarette. So much to do, so many to kill, and it would probably be a good deed to save the kid as well while she's at it since the urchin is, after all, her own flesh and blood.

Delightfully implausible, with lots of explosions, ridiculous escapes, and plenty of funny, sexy rapport.

The Magnificent Seven *(1960)*
Stars: Yul Brynner, James Coburn, Steve McQueen, Charles Bronson, Eli Wallach, Robert Vaughn
Director: John Sturges
Writer: William Roberts, based on the screenplay Shichinin no Samurai *by Akira Kurosawa*

Though it's touted as a classic western, or a clever remake of *The Seven Samurai*, we maintain *The Magnificent Seven* is actually a shameless propaganda film promoting the virtues of tubby suburban husbands while teasing us with sexy, unattainable gunslingers. Given a choice between a chubby, emasculated farmer in white cotton pajamas and the serpentine James Coburn, who can casually fling a knife straight into a target from ten paces, or whippet-thin Yul Brynner, encased in all black, who can calmly sip a whiskey as a bullet passes in front of his eyes, only a male screenwriter would choose the domesticated lunks as the true heroes. All right, we'll be p.c. and root for the asexual farmers, but why hit us over the head with

. . . continued

broad-shouldered Charles Bronson's earnest speech to the boys of the defenseless village about shouldering the burden of responsibility? Nothing against domesticity, but can it really compete with the slapping on of leather gunbelts and a steady hand on a powerful pistol? ▪

In Case of Emergency

All right, so you tried armchair traveling and you're still hell-bent on getting out. But what if after all is said and done you find yourself quoting Dorothy Parker—"What fresh hell is this?"

Try these last-resort In Case of Emergency movies and see if you don't come to a less extreme solution than chucking it all—like, say, a vacation or a shopping spree.

▪ ***Enchanted April*** *(1991)*
Stars: Miranda Richardson, Joan Plowright
Director: Mike Newell
Writer: Peter Barnes, based on the novel by Elizabeth von Arnim

Those who appreciate wisteria, sunshine, and staffed, furnished Italianate castles on the shores of the Mediterranean should luxuriate in this film. *Enchanted April* will convince you that all marital troubles, identity crises, and personal traumas can be cured by a cup of tea and a parasol—and a loooong vacation. As one wearied guest tells herself, "I just want to get my feathers smooth again." Indulge, dearest. Make your reservations now and start preening.

▪ ***Desperately Seeking Susan*** *(1985)*
Stars: Madonna, Rosanna Arquette
Director: Susan Seidelman
Writer: Leora Barish

Look, we know you're sick of her, and if you hear one more time about how cutting-edge she always is, you're going to launch a primal scream. But remember, Madonna-bashing is not proper millennium thinking. We have to replace our feelings of hatred with feelings of light and love. We have to look beyond the current Stevie Nicks incarnation to the heart of the frightened soul beneath, who stands in terror on the precipice of cultural obsolescence. We have to see past the barrettes and the side parts and the self-indulgent spirituality to the restless seeker at her core, and remember what she used to be. We have to hold in our hearts that one brief, shining moment when we all believed that being a boy toy was really cool, and that getting a new "look" meant we were reinventing ourselves, as opposed to recycling.

Of course we wanted a sexy, confident, feminist role model, and how could we foresee that following the Material Girl's example would result in our looking like a bad imitation of Pebbles Flintstone in cheap underwear? We know—you're still recovering from the sight of yourself. But you have to admit, it was fun, wasn't it? And so is *Desperately Seeking Susan*.

Madonna's iconoclasm is forever enshrined in this movie about a bored housewife (Rosanna Arquette) who, through a circuitous plot, takes on the persona of street-smart Susan (you guessed it—Madonna) and becomes sassy, sexy, and self-confident before coming to the realization that she possessed those qualities all along. She only had to click her proverbial ruby slippers—just like you.

> ⚠ Warning Label: *Going in search of your wild self often involves canvasing musty racks of used clothing in tiny boutiques on the Lower East Side of Manhattan and looking like an idiot. Be brave, and remember, you can always burn the negatives.*

Chapter 4

I Know She's My Mom, But She's Driving Me Nuts: Mother-Issue Movies

She did it again, didn't she? Yeah, well, what did you expect? She's always gonna do it. Even though you try to talk to her about it rationally. Even though you've explained in a non-confrontational manner the way you feel when she does it. She's just gonna go right on ahead anyway and do whatever she damn well pleases, just like she's always done. She can't help it. It's practically biological. She's congenitally stubborn. And the worst part is, so are you. And guess what? You're becoming your mother. And you can't help yourself. Maybe you should call her and sort this whole thing out right now. Or maybe you should just go back into denial, pop in one of these mother-issue movies, and forget this whole thing ever happened.

- ***The Glass Menagerie*** *(1987)*
  Stars: Joanne Woodward, John Malkovich, Karen Allen, James Naughton
  Director: Paul Newman
  Writer: Tennessee Williams

Joanne Woodward plays Amanda Wingfield, a faded jonquil of the southern delta, who is obsessed with the idea of finding her daughter a husband. Amanda has gotten it into her Georgia cotton brain that a suitable son-in-law will rescue them all from penury and despair. Amanda's attempts to transform her stutter-tongued, club-footed, butterfly-stomached, glass-animal-identified, never-been-kissed daughter into a memory of her own wasted fecundity threaten to fracture Laura's (played by Karen Allen) fragile bloom entirely. . . . And Laura's cigarette-smoking, bourbon-nipping, overly-ornate-prose-composing daydreamer of a brother (played by John Malkovich in yet another forelock-falling-in-his-face wig) doesn't do her much good either.

This movie is the apotheosis of the daughter-as-ultimate-victim genre, told in the lazy lyricism of the bayou, as only Tennessee can. Celebrate the slaughter! Next time your mother's love threatens to cut you off at the legs, limp on over to your nearest video store, and try this one on for size. If the shoe fits . . . and you know it will . . . watch it!

■ *Postcards From the Edge* (1990)

Stars: Meryl Streep, Shirley MacLaine, Dennis Quaid, Gene Hackman
Director: Mike Nichols
Writer: Carrie Fisher

This coming-of-age-and-out-of-mom's-shadow movie is a loosely fictionalized autobiography of Carrie Fisher's life as the star-stunted daughter of America's sweetheart, Debbie Reynolds. Shirley MacLaine is Doris Mann, a turban-wearing, white-wine-swigging star in decline, who insists on above-the-title billing in her own life as well as her daughter's.

As the movie opens, Suzanne, whose urinalysis reads like the barbiturate section of the *Physicians' Desk Reference*, has nearly died of a drug overdose, and as a result must rebuild her shattered career and stay sober. To make matters worse, she must also find a way to peacefully cohabitate with her mother. As all of us daughters of divas know, this scenario has all the makings of an Elizabethan revenge tragedy, climaxing with the mutilated corpse of the protagonist's self-image strewn across the stage of an antagonistic mother's narcissism. Fortunately, this is the Disney version, and Suzanne manages to find her way out of the heartbreak hotel of her childhood without flights of angels singing her, or anybody else, to their rest.

▪ ***Terms of Endearment*** *(1983)*
Stars: Debra Winger, Shirley MacLaine, Jack Nicholson
Director: James L. Brooks
Writers: James L. Brooks and Larry McMurtry

Shirley MacLaine stars as yet another larger-than-life, self-involved, insatiable mother. The kind who is never happy, no matter who her daughter marries, or what she wears, or how many children she has. Aurora Greenway, a profuse southern peony gone to seed, is so inappropriately attached to the daughter whom she perpetually disapproves of that her daughter, Emma (Debra Winger), must resort to an untimely death just to get her boundary-busting mother off her back.

And then she's sorry. Oh yeah, then she remembers all those little things that Emma used to do for her that went unappreciated, unremarked. And that no-good husband of hers gets a pretty good dose of remorse too. This is a martyred daughter and wife's dream!

Passive Aggressive Mom Moments

DORIS: ***Well, pain is gain.***
SUZANNE: ***No wonder I'm so hefty.***
DORIS: ***Well if you ask me I think you're too thin.***
SUZANNE: ***I was just kidding.***
DORIS: ***I just don't get your generation.***
SUZANNE: ***I don't have a generation.***
DORIS: ***Then I think you need to get one.***

★ Meryl Streep and Shirley MacLaine in *Postcards From the Edge*

Famous Last Words

Oh, I'll change, Mother. I promise. I'll never say mean things to you again.

★ Daughter Veda (Ann Blyth) to her mother, Mildred Pierce (Joan Crawford), in *Mildred Pierce*

■ *'Night, Mother (1986)*

Stars: Sissy Spacek, Anne Bancroft
Director: Tom Moore
Writer: Marsha Norman

In this ode to a doormat, Sissy Spacek stars as Jessie, an epileptic, beleaguered, suicidal daughter of the South. (Speaking of the South, what's going on below the Mason-Dixon line with all these homicidal mothers? Is it something in the water?) Anyway, trapped in a joyless life and an unflattering housedress, she methodically prepares the home she and her mother share to function after she kills herself. She sets all the alarm clocks to 6:04, cancels the newspapers, cleans the science experiments out of the refrigerator, and stocks the cupboards with the most obscene smorgasbord of simple carbohydrates the world has ever seen: sour balls, horehound, licorice, snowballs, toffee, thin mints, peanut brittle, marshmallows . . . the list, like her mother's appetites, is practically limitless. No question about it, Jessie's got precious little to live for, and as if the cloying details of her mother's sugar fixation aren't excruciating enough, she's also got a ruined marriage, a felonious son, and the most volumeless hairdo that ever lay limp and lifeless across the silver screen (although Kathy Bates's hair in *Misery* comes close; as a matter of fact, she played the role of Jessie on Broadway—is this typecasting by hair texture or what?).

As Jessie sticks instructional Post-it notes across the countertops of her mother's life, Thelma (Anne Bancroft) frantically tries to talk her daughter out of her plan, but succeeds only in convincing Jessie, and us, that if given a choice between death and a life spent feeding the relentless appetites of a mother like this, death is probably a much more desirable option.

Faking It: Phony Gal Films That Really Piss Us Off

How to Make an American Quilt *(1995)*
Stars: Winona Ryder, Ellen Burstyn, Anne Bancroft, Maya Angelou, Kate Nelligan, Jean Simmons, Samantha Mathis, Alfre Woodard, Dermot Mulroney
Director: Jocelyn Moorhouse
Writer: Jane Anderson, based on the novel by Whitney Otto

You can't seem to focus on your dissertation, you're feeling pressured by your fiancé to throw away your career and get down to the business of procreating, and so you take refuge among quilting maternal figures. You hear stories of love, heartache, and triumph, and learn that true love and happiness is to be found by following the flight of a blackbird. Hello? Don't bother negotiating with your partner about whether to turn your extra room into an office or a nursery. Just watch for a starling crossing your path and bingo! Resolution.

In your dreams, old women. ■

⚠ Warning Label: *Don't listen to your elders.*

■ ***Frances*** *(1982)*
Stars: Jessica Lange, Kim Stanley, Sam Shepard
Director: Graeme Clifford
Writers: Eric Bergren, Christopher DeVore, and Nicholas Kazan

Jessica Lange shrieks, rages, seethes, and howls her way through this bio-pic about the pugilistic Frances Farmer, an actress with B-list credits and an A-list temper. Frances, who is something like a cross between Marilyn Monroe without the mood adjustors and a post-Symbionese Patty Hearst, takes on the empty glamour of Hollywood, the hypocrisy of small-town American life, the furnace of the American family, and the empty rhetoric of the Group Theatre in an attempt to infuse her life with genuine meaning.

As a consequence of her uncensored style, and a conflicted relationship with her debauched antebellum (yup, she's southern too), homicidal mother (played by Kim Stanley), Frances—and you—are in for the wail of a lifetime.

■ ***This Is My Life*** *(1992)*
Stars: Julie Kavner, Samantha Mathis, Gaby Hoffman, Carrie Fisher
Director: Nora Ephron
Writers: Delia Ephron and Nora Ephron, based on the novel by Meg Wolitzer

It's hard enough for a teenager (Mathis as Erica Ingels) to establish a separate identity from her mother, but when mom's a would-be stand-up comic named Dottie (Kavner), who drapes herself in polka dots ("Dottie"—get it?), flaps about in chicken suits for commercials, and tells placenta jokes, it's time to seriously consider changing your last name.

Frankly, however, Erica's discomfort with "that spotted woman" will be nothing compared to yours as you wince through Kavner's embarrassing stand-up bits. If you can ignore the implausibility of Dottie's getting beyond performing at the Macy's makeup counter on Queens Boulevard with this pathetic material, you may enjoy this tale of a cringe-inducing mother who is perpetually laying an egg. Don't let your own mom watch it, though: It's just the kind of film that'll give her dangerous ideas about new career possibilities.

■ ***Drop Dead Fred*** *(1991)*
Stars: Phoebe Cates, Rik Mayall, Marsha Mason
Director: Ate De Jong
Writers: Carlos Davis and Anthony Fingleton

On their own, Mayall's juvenile antics, which are pure scatology, are enough to inspire a bad case of gas. But don't let it put you off from the story here: Nice girl (Cates), whose overbearing and anal retentive mother has doomed her to a life of being dumped upon, is jilted by her fiancé, fired from her job, and subjected to a mother–daughter makeover so creepy it will strike terror into the hearts of daughters everywhere. When Cates's repressed rage manifests itself as the reappearance of her childhood imaginary friend, she struggles valiantly to put the genie back in the bottle—and find an effective carpet cleaner before Mom gets home and sees what her subconscious rage has done to the brand-new blizzard-white Berber!

■ ***Mommie Dearest*** *(1981)*
Stars: Faye Dunaway, Diana Scarwid
Director: Frank Perry
Writers: Robert Getchell, Tracy Hotchner, Frank Perry, and Frank Yablans, based on the autobiography of Christina Crawford

It's hard to imagine laughing at a film about child abuse, but Dunaway as Crawford is so over the top with her square red lips, mouse-size eyebrows, quarterback shoulders, and camp histrionics ("No wire hangers! No wire hangers everrrrr!") that you'll find yourself snickering at the cheap emotions as well as the cheap production values (check out little Christina's ridiculous wigs, which slip whenever Mommie Dearest starts choking her).

Sinister, stupid, and made-for-TV silly (it's hard to believe the producers were serious about this!), it'll make anyone's mom look damn good by comparison. Watch it with your own mommie dearest—afterward, the two of you can bond with a mother–daughter pruning in the rose garden.

Passive Aggressive Mom Moments

I'm not mad at you! I'm mad at the dirt!

★ Faye Dunaway as Joan Crawford in *Mommie Dearest*

■ ***Aliens*** *(1986)*
Stars: Sigourney Weaver, Paul Reiser
Director: James Cameron
Writers: Walter Hill and James Cameron, based on a story by James Cameron and David Giler

When a money-grubbing capitalist pig (Reiser) endangers innocent colonists by exposing them to the dreaded alien, Ridley (Weaver) has got to clean things up—again.

Honestly, is her work never done? She takes under her wing the sole survivor of the massacre, Newt, a quick-witted, terrified little blond child for whom Ridley will slaughter whatever drooling creature comes near. Donning a machine that makes her monster-like herself, she goes at the alien shrew, whose secretions drip as a phallic appendage rises to spear the male android, slicing him open to expose a flood of gooey white stuff. Bodily fluids spew and maternal instincts rage.

> ⚠ Warning Label: *Not a good film to watch before your overbearing mother picks up the kids for the weekend.*

■ ***Dolores Claiborne*** *(1995)*
Stars: Kathy Bates, Jennifer Jason Leigh
Director: Taylor Hackford
Writer: Tony Gilroy, based on the novel by Stephen King

Why is it that just when your life is in complete turmoil, your piss-and-vinegar mother (who, thank God, is not southern) has to go open her big mouth and get herself investigated for murder, necessitating an incredibly ill-timed trip home to that godforsaken island where they don't have reliable phone lines?

Yeah, it's a fine mess she's gotten herself—and you—into, but somewhere deep down there's a part of you that knows just what she's been hiding. As Mom's homily goes, sometimes being a bitch is all a woman's got, and maybe it's time for a refresher course on the best use of that weapon.

> ⚠ Warning Label: *Do not point this weapon at yourself as it will result in negative drinking behaviors and major career setbacks.*

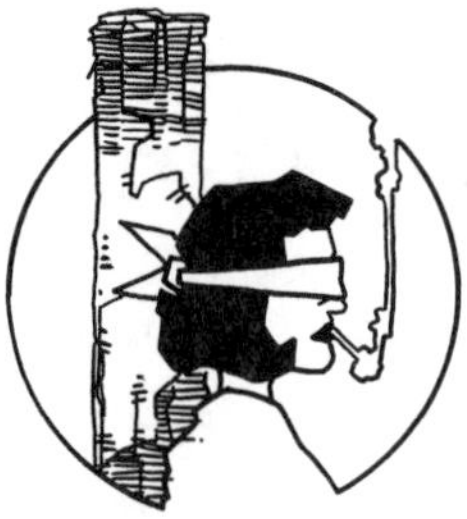

Famous Last Words . . . For Somebody

Sometimes an accident can be an unhappy woman's best friend.

★ Judy Parfitt as Vera Donovan in *Dolores Claiborne*

■ ***Secrets and Lies*** *(1996)*
Stars: Brenda Blethyn, Marianne Jean-Baptiste
Director: Mike Leigh
Writers: Mike Leigh and cast

There are so many possibilities an adoptee imagines when she contemplates her birth mother, but Hortense (Jean-Baptiste), an articulate, poised, recently orphaned black woman seeking her roots, was not exactly picturing a chain-smoking, shrillish Londoner with a bad dye job and an annoying propensity for calling everyone sweetheart, a pasty white woman who is, well, a few pickles short of a ploughman's lunch. First there's the initial mutual shock of discovery, there's the emotional triage to be performed after mom Cynthia's less than diplomatic way of breaking the news to the in-laws, and the matter of how to hammer out a relationship between the two women who are virtual strangers from opposite worlds. Then, too, the appearance of Hortense churns up the waters of Cynthia's entire family, bringing a lot of silt to the surface, exposing secrets that everyone wishes would just go away so they can continue with their dysfunctional status quo.

A great reminder of the power of secrets over lies. Now that it's all out on the table, too bad it doesn't neatly wrap up in one happy family package. But then, what would your therapist do for a living?

■ ***Autumn Sonata*** *(1978)*
Stars: Ingrid Bergman, Liv Ullman
Director: Ingmar Bergman
Writer: Ingmar Bergman, translator Alan Blair

You haven't seen her for seven years, and now you're thinking how terrific it will be to have her come for a nice long visit, so you can really know each other like you never did before, and develop that deeply fulfilling mother–daughter bond you've been missing.

Yes, you are suffering from a selective sort of amnesia in which memories of Mother's neglect and narcissism are successfully repressed, leaving you with serious intimacy issues and an identity crisis so severe that you've taken to wearing braids, granny glasses, and Peter Pan collars—or maybe that's just the Swedish version of this affliction.

Liv Ullman plays the dutiful daughter opening her arms and her home to her concert pianist mother (played by Ingrid Bergman), only to find that all those buried resentments—about dashing off to do the Mozart concerto or to have an eight-month fling while leaving her children and husband to fend for themselves—rise to the surface, thanks to insomnia and an extra glass of wine. And you think you have it bad? Try trading places with the sister with MS, who's no longer physically able to confront Mom except through desperate incoherent cries that go unheard from her bedroom down the hall.

Painful, raw, full of blotchy-skinned and visceral confrontations, with plenty of lines that will cut to the core of all your mother issues. What's worse, this is a Bergman film, so nothing moves, including the time. The writer attempts to generate some emotional activity by making Mom a fully dimensional, sympathetic character, so you'll have to throw guilt into the pot of your churning emotions and face the possibility of forgiveness.

Best watched early in the evening—this one isn't exactly warm milk before bed.

World-Class Wrecks

CYNTHIA: *I can still turn a few heads.*

ROXANNE: *. . . and a few stomachs!*

★ from *Secrets and Lies*

Chapter 5

But He Has Such Potential, and I Know That He Can Change: Earth Mother Movies

If only there wasn't so much pressure on him. If only he had more confidence in himself. If only he could let go of his anger and enjoy life a little. If only the power of your womanly love could heal him. If only pigs could fly and you could put aluminum foil in the microwave.

At least for a few hours, why not foster the fiction that men will change? Check out one of these Earth Mother movies and pretend that with just a little of your time and patience, any fellow who has lost his way in the world can be magically transformed into a whole, well-rounded man, glowing with inner peace and ready for the perfect relationship.

▪ ***Prince of Tides*** *(1991)*
Stars: Barbra Streisand, Nick Nolte, Blythe Danner, Kate Nelligan
Director: Barbra Streisand
Writers: Becky Johnston and Pat Conroy, based on the novel by Pat Conroy

Tom (Nick Nolte) comes from an abusive family and is woefully out of touch with his emotions as a consequence. He despises his mother, has a fractured relationship with his abusive father, and ignores his wife. He makes a joke out of everything, argues with his hat, and is subconsciously haunted by repressed memories of a childhood rape.

In other words, this guy is a real *mess*!

After his poetess sister, who is also a mess, attempts suicide (again), he goes to New York to try to help the psychiatrist (Barbra Streisand) get to the root of Savannah's pain. Not surprisingly, they end up spending a lot more time dealing with Nick's roots.

Lowenstein's psychiatric technique is characterized by catlike pacing across the confines of her office while she flexes her long, impeccably toned legs and wrings her perfectly manicured hands with concern.

The treatment works like a charm, and Tom is able to love again in no time. Unfortunately, there is still the little matter of his other family to deal with, and in the end Lowenstein, too, must learn that more than just salt water rolls in with the tide, no matter how close you are to the prince.

▪ ***Edward Scissorhands*** *(1990)*
Stars: Johnny Depp, Winona Ryder, Dianne Wiest
Director: Tim Burton
Writer: Caroline Thompson, based on a story by Tim Burton and Caroline Thompson

The bad news is, the man that this girl wants to rescue looks like a mime. The good news is, the mime is played by Johnny Depp, and if anybody could make a Marcel Marceauian sexy, it's Johnny.

Edward Scissorhands is a futuristic allegory about a New Age Frankenstein monster, with soulful eyes, drop-dead dimples, and garden shears for hands who spreads love and tasteful styling tips everywhere he goes, but cannot hold hands with his lady love (Winona Ryder) without causing permanent scarring. Mangled by circumstance, and the untimely death of his mad creator (Vincent Price), not to mention the evil genius of the film's mad director (Tim *Nightmare Before Christmas* Burton), Edward is doomed to a life without physical human contact. But then he is rescued from his isolation, like a maiden from the tower, and delivered to the suburbs by an Avon lady turned mom in shining armor (Dianne Wiest). There he spreads the gospel of kindness and asymmetrical hairdos.

And who needs hand-holding when you've got a guy who is gorgeous, sensitive, and causes women throughout the neighborhood to see God every time he layers and feathers? And hey—he does hedges too.

■ ***Dogfight*** *(1991)*
Stars: River Phoenix, Lili Taylor
Director: Nancy Savoca
Writer: Bob Comfort

When a good-looking, seemingly well-mannered marine nicknamed Birdlace (Phoenix) comes into her mother's restaurant and rescues her from an evening of marrying condiments, the painfully vulnerable Rose (Taylor) searches frantically through umpteen hideous 1963 party dresses and backcombs furiously—only to discover that the party he's invited her to is a viciously ugly prank. Rather than slink away, the outraged Rose, empowered by a clear inner beauty, lectures the jarhead on basic human decency. Chagrined, he spends the evening making it up to her and learns about the beauty of honor, respect, and truth—unfortunately, too late to get out of his stint slaughtering the Viet Cong, torching villages filled with innocents, and permanently wounding his mortal soul. Clearly, having a female folksinger in the White House could've prevented a major blight on America's conscience.

Swooningly romantic whenever the sweetly genuine Phoenix leans in for a kiss or Joan Baez begins singing in the background, *Dogfight* is a moving testament to the civilizing force of the feminine.

■ ***On the Waterfront*** *(1954)*
Stars: Marlon Brando, Eva Marie Saint, Karl Malden, Lee J. Cobb, Rod Steiger
Director: Elia Kazan
Writer: Budd Schulberg, based on a story by Budd Schulberg and magazine articles by Malcolm Johnson

You know the story: Young guy (Marlon Brando) works as a longshoreman down on the docks. Big strong arms, tattoo of a dragon or something on his left tricep, wounded, soulful eyes. He's a little bit punch-drunk from the blows he's taken on the chin, but he's sweet as honey, and he is all man.

And he's got so much potential. You know he does. You've watched him grow up in your neighborhood. You've seen the good in him and you remember when he was young and hopeful. And you've seen that light in him slowly start to flicker. If only he could believe in himself. If only he'd realize that everybody gets a second chance, even a second-rate club fighter who agreed to take a dive on his first title match because his brother told him to and wound up a loser, when he could have been a contender. If only he could get away from those horrible friends of his, that no-good brother, and that awful boss, Johnny Friendly (Lee J. Cobb).

Maybe if you get the priest (Karl Malden) involved. He respects the Church. Maybe the Father could get him to take a stand, and help him to redeem himself from a life of self-contempt.

In real life, a narrative logic such as this is a recipe for disaster, but in this movie, all the codependent passive aggressive tactics work, and Marlon Brando is healed by the power of his woman's love. . . . Only in the movies, gals . . . only in the movies.

■ ***Making Mr. Right*** *(1987)*
Stars: John Malkovich, Ann Magnuson
Director: Susan Seidelman
Writers: Floyd Byars and Laurie Frank

In this feminist retelling of the Pygmalion myth, Ulysses, an anatomically correct robot (played by John Malkovich in a bouffant platinum forelock-falling-in-his-face wig) is created to test the psychological effects of deep space upon the male psyche. But before he can go where no man has gone before, Ulysses must learn how to dress tastefully, how to behave in public, and how to experience real emotions.

In other words, he needs a girlfriend.

Enter Frankie Stone, a breezy, eighties-style lady ad executive (Ann Magnuson), who has freckles and panache to burn. She carries her Rolodex like a trendy clutch purse, and drives her vintage Mercury through an L.A traffic jam with a cellular in one hand and a

The Handy Hunk Chart Key

Hunk Ratings:

All-American Boy

The Wounded Soldier

BE = *Bedroom Eyes* **DMCA** = *Devil-May-Care Attitude* **FSG** = *Feckless Schoolboy Grin* **PBE** = *Piercing Blue Eyes* **RGH** = *Really Good Hair* **RUM** = *Raw Unpredictable Masculinity* **SIN** = *Smoldering, Inscrutable, and Noble* **TSHT** = *That Sexy Homicidal Thing* **UGB** = *Urban, Gritty, and Brooding*

The Handy Hunk Chart

Robert Redford

DMCA, FSG, PBE, RGH

Robert Redford is like the ur-Brad Pitt, the Alpha Hunk. The most gorgeous uptight WASPy guy to look into a lens and say cheese. Redford brilliantly straddles the fence, and how we'd love to be that fence. He's mischievous but never bad, questionable but never shady, heedless but always just this side of unpredictable. And, of course, there's that face. One could compose sonnets to his cheekbones, although they've grown a bit craggy of late. But in his prime they crowned his face like the Indian peaks, mirroring one another at dawn, calling to each other from east to west across the bridge of that cute button nose. He's the fair-haired boy next door grown up, honed to a little bit of an edge by the same high-altitude western sun that kissed his cheeks with that sunset glow. Oh my God . . . we can't go on. We know you'll understand and forgive us. ■

. . . *continued*

Paul Newman

DMCA, FSG, PBE, TSHT

Okay, so he's gone a little gray around the temples, and we think of him most often now in relation to popcorn or salad dressing, but there was a time . . . in the halcyon days of yore . . . when Paul's eyes flashed as he sped around some racetrack, smiling that hundred-mile-an-hour smile and slipping into high gear. And those skimpy government-issue T-shirts he'd parade around in would cling to his sinewy frame like sweat to a Budweiser can in the dog days of August. . . . And that wink that seemed to say "Yes, I know, I'm impossible, but you can't resist me because my eyes are as blue as the azure skies of deepest summer and I can elevate the consumption of a hardboiled egg to a religious experience." Say "uncle." Next time you're feeling protein-deprived, check out a Paul Newman movie and remember when. ■

Marlon Brando

BE, RUM, SIN, UGB

Marlon Brando is not just a hunk, he's a force of nature, like continental drift or the principles of fusion physics. This original bad boy doesn't just smolder, he combusts. Now, granted, it's kind of hard to think of that weird guy who was Superman's father on Krypton as a conductor of sufficient sexual energy to motivate a tectonic shift. In his day, though, Brando was the Big Bang theory all wrapped up in a flimsy T-shirt just waiting to explode and create new universes. Try out one of those early flicks and learn why they paid him a gazillion dollars just to be elemental, back in the days when he could make you feel the earth move through the force of his screen presence, rather than his lumbering girth. ■

mascara brush in the other, and the steering wheel between her knees, and all in time with an upbeat, seventies soundtrack . . . is she a cool chick or what?

Frankie is brought on board to make a man out of the boy robot. She is impeded in her efforts by Ulysses' nerdy creator, Dr. Jeff Peters (also played by John Malkovich in a limp and lifeless, forelock-falling-in-his-face wig), who has difficulty relinquishing his adolescent alter ego to the civilizing influences of the metaphorical mother.

This movie is a caregiver's dream come true. Not only does the guy change exactly according to specification, but he's slated to be propelled into hyperspace before he has the chance to revert back to his old behavior.

▪ ***Jacknife*** *(1989)*
Stars: Robert De Niro, Kathy Baker, Ed Harris
Director: David Hugh Jones
Writer: Stephen Metcalfe

A bearded, baseball-hatted Robert De Niro stars as Megs, a Vietnam vet living with a world of hurt inside. Megs is prevented from moving forward in his life by his terrible memories of war and the loss of his brother-at-arms, Bobby. He earns the name Jacknife because he drives his truck the same way that he lives his life, pushing himself, and his cargo, to the brink of total destruction.

Martha, a timid schoolteacher who has been so busy taking care of her brother, Dave, that she has no time to find the right shade of lipstick to bring out her eyes, falls in love with Megs. Through his ministrations, she gets to go to the prom she never attended, and through her love and concern, his wartime wounds are healed. Together they join forces to save Dave.

This is a sweet, naturalistic love story, with the uplifting message that love can cure all, even Vietnam-inspired post-traumatic stress disorder, alcoholism, and partial paralysis. He even shaves for the prom! Wouldn't it be nice . . .

■ ***The Best Years of Our Lives*** *(1946)*

Stars: Frederic March, Myrna Loy, Teresa Wright, Dana Andrews, Virginia Mayo, Cathy O'Donnell, Harold Russell
Director: William Wyler
Writer: Robert E. Sherwood, based on a novel by MacKinlay Kantor

Three men come back from the Good War and struggle to adjust to peacetime with the help of three nurturing, stoic, and beautiful ladies (Loy as the Wife, Wright as the Daughter/Girlfriend, O'Donnell as the Fiancée). Their emotions are as gentle and controlled as their carefully curled coifs, but you'll weep when armless Homer (Russell), a sweet boy next door, dares his loyal fiancée to continue loving him in spite of his helpless moments late at night. You'll sneer at those awful Rosie the Riveters who keep the fellas from finding quality employment that will pay enough to buy a little prefab and a yard for the 2.4 kids and the dog to play in someday. Boo! Hiss! And what about that shallow bitch who married poor Fred just because she loved his uniform, denying Teresa Wright, who has no time for teenage indulgences, a chance to settle down and be a supportive and adoring wife? Well, hanging's too good for her.

The woman-as-healer message is thoroughly shameless, but this classic piece of home-front propaganda will draw you in completely.

■ ***Four Weddings and a Funeral*** *(1994)*

Stars: Hugh Grant, Andie MacDowell, Kristin Scott Thomas
Director: Mike Newell
Writer: Richard Curtis

Lesson for the day: The surest way to make a man commit is to be a free spirit with a list of ex-lovers in the mid–two digits—and to have the good fortune of bumping into him at weddings where a man can't help but contemplate the possibility of his own matrimony. Of course, Andie MacDowell isn't that calculating, but then when you're Andie MacDowell, you don't have to be. Hugh Grant is at his stuttering best here—try to repress the memory of that prostitution scandal and his innocent vulnerable act will work a lot better for you.

■ ***Coming Home*** *(1978)*
Stars: Jon Voight, Jane Fonda, Bruce Dern
Director: Hal Ashby
Writers: Robert C. Jones and Waldo Salt, based on a story by Nancy Dowd

Talk about a bad first impression—his catheter bag spews urine on her crisp summer dress while he rages from his gurney, madly swinging a cane at whoever comes near. But that's just the sort of honest, raw detail that makes this love story between an angry Vietnam vet and a naive military wife so real and compelling. John Voight, looking *très* Boulder in a wispy blond seventies do with beard and macho choker, plays a troubled and crippled vet who is inspired by the sweetly awkward gal next door (Fonda) because of her kindness toward the forgotten warriors. He finds his path, she finds herself, and we find out that it was all one goddamn, raw, spewing catheter mess of a war that's going to take a lot more than a bucket and a sponge to clean up.

■ ***The King and I*** *(1956)*
Stars: Yul Brynner, Deborah Kerr
Director: Walter Lang
Writers: Margaret Landon and Ernest Lehman

Well, he may be the king of Siam, but that is no excuse for breaking promises regarding housing arrangements. Huffy over such power plays, the fiery British governess (Kerr) sets out to civilize the king (Brynner) of this backward, if exotic, country and teach him a thing or two about refinement, as defined by the British Empire: proper accommodations for guests, which fork to use, the importance of corseting women, and the superiority of imperialism, which obliterates the indigenous culture, creates a class structure that dooms the native to near poverty for generations to come . . . et cetera, et cetera, et cetera.

Luckily, the king's an eager learner, and if he refuses to don proper footwear, it's easy to forgive a man who waltzes so divinely when barefoot. He may be headstrong, but clearly our lovely ambassador has the ability to secure his crown jewels for Britain, thereby ensuring the domination of the monarchy in yet another third-world country.

Marvel over the delicious sight of a half-nude, buffed Brynner strutting his stuff, and pretend that an arrogant, jealous, and petty man would give it all up with a few scoldings from you.

Chapter 6

Going Postal: Working Girl Blues Movies

It's not just a job, it's twelve to fourteen hours a day, six to seven days a week, twelve months a year, for the rest of your life. Don't fret! Sometimes a gal's workaday dreams can come true: a job that's a calling and has a profound impact upon the world, a chance to prove oneself against daunting odds, maybe a fling with a co-worker that makes the daily grind a little more bearable. Kick back and try on someone else's career for a while. Then again, given what some of these women have to suffer, maybe late-night faxes to the coast or marrying condiments doesn't seem so bad after all.

- ***Nine to Five*** *(1980)*
  Stars: Jane Fonda, Dolly Parton, Lily Tomlin, Dabney Coleman
  Director: Colin Higgins
  Writers: Colin Higgins and Patricia Resnick

This movie is an administrative assistant's wet dream. They say that now, you know . . . administrative assistant. Nobody says secretary anymore. And if they do say it, it's muttered, in low tones . . . like the word has been forever enclosed in quotes, and it's all on account of a bunch of stupid men who treat their jobs like a strap-on.

But all tyrannies crumble. There's no free lunch. And in this movie, the guy in the big office who gets caught with his hand in the cookie jar starts paying for all those empty calories, in spades.

Recently divorced Judy Bernly (Jane Fonda) reenters the workplace for the first time since marrying her husband some ten years earlier and plunging herself into domestic isolation and personal stasis. (Ringing any bells, Mrs. Turner?) Judy befriends Violet Newstead (played by a Mondrianesque Lily Tomlin), a seasoned veteran of the steno pool who's bucking for a promotion into management. Violet and Judy bond with Doralee Rhodes. While Violet and Judy are at first suspicious of Doralee (played by a Rubenesque Dolly Parton) because she's the boss's "secretary" and is suspected of sleeping her way to the top, the trio bonds over many after-work beers and hard-luck stories. Ultimately, they become partners in crime when they inadvertently kidnap the head honcho.

Nothing better than a few close-ups of some white-collar plutocrat chained to a dog run to cheer you up after a hard day in the salt mines, right?

▪ ***Silkwood*** *(1983)*
Stars: Meryl Streep, Kurt Russell, Cher
Director: Mike Nichols
Writers: Alice Arlen and Nora Ephron

Meryl Streep stars as Karen Silkwood, a nuclear-plant worker who, in 1974, blew the whistle on the dangerous conditions at Kerr-McGee in Oklahoma, and then died suddenly, under circumstances that are still suspect. This movie is like one long bad day at the office. First off, Karen gets scheduled to work on a day she needs off to visit her daughter. It takes her forever to find someone to take her shift, and when she finally does, that person doesn't have to work anyway because the plant closes down on account of a nuclear contamination, which they then blame on Karen because she wasn't on her shift. Talk about Murphy's Law!

Then there's the internal radioactive contamination, the daily urine tests, the involuntary showers with a wire brush, the contempt of your co-workers, and those weird guys with the Geiger counters and the paint scrapers, and, of course, that pair of anonymous headlights, approaching in the distance, right in the middle of the final a capella verse of "Amazing Grace."

A great reminder that while your job may be trying at times, at least your workplace irritations aren't going to cause you to glow in the dark. After all, if you can pee in a cup without a radioactive alarm going off, you're doin' okay.

> ⚠ Warning Label: *If your workplace irritations are causing you to glow in the dark, turn off the damn TV and start looking for a new job.*

■ ***Working Girl*** *(1988)*
Stars: Melanie Griffith, Sigourney Weaver, Harrison Ford, Joan Cusack
Director: Mike Nichols
Writer: Kevin Wade

You say you're underpaid, overworked, and the 401K contribution match doesn't make up for that bitch-on-wheels boss (Sigourney Weaver) who steals your ideas and takes credit for all your hard work? Well, toss aside those magazines full of ponderous career advice and take a cue from perky underling Melanie Griffith: Seize the first opportunity to abscond with the evil one's Rolodex and work it, babe (the Rolodex, that is; the half-nude dance with a vacuum cleaner is entirely optional and will not necessarily result in career advancement). Remember, you can overcome any second-act setbacks with the help of a faithful office pal (Joan Cusack in all her big-haired eighties glory) and a handsome client (Harrison Ford in a reversed-gender, girl-love-interest role), who'll ensure that you end up with a corner office and a real salary.

While you're busy putting in several years real time, and suffering plenty of stress-related illnesses along the way, you'll enjoy this condensed version of a lackey's triumph over corporate hell.

■ ***Working Girls*** *(1986)*
Stars: Louise Smith, Ellen McElduff, Amanda Goodwin
Director: Lizzie Borden
Writers: Lizzie Borden and Sandra Kay

Molly (Louise Smith) just hates having to pull a double shift. Of course, when a double shift means another six hours of sex with every scumbag with an itch to scratch who shows up at the brothel where you're employed, *grueling* does not begin to describe the experience. But unfortunately, for this single mom and lesbian with a decent education and a first-class mind, prostitution is the best job open to her at the moment. This means hour after hour of having to act charming around jerks who ought to be home getting intimate with an old gym sock, but Molly's dry-witted detachment and unshakable sense of self ensure that however soul-crushing her day, she's not going to be putting up with this for long—and she won't need Richard Gere to rescue her either.

■ ***To Die For*** *(1995)*
Stars: Nicole Kidman, Matt Dillon, Joaquin Phoenix
Director: Gus Van Sant
Writers: Buck Henry and Joyce Maynard

Loosely based on the Pamela Smart murder case, this scathing indictment of the media age stars Nicole Kidman as Suzanne Stone Moretto, a blond, blue-eyed, telegenic bimbo who dreams of being a broadcast journalist. Suzanne speaks in sound bites, dresses in pastel plaids, and dwells in a perpetual sweeps week, pulling out all the stops, even the ones put in place to prevent antisocial behavior—like, say, a conscience—in a desperate attempt to garner ratings.

Nothing, but nothing will get in the way of Suzanne's nineteen-inch vision of herself, including her sweet galoomph of a husband (Matt Dillon), who winds up paying a pretty stiff price for his more traditional views on women in the workplace.

Despite the fact that Suzanne is an entirely vacuous, chromatically challenged, morally corrupt hologram of a human being, whose biggest fans are a group of malcontented, latently homicidal adolescents with skin problems, she succeeds in making her media dreams come true. But at what cost?

Next time you start hungering for your fifteen minutes of fame, watch this movie and count the blessings of anonymity.

Blind Ambition

All I want to do is graduate from high school, go to Europe, marry Christian Slater and die.

★ Buffy in *Buffy the Vampire Slayer*

My name is Judy! J-U-D-Y Judy and I'd like somebody to call me by my name! Oh, okay I took my life in my own hands, I made a mistake fine I'm sorry! I'll never do it again! I wanna wear my sandals . . . I wanna go out to lunch. I wanna be normal again!

★ Judy Benjamin in *Private Benjamin*

I just love finding new places to wear diamonds.

★ Lorelei Lee in *Gentlemen Prefer Blondes*

I'm late for a jean folding seminar. Let's locomote!

★ Vickie Miner in *Reality Bites*

- ***Suspect*** *(1987)*
  Stars: Cher, Dennis Quaid, Liam Neeson
  Director: Peter Yates
  Writer: Eric Roth

When a judge commits suicide, and his secretary is found murdered, Carl Anderson (Liam Neeson), a homeless deaf-mute, is arrested and charged with the crime. Kathleen

Faking It: Phony Gal Films That Really Piss Us Off

Pretty Woman *(1990)*
Stars: Julia Roberts, Richard Gere
Director: Garry Marshall
Writer: J. F. Lawton

We've never understood the romantic appeal of a money-grubbing corporate raider taking up with a streetwalker he's hired to give him a blow job. We never bought that a young woman becomes a prostitute for the same reason she might become a grocery checker or drugstore clerk—gosh, it seemed like a good job at the time. And we never bought that a woman who looks like Julia Roberts would be picking up johns on the corner of Hollywood and Vine.

Julia Roberts's dazzling smile and the vicarious thrill of a Rodeo Drive shopping blow-out can't make up for this ugly mess of a movie, with its absurd story and decade-of-greed morality. We've got to agree with Romy and Michele:

MICHELE: ***You know, even though we've watched*** **Pretty Woman** ***like, thirty-six times, I never get tired of making fun of it.***
ROMY: ***Oh, I know. . . . Aw, poor thing—they won't let her shop. Yeah, like those salesgirls in Beverly Hills aren't bigger whores than she is.*** ■

Riley, a beautiful, raven-haired public defender with really good cheekbones (Cher), is called upon to defend the lumbering vagrant, who at first glance seems like a violent homicidal psychopath, but as a result of Kathleen's compassionate ministrations turns out to be a real teddy bear of a guy.

Kathleen is assisted in her battle to save the falsely accused hobo by Eddie Sanger (Dennis Quaid), a be-dimpled lobbyist from Wisconsin with six-pack abs and a feckless frat boy grin, who is leaking insider knowledge to Kathleen while simultaneously sitting on her jury, in an attempt to lead her to the real killer.

So you think you had a tough day? Try representing an innocent deaf-mute with violent tendencies, in front of a corrupt judge, while simultaneously discouraging the very welcome advances of the cutest lobbyist ever to emerge from America's heartland, because if you go to bed with him, you'll get accused of jury tampering. That squabble with your co-worker by the water cooler isn't looking so bad now, is it?

■ ***Rush*** *(1991)*
Stars: Jennifer Jason Leigh, Jason Patric
Director: Lili Fini Zanuck
Writer: Peter Dexter, based on a book by Kim Wozencraft

Raynor and Kristen (Jason Patric, Jennifer Jason Leigh), two very young, very good-looking, very intense, very Stanislavsky-system narcotics cops, go undercover to catch a kingpin drug dealer. Because they are devout students of the Method, however, they can't just pretend to use drugs in order to ensnare pushers. No, that wouldn't be organic. They actually have to actually use the stuff; otherwise, the dealers might realize that their performance is pure craft, without any grounding in emotional reality.

Consequently Raynor and Kristen, like many Method actors before them, descend into a fog of dangerous addiction, and ultimately sacrifice their professionalism. So you see, it could be worse.

> ⚠ Warning Label: *Don't attend to tasks outside your job description if they encourage physical or psychological addictions.*

■ ***Baby Boom*** *(1987)*
Stars: Diane Keaton, Harold Ramis, James Spader, Sam Shepard, Sam Wanamaker
Director: Charles Shyer
Writers: Nancy Meyers and Charles Shyer

We know you wouldn't dream of leaving a baby with a coat-check girl, or securing her diapers with electrical tape, or serving the kid linguine without the benefit of a room-size tarp and a cleaning lady standing by. But career woman J. C. Wiatt (Keaton) doesn't have a lot of choices, having just unexpectedly inherited the ultimate family heirloom—a baby.

Diane Keaton is at her flustered, comedic best here, trying to balance a high-powered job in an advertising agency with responsible parenthood. As baby starts cramping Mom's style big time, it's clear J.C. needs that one invaluable accessory not available at upscale baby boutiques—namely, a wife. Unfortunately, she's a woman, so she'll have to redirect her creative energies and resources toward solving her own problem outside of the corporate structure, kiss off any hope of help from governmental or social institutions, and thank God that she's got an education and a huge financial cushion to keep her afloat until she comes up with a solution. 1987, eh? Too bad it's the yuppie baby food in this movie that seems outdated, not the dilemma.

■ ***Woman of the Year*** *(1942)*
Stars: Spencer Tracy, Katharine Hepburn
Director: George Stevens
Writers: Ring Lardner, Jr., and Michael Kanin

Katharine Hepburn plays Tess Harding, a high-spirited gal who is not only the most influential columnist in America but a world traveler with friends in high places, a sophisticated New Yorker with a fantastic Fifth Avenue apartment, and a witty and intelligent feminist who speaks several languages fluently. Her fellow columnist at the paper, Sam Craig, knows a lot of baseball stats. After they've torn each other up in their mutual columns because of Tess's disdain for the great American pastime, they finally meet in the editor's office. Oh, the boss has something important to say about team efforts and such, but Tracy and Hepburn are too busy taking in each other's pheromones and burning up the screen with their electricity to pay much attention. Which pretty much describes this whole movie. Sure, we can appreciate the cute lines, the classic ballpark scene in which Tracy tries to explain the rules of baseball to Hepburn, and the darling scene in which the hopelessly undomestic Hepburn tries to work a toaster and control the beast that lives in the waffler maker. And true, there are passing nods to the difficulties of a woman having it all, a dilemma neatly sidestepped in the end, just as the troubling notion of Tracy's feeling entitled to an old-fashioned wife is relegated to a mere plot device. But this is less a film about balancing work and home than an excuse to watch this classic screen couple in their first outing as they flirt outrageously with each other and practically melt the cameras with their combustible chemistry. Don't you wish you had an ogling charmer to come home to after a hard day saving the world?

Great Pickup Lines Featuring New Jersey

Why don't you go get your hat and we'll go and get lost in New Jersey?

★ Spencer Tracy to Katharine Hepburn in *Woman of the Year*

■ ***Female*** *(1933)*
Stars: Ruth Chatterton, George Brent, Lois Wilson, Johnny Mack Brown
Director: Michael Curtiz
Writers: Gene Markey and Kathryn Scola, based on a story by Donald Henderson Clarke

This little gem of a movie about a high-powered female business executive, circa 1933, may be hard to find, but boy, is it worth a viewing.

Alison Drake (Ruth Chatterton) has it all—almost. She runs her own major car-manufacturing company, she's got an amazing house, a full staff of servants to bring her Russian vodka to fortify the courage of the gentlemen she entertains, and a string of young studs from the office to service her after five o'clock. Should any of them get jealous or moody, she'll just banish them to the Montreal branch—"From now on, I'll have nothing but women secretaries," she vows when one moon-eyed male secretary declares his love for her. "Get me two sensible women!" she barks to her assistant. "And it takes more than flat heels and glasses to make a sensible woman!"

Of course, the one thing Alison can't seem to find is her match, a man who is worthy of her brains, skills, and sharp tongue. By a stroke good fortune, he (George Brent) ends up being her underling as well. Yet when she tries her well-rehearsed and effective sexual harassment moves on him, he'll have nothing of it. Yes, he's definitely the fellow for a tumble on the white fur rug—now she's just got to win him over without having to sacrifice her ball-busting ways.

> ⚠ Warning Label: *The last few seconds of this flick will disappoint you, but you'll be surprised how much this sexy and sophisticated comedy resonates even now, sixty-odd years later.*

■ *Miami Blues* (1990)

Stars: Alec Baldwin, Jennifer Jason Leigh
Director: George Armitage
Writer: George Armitage, based on the novel by Charles Willeford

Jennifer Jason Leigh stars in this noir classic as Susie Waggoner, a novice prostitute with a heart full of gold and a head full of air. Her first assignment takes her to the hotel room of sociopath Fred Frenger (Alec Baldwin), a staggeringly handsome, blue-eyed thief, who is as untalented at armed robbery as Susie is at turning tricks.

Bound by their mutual incompetence, Susie and Fred join forces, and in another dreadful career move, Susie decides to tag along for the ride when Fred strikes out toward Florida to make a fresh start. Susie, whose nickname is Princess Not So Bright for a very good reason, is thrilled with Fred's every gesture, and goes about forging a vision of her domestic ideal from the raw material of their tawdry Florida hideout.

Unfortunately, Fred isn't any better at being Ward Cleaver than he was at being Clyde Barrow. Frustrated at every turn by a quirky cop in a whiplash collar (Fred Ward), Fred ultimately throws up his hands and unleashes himself on this sleepy retirement community in a brutal one-man killing spree, which ultimately leaves Susie sitting Cinderella-like amidst the ashes of her domestic utopia, carefully considering her next career move.

Doesn't your resumé look a little more impressive to you now?

▪ ***Claudine*** *(1974)*

Stars: Diahann Carroll, James Earl Jones, Lawrence Hilton-Jacobs
Director: John Berry
Writers: Lester and Tina Pine

Then again, you could be on welfare, couldn't you? Diahann Carroll plays a harried inner city mom trying to raise her six kids, keep her sanity, and hide the television and the new iron from the nosy welfare worker (the kids play Paul Revere whenever she pops by to make sure the family is living in wretched misery as they ought). Maybe, just maybe, Mom can find a little romance with the sweetly sexy garbage man (Jones) who draws bubble baths for her (albeit with Joy dishwashing detergent—clearly Claudine is thick-skinned in more ways than one). Dare she dream of a life for herself?

With Gladys Knight crooning in the background, you know that eventually peaceful waters will flow and Claudine's midnight train will come in—at least until "tough love" welfare reform kicks in.

▪ ***Fierce Creatures*** *(1997)*

Stars: Jamie Lee Curtis, Kevin Kline, John Cleese
Directors: Robert Young, Fred Schepisi
Writers: John Cleese and Iain Johnstone

This farcical metaphor for the ravaging of American business by capitalist piggies who are all power and no soul, which is also a thinly disguised attack on media Satan Rupert Murdoch and his ilk, will make any corporate slave cheer. Jamie Lee Curtis, a ball-busting powerhouse, shows up at work only to find her boss (Kline) has sold off the company she was to run. No prob—he'll just buy up another one by the end of the day (in this case, a zoo), install the pretty gal as CEO, give her an arbitrary profit margin to meet, and let her destroy all that the organization stands for that is decent and honorable. A displaced manager desperate to hang in long enough to get his pension (Cleese) and the whorish son of the big guy (Kline in a dual role) complicate matters. Will the zoo creatures and gentle keepers turn the hearts of Kline and Curtis and successfully fend off corporate evil? Can anyone really re-engineer the corporation? Or will the entire industry fester like a boil then disintegrate before your eyes, forcing you to go freelance?

Have a laugh and make some networking drinks dates *now.*

■ ***A Star Is Born*** *(1937)*
Stars: Janet Gaynor, Fredric March, Adolphe Menjou
Director: William A. Wellman
Writers: Dorothy Parker, Alan Campbell, and Robert Carson, based on a story by William A. Wellman and Robert Carson

Wide-eyed farm girl Esther Blodgett (Gaynor), a redheaded Betty Boop with stars in her eyes, moons over Norman Maine at the picture show and dreams of conquering Hollywood. Her aunt and uncle think all she needs is a good dose of sulfur and molasses, but pioneer Granny, who buried her husband out on the prairie with her own hands after some durned Injun drove a tomahawk into him, exhorts Esther to follow her dream—"If you've got one drop of my blood in your veins, you won't let Matty or any of her kind break your heart. You'll go right out there and break it yourself! That's your right!"

Bolstered by Granny's cash and dubious words of encouragement, Esther blows into that metropolis of make-believe, finds a cheap flophouse, registers with Central Casting, and awaits her big break. It's provided by a chance meeting with Norman Maine himself—handsome as the devil and drunk as Bacchus—who becomes smitten with her and nabs her an agent (Adolphe Menjou) and a leading role. Soon she's starlet Vicki Lester, also known as Mrs. Norman Maine, cheerily frying eggs in the back of a camper on their honeymoon, convinced she can combine career, love, and domestic tranquillity. Alas, her husband is a sullen, self-pitying, long-past-his-prime leading man whose drunken exploits have become far more entertaining than his pictures. While Hollywood licks its lips awaiting Norman's final humiliating and pathetic descent into total debasement, Vicki stubbornly clings to her dream that the man she loves can share in her happiness, a dream that seems far less attainable than a kid off the farm earning a star in front of Grauman's Chinese Theatre.

Viewer's Note: The Judy Garland/James Mason version isn't nearly as much fun without those nasty cracks about Hollywood that make the original so delicious, and the emotional thread keeps being interrupted by show-stopping Garland numbers or pan shots of stills where the original piece of film is missing. But Garland is brilliantly vulnerable and sings from the heart. As for the seventies Kris Kristofferson/Barbra Streisand remake, can you really stomach Kristofferson's perpetually off-key singing and the intimidating specter of Barbra's epic bouf?

▪ ***Desk Set*** *(1957)*
Stars: Katharine Hepburn, Spencer Tracy, Gig Young, Joan Blondell
Director: Walter Lang
Writers: Phoebe and Henry Ephron, based on a play by William Marchant

Automation, in the form of an original-series-*Star-Trek*-like room-size computer with lots of cheesy flashing lights and a cute nickname, threatens to displace the gals in the research department at the TV network, who've looked up so many arcane facts over the years that they can recite Ty Cobb's batting average, the names of Santa's reindeer, or the entire *Song of Hiawatha* in their sleep. The genial but penny-pinching efficiency expert (Tracy), hired to secretly determine the feasibility of one of these newfangled "thinking machines," finds that no IBM product—particularly this monstrosity whipped up by a woefully underfunded scenery department—can possibly match the mind, wit, and creativity of Katharine Hepburn. Yeah, no kidding—even Yahoo and Altavista can't match the entertainment value of the impossibly professional, funny, and clever Hepburn at work, much less the sparkling scenes featuring her and Tracy. She does have a noncommittal beau in another department of the company, but savvy and hyperefficient career women don't have to settle for just any man, do they?

Enjoy the gals' camaraderie, the champagne-infused Christmas party, and their outrageously smart pre-casual-Fridays office wear (and don't envy them their figures: remember, they had some *serious* foundation garments in those days).

▪ ***Up the Down Staircase*** *(1967)*
Stars: Sandy Dennis, Patrick Bedford, Eileen Heckart, Ruth White, Ellen O'Mara
Director: Robert Mulligan
Writer: Tad Mosel, based on the novel by Bel Kaufman

Sandy Dennis lisps, sputters, and twitches her way through her performance as Miss Barrett, an endearingly awkward first-year English teacher in a New York City public high school. With her blond flip, a darling overbite, and an awe-inspiring panoply of nervous tics, she's got *pushover* written all over her. Desperately trying to keep track of latenesses, requisitions orders, something called Delaney cards, and which is the "up" staircase and which is the "down," Miss Barrett is rattled by the pointless bureaucracy and the petty squabbles among her cynical colleagues. This makes it difficult to concentrate on leading her students into intelligent discussions about literature. To complicate matters, she's got a low-rent James Dean baiting her and a Sylvia Plath wannabe looking to her for an explanation of the meaning of life. Even if you aren't in a female-dominated, altruistic, grossly underpaid position, you'll identify with this story of a woman on her first job, discovering her own style and confidence . . . not to mention her own limitations.

■ ***Gorillas in the Mist*** *(1988)*
Stars: Sigourney Weaver, John Omirah Miluwi as Sembogare the guide
Director: Michael Apted
Writer: Anna Hamilton Phelan

What would drive a woman to devote her life so utterly to her cause—the protection of the mountain gorillas—that she would risk her life offending governments, poachers, and even fellow researchers and go so far as to threaten little children who get in her way? Yup, Dian Fossey (played by the resolute-jawed Sigourney Weaver) was a megabitch, but she made progress, didn't she? Remember that the next time someone accuses you of megalomania, blackmail, bribery, dishonesty, and highly questionable ethics. Then again, Fossey's cause wasn't an improved quarterly profit: she would stop at nothing to protect her beloved gorillas from being captured for zoos or slaughtered to create ape-hand ashtrays, for she was determined to protect their fragile ecosystem and carefully balanced social systems, which make allowances for the young, the old, and the infirm. And your annual stated goal this year at the office was what?

Even if you aren't a PETA member, you'll be deeply moved by this story of a woman who found her calling and pursued it no matter what the cost.

> ⚠ Warning Label: *This movie will also raise some hard questions about the ultimate purpose of your own work—and about the primates in your office.*

Them's Fightin' Words

This time I have bought a gun and if any civil war comes my way it had better watch its ass.

★ Sigourney Weaver as Dian Fossey in *Gorillas in the Mist*

▪ ***Ermo*** *(1994)*
Stars: Ailiya, Liu Peiqui, Ge Zhijun, Zang Haiyan
Director: Zhou Xiaowen
Writer: Lang Yun, based on a story by Xu Baoqi

Watching the opening sequence as Ermo (Ailiya) prepares noodles to sell on the streets of the nearest big city, sweating and grunting as she kneads the dough with her feet and hangs the steaming noodles, you're likely to have two thoughts: (1) Thank God we've got air-conditioning at the office, and (2) does the health department know about her preparation methods? *Mental Note:* Don't eat food from street vendors!

Anyway, entrepreneurial Ermo may be laboring in drudgery, but she's determined to build herself up financially until she can achieve her ultimate goal. Financial security in the form of a hefty SEP–IRA spread over aggressive-growth mutual funds and a smattering of bonds? Naaah. Improved living conditions? Naaaah. A fabulous wardrobe? Hey, this is China—even Manolo Blahnik shoes aren't going to enhance your work outfit. No, she wants the zenith of consumer goods: a huge color TV, bigger than her neighbors', despite the fact that the programming in China makes UPN and E! look exciting.

As Ermo doggedly pursues her seemingly frivolous goal, you'll start thinking about your own slavish devotion to the acquisition of consumer goods and other dubious symbols of achievement.

> ⚠ Warning Label: *Rent this one with* Gorillas in the Mist *and you'll really have a career crisis.*

■ ***The Silence of the Lambs*** *(1991)*
Stars: Jodie Foster, Anthony Hopkins, Scott Glenn
Director: Jonathan Demme
Writer: Ted Tally, based on the novel by Thomas Harris

Despite the pressure to think and act like a man in order to fit into your male-dominated work environment, it's good to be reminded that female ways of operating can add an important dimension to the workplace, and that there are many ways to skin a cat. Keep that image in mind and you may guess the ending to this story of a wet-behind-the-ears FBI agent, Clarice Starling (Foster), trying to discover the identity and motive of a serial killer before his next victim shows up in the river, her throat clogged by an object of metaphorical value that a literalist masculine mentality cannot possibly decipher. Luckily, Clarice, who is struggling to fit into the masculine FBI culture, has a poet helping her out—not her boss (Glenn), who debriefs her with just the facts, ma'am, but her mentor, Dr. Hannibal Lecter (Hopkins). Lecter's a man with an appreciation for art, literature, and fine wines, and a deep understanding of human nature—a man whose brilliance, creativity, and insight ensure that he always gets his way in the end because of his killer instinct. You know, it's too bad he's a brutal psychopath and known cannibal; they could've had something. But then again, office romances are always fraught with complications, aren't they?

■ ***Adam's Rib*** *(1949)*
Stars: Spencer Tracy, Katharine Hepburn, Judy Holliday, Tom Ewell
Director: George Cukor
Writers: Ruth Gordon and Garson Kanin

Tracy and Hepburn play a married couple, both lawyers, who end up opposing each other on a case, not some mundane insurance fraud thing, mind you, but a notorious murder case that brings to light all sorts of important issues about equality between the sexes and marital obligations. They both plead passionately in court about how men and women ought to act, then go home to fabulous dinner parties and their usual loving and witty repartee before climbing into bed—separate twin beds, that is (aren't the fifties *annoying*?). Oh, they have a few spats, but they quickly make up for them with apologies and little gifts and gentle acts of kindness, and we know that no matter how ugly it gets in the courtroom, they'll sneak a momentary flirtation between examination and cross and patch it up in the end.

Isn't it inspiring, the ideal marriage this onscreen couple creates? Of course, the screenwriter was able to write out Spence's staunch Catholicism and aversion to divorce, Mrs. Tracy back home, and Kate's consequent inability to have marriage and a family to go along with her brilliant career, not to mention all the petty complications that pile up in real-life relationships, like housework and in-laws, that make career conflicts all the more taxing. And though both are lawyers, neither is a greedy snake, or a workhorse trying to make partner, or a prisoner of the law library. They don't even have to scrounge to pay off their law school debt. Don't you wish married life were this easy?

▪ ***His Girl Friday*** *(1940)*
Stars: Cary Grant, Rosalind Russell
Director: Howard Hawks
Writers: Ben Hecht and Charles MacArthur, based on their play The Front Page

She's a reporter, he's her former boss, and she just wants to fill him in on her plan to marry Egbert—or whatever his name is—and settle down to raise a family. All of which, of course, is simply a sturdy wooden match that sparks Cary Grant to action. After all, he's scored far too many scoops to let the chance to reunite with a go-get-'em gal like Rosalind Russell go up in smoke. Sure, she's just a short train trip away from getting hitched, and the two of them are, after all, divorced, but this is the movies, where divorce is merely a first-act plot point to provide an obstacle to the obvious couple's getting together. Anyway, Cary Grant knows that a controversial death-penalty case, which is just screaming for an investigative reporter to uncover deadly political shenanigans, will provide the perfect spark to re-ignite the smoldering embers of their love affair and inspire her to forget this domestic nonsense and go back to being an ace reporter.

Watch the fireworks, rewind to catch that rapid-fire dialogue, and pretend that guys like Cary Grant who love working women can actually be found in offices where real women can meet them. We wish!

■ ***Norma Rae*** *(1979)*
Stars: Sally Field, Ron Liebman, Beau Bridges
Director: Martin Ritt
Writers: Irving Ravetch and Harriet Frank, Jr.

Weekend plans? Sure. Soaking her feet. And maybe some cheap hotel sex with a married man—George, a local nobody whose finest quality is his ability to spring for a steak dinner. That's what a gal's got to look forward to when she works in a nonunionized textile mill in the South. It's only when a labor organizer from New York City (Liebman) shows up in town with plenty of handbills and optimism that Norma Rae Webster considers the possibility that her rebellious nature, which until now had manifested only in demands for more Kotex machines in the ladies' room at the mill, might have an even more productive outlet. Her husband (Bridges) isn't exactly keen on her new priorities—laundry and grocery shopping having taken a backseat to using the Xerox machine and making phone calls to would-be union supporters—but that's just too damn bad, isn't it? Norma Rae's headed for a showdown, and her life will never be the same again.

Here's one climax that can't be written off to starry-eyed Hollywood screenwriters—it's a true story, and one that may convince you to do a little cage-rattling yourself.

Chapter 7

I Just Washed My Hair and I Can't Do a Thing with It: Bad Hair Day Movies

Have you got the psychological equivalent of hat head? Are your emotional ends splitting? Do you feel dry, limp, lifeless, and in need of deep conditioning? Well, slather a hot-oil treatment on that tonsorial disaster and tune in to one of these Bad Hair Day movies, featuring wallflowers, chronic neurotics, and other bad-hair babes who manage to land the leading man anyway.

- ***Hairspray*** *(1988)*
  Stars: Ricki Lake, Divine, Sonny Bono, Debbie Harry
  Director and Writer: John Waters

Where else but in a Bad Hair Day movie would a chubby girl from Queens named Tracy Turnblad (Ricki Lake) win a beauty contest and go on to inspire a hip line of plus-size fashions, a dance craze, and a bouffant Jackie O–like hairdo doused with so much stiff stuff that it would retain its flip in a gale-force wind?

And it gets better. Her mother, Edna Turnblad, is played by transvestite Divine, who is always ill-tempered, always barefoot and in a bad wig, and always ironing. Sonny Bono and Debbie Harry also make appearances as Velma and Franklin Von Tussle. Debbie Harry's beehive in these scenes is epic in scale. And Sonny . . . well, he's wearing a vest, I think.

This is also the movie that catapulted a real-life bad-hair babe, Ricki Lake, into the cultural dialogue, and popularized the notion that the term *bigger is better* applies to more than just shopping malls.

■ *Bringing Up Baby* (1938)

Stars: Katharine Hepburn, Cary Grant, Virginia Walker
Director: Howard Hawks
Writers: Dudley Nichols and Hagar Wilde, based on a story by Hagar Wilde

Bespeckled paleontologist David Huxley (Cary Grant) may be engaged to a fiercely dull and left-brained woman (Virginia Walker) who believes domesticity and children will be a distraction to their important scientific pursuits, but he won't be for long when the high-spirited and decidedly nonlinear Susan (Katharine Hepburn) shows up and literally sweeps him off his feet (courtesy of a bar trick with an olive that evidently requires much more practice). You see, Susan's sense of gravity, both literally and figuratively speaking, is precarious, which is why before he knows it David's baby-sitting a leopard named Baby, wearing a ladies' filmy wrap and jumping up and down declaring "I've suddenly gone gay!" and desperately digging up dirt trying to find a priceless brontosaurus bone that Susan's pooch has buried out back. He'd like to escape, but Susan's connection to a potential patron and her pre–Lucy Ricardo hijinks have him embroiled in one farcical scenario after another. Meanwhile, the hopelessly neurotic Susan merely lets loose her Woody Woodpecker laugh and reassures him that everything will be just fine. Of course it will be, but it's a deliriously daffy ride until then.

▪ ***A Stolen Life*** *(1946)*
Stars: Bette Davis, Glenn Ford
Director: Curtis Bernhardt
Writers: Catherine Turney and Margaret Buell Wilder, based on the novel Uloupeny Zivot *by Karel J. Benes*

Painter Kate (Davis) is delightfully, refreshingly forward and honest, and thereby destined to be kicked in the ass by the man she loves. Despite her brave seduction of the dreamy lighthouse keeper (Ford), Kate discovers her evil twin sister, Pat (Davis again), has edged in on her beau. Poor Kate is just too Milquetoast and seems destined for a life of painting third-rate pictures and being verbally abused by a snotty painting partner she's employed as her own personal cat-o'-nine-tails. Will she discover the tigress within and wrest her man away from her bitch of an alter ego? Or will she be forever stuck in sensible suits, helping her beloved Bill choose lingerie for swinish sis, who always manages to come out ahead despite being cursed with just as awful a 'do as Kate? (What is *with* those *bangs?*). Our downtrodden heroine's inner turmoil causes plenty of foggy storms off the Vineyard, which generate a soap opera plot twist, providing a chance for her to nab that fella once and for all.

Classic Bette Bytes

I'll admit I may have seen better days . . . but I'm still not to be had for the price of a cocktail, like a salted peanut.

★ Bette Davis as Margo Channing in *All About Eve*

▪ ***Marty*** *(1955)*
Stars: Ernest Borgnine, Betsy Blair
Director: Delbert Mann
Writer: Paddy Chayefsky, based on his TV play

You know you've got to start working on those esteem issues when you find yourself identifying with Ernest Borgnine. Well, he is brilliant in this raw portrayal of two losers who ain't such dogs after all, even if they do get ditched and dissed right and left. When Marty, a Brooklyn butcher, rescues a not so fair damsel in distress (Blair) at the Stardust Ballroom, he realizes that maybe happiness will not elude him forever, despite his painfully honest declaration to his worried mama that he'll never get married—"I'm a fat, ugly little man!" he cries (uh, no argument there). Okay, the girl ain't no prize, but she's a nice girl, she is. And in that moment when Marty gulps, opens his frog eyes wide, and asks, "Are you . . . a Catholic?" you realize that this odd pot has found its lid, just like Ma promised.

Brutal and beautiful. We suggest you do a mud mask and manicure and put a six-week rinse in your hair while you're watching—and avoid all mirrors lest you unleash a crying jag.

■ ***The Snake Pit*** *(1948)*
Stars: Olivia de Havilland, Mark Stevens, Leo Genn
Director: Anatole Litvak
Writers: Frank Partos and Millen Brand

Oh, it's all so confusing. Who are these women? And why are we walking into this building? And—oh! Those are locks! and chains! and straitjackets! Oh, dear. This is not good.

Poor Olivia de Havilland wears huge dark circles under her eyes here as she struggles to wrap her thin little cardigan across frail shoulders. If only she could remember who she is and what has happened to land her in the Juniper Hill State Hospital, where the standard treatment for a lost little soul is electroshock therapy and immersion in a snake pit full of women who are dancing madly or staring catatonically. But a very nice man with a soothing voice is going to help her, he promises, and soon she remembers that day, that terrible day that Daddy . . .

Well, you get the point. Transference, the talking cure, and tiny Mrs. Cunningham will soon be reunited with Mr. Cunningham, who will wrap his arms around her and never, ever leave her, because she's a good girl.

And you thought you weren't dealing with *your* issues.

■ ***The Truth About Cats and Dogs*** *(1996)*
Stars: Janeane Garofalo, Uma Thurman, Ben Chaplin
Director: Michael Lehmann
Writer: Audrey Wells

One of the truths about cats and dogs is there are cat people and there are dog people, just as there are Uma Thurman people (those would be called "men") and Janeane Garofalo people (that would be "women"). Of course, the sweet, sexy, and hopelessly obtuse guy (Ben Chaplin) thinks that a Janeane Garofalo personality can come in an Uma Thurman package, which is about as plausible as his blind stumblings through this mistaken-identity farce. Still, it's worth suffering through the silliness so you can enjoy Garofalo's cantankerous observations on men and love. Plus, Uma Thurman is thoroughly believable as a flustered, lovable bimbo who has self-esteem issues and, of course, aspirations for a career in news journalism (what else?).

Words to Live By

Anything you can do to draw attention to your mouth is good.

★ Alicia Silverstone as Cher in *Clueless*

■ ***White Palace*** *(1991)*
Stars: Susan Sarandon, James Spader, Eileen Brennan
Director: Luis Mandoki
Writers: Ted Tally and Alvin Sargent, based on the novel by Glenn Savan

She works at a White Castle. She wears a hair net. She's covered in a perpetual layer of french fry grease. She smokes like a chimney, doesn't own a vacuum, drinks a little too much and doesn't know how to cook . . . and still she lands a Wall Street executive with a six-figure salary and the most amazing bedroom eyes you've ever seen on a WASPy rich boy. How does she do it?

Susan Sarandon stars as Nora Baker, one of the most successful bad-hair babes of all time, in this mismatched love story about a disillusioned fast food waitress and a grieving Wall Street executive who find comfort and love in each other's unlikely arms.

Nora Baker and Max Baron are two lost souls from opposite sides of the tracks. They're both searching for a moment of release from their private sorrows, and find it in each other, so long as they are safely ensconced in Nora's ramshackle bungalow in the wrong part of town. But when they try to cross over into Max's co-oped world, it becomes clear that Nora just doesn't fit in.

Their lack of cultural and sanitary symmetry threatens to come between them, when Max starts doing passive aggressive things like giving Nora a vacuum cleaner for her birthday. When Nora suggests an alternative use for the brush attachment and storms out, it becomes clear that this bad-hair babe is going to be taken on her own terms, or not at all.

■ ***Autumn Leaves*** *(1956)*
Stars: Joan Crawford, Cliff Robertson, Lorne Greene, Vera Miles
Director: Robert Aldrich
Writers: Jack Jevne (front for blacklisted writers Jean Rouverol and Hugo Butler Lewis), Lewis Meltzer, and Robert Blees

He doesn't mind that she's a good twenty years older than he is, or that her thighs are a bit heavy peeking out of her bathing suit. He doesn't even mind that she practically drowns on their beach date because she was too embarrassed to admit she can't swim. Even after she, afraid that his infatuation with her will fizzle out, insists he go away and find someone his own age, he shows up at her door, proposing marriage.

She's thrilled, and terrified. After all, it's been ten years since she's been laid, and that's assuming she got down with her last boyfriend. So, in an empowering act of bravery, she takes the plunge. Isn't it nice to know that it's never too late for love?

Except for one small problem—he's a pathological liar. Well, that, and he appears to be on the edge of a complete mental breakdown and is lashing out at her. Damn, this is what happens when it's a Joan Crawford vehicle. Nothing can be easy, can it? Noooo. She's got to draw on every ounce of fortitude and go to hell and back for him. How come Grace Kelly never has to deal with this crap?

Well, it may be a battle, but even when you're stuck in a series of 45-degree-angle shots underscored by dissonant piano chords, be assured that a happy ending is in sight.

Faking It: Phony Gal Films That Really Piss Us Off

Frankie and Johnny *(1991)*
Stars: Al Pacino, Michelle Pfeiffer
Director: Garry Marshall
Writer: Terrence McNally

Al Pacino, still wearing that red bandanna from that silly movie about the Spanish revolutionaries, plays Johnny, a short-order cook recently released from jail. He has his eye on Frankie, a beautiful and ethereal blond waitress (Michelle Pfeiffer, of course. Who else do you think of when you string the words blond and ethereal together?).

Now this is the thing. This movie is taken from a play, *Frankie and Johnny in the Claire de Lune,* by Terrence McNally, who is one of this country's premiere playwrights. In play form, the way I read it, this is supposed to be a story about two misfits who find love in each other's arms, proving that genuine affection can overcome anything, even a rap sheet and a babe whose life is one long bad-hair day.

But then Hollywood got hold of it, and while Pacino and Pfeiffer give excellent and compelling performances, they're both drop-dead gorgeous, which changes *everything* in this culture. Okay, Al's a little bit short, and Michelle's a little bit skinny, and they put her in bad gym shoes and stupid-looking socks. But she's Michelle Pfeiffer for God's sake, with that angelic halo of hair, that translucent skin, that delicate strand of seed pearls she calls teeth, and that inner glow that radiates from within like the rosy blush of first dawn. C'mon now . . . ▪

■ ***Blue Sky*** *(1994)*
Stars: Jessica Lange, Tommy Lee Jones
Director: Tony Richardson
Writers: Jerry Leichtling, Arlene Sarner, and Rama Laurie Stagner, based on a story by Rama Laurie Stagner

Carly Mitchell (Jessica Lange) is not exactly your typical military wife. When she's not frolicking topless in the surf and waving up coquettishly at the helicopters overhead, she's doing her best Blanche DuBois crazy southern gal act: slinking about in skintight sheaths, dirty dancing with her husband's colleagues, and draping scarves over lamps like Stevie Nicks run amock. She may be a loose woman, but she is madly in love with hubby Hank (Tommy Lee Jones). Hank anchors her in her furniture-breaking fits of pique, which she's prone to throw since a woman who is quite sensitive to the aesthetics of her surroundings isn't going to be at one with her environment in prefab housing on a military base. Her daughters resent Carly's diva-like behavior and her powerful hold over Daddy and feel compelled to confront their father with their psychoanalysis of their parents' relationship (this despite the fact that it's the early sixties and real-life kids wouldn't have thought of addressing their officer daddy without calling him sir—oh well, you know how annoying it is to get down those period details).

When Carly takes her free-form sexuality a step too far, it serves as an easy excuse for the military to railroad nuclear-testing specialist Hank, who is threatening to expose the army's complete disregard for human life—well, that's a news flash, isn't it? Ironically, it's up to this hothouse flower to find the inner strength to be Hank's rock. But will such a role reversal destroy their carefully choreographed dance of interdependence?

■ ***Possessed*** *(1931)*
Stars: Joan Crawford, Clark Gable
Director: Clarence Brown
Writer: Adaptation and dialogue continuity by Lenore J. Coffee, from the play The Mirage *by Edgar Selwyn*

She may just be another kid from some faceless small town where the best a girl can hope for is a job in the Acme Paper Box Company and a husband in overalls who thinks melted ice cream, a shabby little house, and happiness on the installment plan are just peachy. But Marian (Joan Crawford) wants more. More, do you hear me? More! And so she slouches toward the tracks with her melancholy pout and foot-dragging ennui, and when a passing luxury passenger train gives her a glimpse at how the other half lives, she's outta there. Donning a jaunty little tam, a sensible suit, and a happy bow tie, she's off to conquer New York City, or at least the first wealthy bachelor she meets.

On Park Avenue, she spots a prime target—lawyer Mark Whitney (Clark Gable), a man with broad shoulders, a double-breasted suit, and a gaze that could melt more than just ice cream (even if he is cursed with an eye-makeup job that looks frightfully Liz Taylor–like—it's that stagey 1932 thing). Mark takes her in and teaches her the proper temperature at which to serve Chablis, how to order in French without ending up with some unspeakably disgusting part of a creature's anatomy on one's plate, and, in short, how to be a proper mistress to an up-and-coming politician.

But Marian's lack of pedigree makes her seem destined to be a kept woman instead of the adoring and adored wife. Will he marry her? Or will her apple pie heart be broken as she settles for slinky sequined gowns by Adrian, diamond baubles, dinner parties with diplomats, and sex with Clark Gable?

Hmmm . . . and the downside would be?

The Handy Hunk Chart Key

Hunk Ratings:

A Man's Man

The Wounded Soldier

Knight in Shining Armor

ASD = *Aristocratic, Suave, and Debonair* **BE** = *Bedroom Eyes* **DD** = *Drowsy Drawl* **DMCA** = *Devil May Care Attitude* **EMT** = *Eyes Moist with Tears* **RGH** = *Really Good Hair* **RUM** = *Raw Unpredictable Masculinity* **SIN** = *Smoldering, Inscrutable, and Noble* **TWL** = *That Wounded Look*

The Handy Hunk Chart

Johnny Depp

BE, EMT, RGH, SIN, TWL

Top Drool Pics: *Don Juan DeMarco, Donnie Brasco, Edward Scissorhands, What's Eating Gilbert Grape*

We have Johnny Depp to thank for elevating cheekbones to the level of the sublime. Those twin peaks of his imbue one with a kind of classic calm that transcends time and space. Lifetimes could pass as one stands in rapt contemplation of those delicately chiseled planes, those pulsing temples and those astounding dimples, swaddled in the lush hollows of his mastic meadows. Depp is more than beautiful, he's a triumph of evolution, a human expression of the Hellenic conception of aesthetic perfection. And on top of all that he can, on occasion, act. It is unfortunate that his shoulder was accidentally chipped during transport, but the resultant rage adds an element of unpredictability that makes him even more attractive . . . unless you're the owner of a toney hotel on the Upper East Side, or the poor schmuck who gets stuck with the check at the Viper Room. ■

Alan Rickman

ASD, BE, DD, RGH, SIN

Top Drool Pics: *An Awfully Big Adventure, Rasputin, Robin Hood: Prince of Thieves, Sense and Sensibility, Truly Madly Deeply*

It's the drawl, isn't it? That slow, drawn-out baritone, resonant and weighty, betrays an intense passion only hinted at by those sleepy eyes under bashful blond bangs. And it's the leisurely grin that works its way skyward in

. . . *continued*

sync with one's own hormone level, not to mention, well, you know. Yes, whether he's stoically waiting for a woman to recognize his undying devotion, ordering ladies about as if they existed only for his pleasure, lifting his chin in dignified resignation as he lets loose his beloved to face a life without him, grimacing in the intensity of lovemaking, or curing small children of congenital birth defects, his British reserve barely conceals the smoldering embers within that threaten to leap forth in a plume of all-consuming desire.

Clark Gable

DMCA, RGH, RUM

Top Drool Pics: *China Seas, Gone With the Wind, It Happened One Night, Mutiny on the Bounty, No Man of Her Own, Possessed, Red Dust, Saratoga*

Possessed of shoulders so broad that they strained the most well-made of suits, a debonair mustache that would make a lesser-boned man look fragile, strong hands that were equally adept at gripping the shoulders of a woman near swooning at his kiss or swatting the derriere of a grateful gal in need of a little naughty horseplay, Gable was the man every man wanted to be and every woman wanted to be with. Who could forget the sight of him at the bottom of that sweeping double staircase in *Gone With the Wind*, looking like a man well versed in the secrets hidden underneath petticoats and pantalettes, or smirking as he towered over yet another angry woman whose temper was tamed by a man who knew what she wanted at that moment—an obliterating kiss that would wipe out all memory of three-dimensional existence. Oh, we know that angry gallop up those red-carpeted stairs wasn't something to sing about the next morning, but let's face it, somehow, with Gable, it worked. ▪

▪ ***While You Were Sleeping*** *(1995)*
Stars: Sandra Bullock, Bill Pullman, Peter Gallagher
Director: Jon Turteltaub
Writers: Daniel G. Sullivan and Fredric Lebow

She's a single woman who is overly attached to her cat, her best romantic prospect is the lunk next door whose ego is as big as his belly, she's got no friends or family to spend Christmas with, and she is obsessed with a man whose only interaction with her is to say "One please" each morning when he buys a train token at her booth. But she is Sandra Bullock, who looks adorable in untrimmed bangs and a messy ponytail, and who can take off a knit cap and not have hat head much less flyaway. Ahh, movie magic.

Through a ridiculous turn of events, Lucy (Sandra Bullock) is taken in by the family of Peter Callaghan (Peter Gallagher), the man she has a crush on. She plays along with their false assumption that she is Peter's fiancée. Lucy knows that once Peter comes out of that coma (it's complicated, okay?), she's going to have to deal with the reality that he doesn't even know her, and meanwhile his unsettlingly cute brother (Bill Pullman) is falling for her, taking her on romantic long walks along the Chicago River (in December . . . hatless . . . with no signs of chill or frostbite. Now that's *real* movie magic). But of course she'll end up with the right guy, and she'll get the perfect in-laws either way.

▪ ***My Fair Lady*** *(1964)*
Stars: Rex Harrison, Audrey Hepburn, Stanley Holloway
Director: George Cukor
Writer: Alan Jay Lerner, based on the play Pygmalion *by George Bernard Shaw*

Destined for a hard-knock life as a poor flower girl, that's what she is, and all because of her lower-class accent. Linguistics professor Henry Higgins bets he can fix that right up and pass her off as a duchess in six months time. Certainly he can polish her exterior quickly enough—only in a fanciful musical would the director think Audrey Hepburn could look like a foolish street urchin merely by donning a ragged dress, pulling a few strands loose from her bun, screeching in Cockney, and popping her eyes wide in amazement at the professor's erudite pronouncements. Guess the makeup department couldn't do anything about that exquisite bone structure.

But then this movie calls for a lot of suspension of disbelief, not to mention the acceptance of male arrogance, verbal abuse, and pimping as cute and funny. Professor Henry Higgins heaps it on Eliza, calling her "deliciously low, horribly dirty" and a "draggled-tailed guttersnipe," of use to nobody but him and devoid of human feeling—and threatens to wallop her. But ya gotta admit, he does look awfully good doing it, with that dimple and those twinkly eyes. And you know once Audrey Hepburn puts on that inevitable tiara (Quick! Name an Audrey Hepburn movie in which she does not wear a tiara!) and gives him a verbal thrashing, he'll clean up even better than she did.

⚠ Warning Label: *If you're feeling ornery, avoid this one.*

Chapter 8

Hell Hath No Fury: Dumped and Out-for-Blood Movies

Who needs him anyway? He was an insensitive clod completely incapable of genuine intimacy. If only you could be as self-involved as he is. If only you could drink him dry and then leave him, cold, alone, and implicated in a crime he didn't commit. But you can't, can you? No. And do you know why? Because you're too *nice*!!! But he'll get his. One day he'll wake up in his emotional cave and realize that he's become an embittered and lonely old man. Then he'll be sorry. Then he'll wish that somewhere in the depths of inner isolation he'd managed to locate a pay phone and call you. The self-centered jerk! But until that day, choose one of our Dumped and Out-for-Blood movies and watch men get a taste of their own medicine.

■ ***Body Heat*** *(1981)*
Stars: William Hurt, Kathleen Turner
Director and Writer: Lawrence Kasdan

This is a classic selection from the woman-as-spider/man-as-fly genre. Ned Racine (William Hurt) is a marginal lawyer with questionable principles, who hails from some sinkhole or another on the coast of Florida. Wandering the pier in search of a breeze one torpid summer evening, he runs into the humid Matty Walker (Kathleen Turner), who is also out trolling for ventilation to ease her languor. She's wearing this gauzy sort of slip thing, that kind of sticks to her in all the right places, and there's a long chiffon scarf that trails for yards behind her, dancing crazily in the hot breath of the trades.

Like most things have a tendency to do during a heat wave in southern Florida, Matty and Ned stick to each other. They lounge on the verandah of her palatial summer cottage, owned by Matty's rich but ultimately inconvenient husband. Mostly they make love, backdropped by the southern Atlantic, and the tinkle of countless wind chimes.

And then, when her prey is sated and self-satisfied, Matty the spider casts her web. And by the time she's done, Ned is ensnared in a weave so intricate, and so masterfully executed, that he can do nothing but dangle and wait for the kill.

> ⚠ Warning Label: *This movie is slow torture, and it hurts soooo good.*

Words to Live By

There's nothing tragic about being fifty—not unless you're trying to be twenty-five.

★ from *Sunset Boulevard*

■ ***She-Devil*** *(1989)*
Stars: Meryl Streep, Roseanne Barr, Ed Begley, Jr.
Director: Susan Seidelman
Writers: Mark R. Burns and Barry Strugatz, based on the novel by Fay Weldon

Meryl Streep is a vision in pink as a husband-stealing, chintz-draping, cockatoo-toting romance writer who breaks up Ruth's (Roseanne Barr) marriage to her husband (Ed Begley, Jr.), who is wallowing in the depths of a midlife crisis. Ruth, a suburban wife and mom who looks more at home in blue jeans and flannel than lace and pink chiffon, vows to get even.

What ensues is just one world-class ball-busting maneuver after the next as Ruth devotes herself to a systematic dismantling of her husband's new life with the most cloying creature that ever put purple pen to page. You'll be Bronx-cheering right along with Ruth as she reduces her rival to a quivering mass of pink Jell-O, and teaches her husband in a very visceral way that when you play with fire . . . you're gonna get burned.

■ ***The War of the Roses*** *(1989)*
Stars: Michael Douglas, Kathleen Turner, Danny DeVito
Director: Danny DeVito
Writer: Michael Leeson, based on the novel by Warren Adler

Barbara (Kathleen Turner) and Oliver (Michael Douglas) Rose are the ideal American couple: two good-looking people, in a good-looking house, with good-looking futures in their respective, upwardly mobile, careers. And like many such ideal couples, way down deep they can't stand the sight of each other. It takes only the smallest spark to send the whole kit and kaboodle up in a blaze of 100-proof hatred.

They decide to divorce but an amicable parting is out of the question. For the rest of the movie, they do nothing but go at each other, hammer and tongues, with the aid of their respective attorneys, one of which is a diminutive dictator in pinstripes played by Danny DeVito during his Louie DePalma phase.

This movie is a veritable banquet of bad feeling. Watch it with someone you love to hate.

World-Class Wrecks

I think . . . no, I am positive . . . that you are the most unattractive man I have ever met in my entire life. You know, in the short time we've been together, you have demonstrated every loathsome characteristic of the male personality and even discovered a few new ones. You are physically repulsive, intellectually retarded, you're morally reprehensible, vulgar, insensitive, selfish, stupid, you have no taste, a lousy sense of humor and you smell. You're not even interesting enough to make me sick.

★ Cher as Alexandra Medford in *The Witches of Eastwick*

■ ***Extremities*** *(1986)*
Stars: Farrah Fawcett, James Russo
Director: Robert M. Young
Writer: William Mastrosimone

The searing central image of this film is Farrah Fawcett, in her frosted and feathered years, fire poker poised in her hand, threatening her would-be rapist, whom she has chained behind the screen in the fireplace. They spend most of the film with both of their lives on the line, ready to spring at each other at the first opportunity. Nothing blows up in this film, or catches fire. No car chases or love scenes . . . but it's heart-stopping action, nonetheless.

The thing is, Farrah Fawcett is a really good actress, but she never got her shot at legitimacy because of that ice-pink patina of hers. When somebody's throwing off a glare like that, it's sort of hard to take them seriously. And so she languished, an opalescent oddity in a matte finish world. And then she married that cute Ryan O'Neal, who turned immediately to bloat. No question, Farrah hasn't had an easy life, but for one brief and, yes, shining moment, in this film, Farrah gets hers!

■ ***Diabolique*** *(1996)*
Stars: Sharon Stone, Isabelle Adjani, Chazz Palminteri, Kathy Bates
Directors: Jeremiah Chechik
Writers: Henri-Georges Clouzot, Jérôme Géronimi, and Don Roos, based on the novel Celle qui n'était plus *by Pierre Boileau and Thomas Narcejac*

The virgin wife (Isabelle Adjani) and magdalene mistress (Sharon Stone) of the sadistic headmaster of an exclusive boys' school team up and plot to drown their tormentor in a bathtub. They wrap the body in a shower curtain and submerge it in a murky pond on campus, but mysteriously, when the pool is drained, the body has disappeared! Pushed to extremes by the severity of their circumstances, Adjani begins an emotional penance that nearly drives her to martyrdom, and Stone metamorphoses into a siren from hell, albeit one with a very large wardrobe budget. As the women scramble to find the body, they are pursued by a quirky menopausal detective (Kathy Bates), who begins to unravel the intricate ties that bind them.

Next time you come face-to-face with the madonna-whore complex, check out this movie and watch what happens when the two Marys get together and unleash the awesome power of the female archetype.

World-Class Wrecks

I could peel you like a pear and God himself would call it justice!

★ Katharine Hepburn as Eleanor of Aquitaine in *The Lion in Winter*

Power Cuts and Transformational Color

What is it about women and their hair? Major emotional crises and rites of passage seem to demand a ritualistic shearing or dyeing of locks. These movie moments will remind you that tonsorial rebellion can be a liberating expression of the new you:

❍ In *Roman Holiday,* princess Audrey Hepburn escapes the stultifying palace, puts on a simple skirt and blouse, walks into the nearest hairdresser's, and emerges with an awesome gamine cut.

❍ In *National Velvet,* teenage Elizabeth Taylor asks Mickey Rooney to scissor off her long hair so she can pass as a boy jockey and win the Grand National.

❍ In *The Accused,* Jodie Foster plays a rape victim whose visceral act of haircutting returns to her a sense of power over her own body.

❍ In *Coming Home,* the politically and sexually awakened Jane Fonda cuts it short, and husband Bruce Dern, returning from Vietnam, isn't sure he likes the change.

❍ In *Blue Sky,* the newly empowered Jessica Lange switches her hair color from a sexy but vulnerable Marilyn Monroe blond to a bold and gutsy Liz Taylor black.

❍ In *Educating Rita,* hairdresser Julie Walters decides that a softer, classier look is more in keeping with her new upscale choices in literature.

❍ In *Little Women,* Jo sells her hair to help out her family, bravely faces the prospect of being the only short-haired girl in town, and discovers that individuality ain't such a bad thing after all.

❍ In *Moonstruck,* Cher lets it loose, covers the gray, and frees herself up for a wild affair with a passionate Italian.

. . . continued

And in the "Don'ts" department:

○ In *The Brady Bunch Movie,* Jan Brady tries out a wig but realizes everyone sees the same old neurotic middle child—probably because she's a California blonde who's chosen an Afro look that would put the seventies' Billy Preston and Angela Davis to shame.

○ In *Play Misty for Me,* Jessica Walters decides she's not the one who needs the radical new look—her rival is. Look out! ■

■ *Something to Talk About* (1995)

Stars: Julia Roberts, Dennis Quaid, Gena Rowlands, Robert Duvall, Kyra Sedgwick
Director: Lasse Hallström
Writer: Callie Khouri

Savaged by critics after her hard-hitting Thelma and Louise got bloody revenge against the worthless and despicable men in their lives, screenwriter Callie Khouri tones it down a bit here and lets the guy get off with no more than one powerful knee to the groin, courtesy of the protagonist's sister (played by Kyra Sedgwick). Why is it that the wronged woman can't just get in a few punches at least before her friend strikes a righteous blow? Sheesh.

Anyway, Julia Roberts plays a wronged woman, Grace, a French-braided, wholesome southern gal who's got an adorable daughter nicknamed Doodlebug and an equally adorable husband named Eddie (Quaid), whose nickname in college was Hound Dog, which should've tipped her off to the inevitability of finding him smooching a red-clad bleached blonde someday. Despite Mom's (Gena Rowlands) exhortations to handle these "family matters" privately and forgive Eddie for his "little slip," and Dad's (Robert Duvall) demand that she patch things up before she blows a big business deal for him, Grace isn't about to be gracious about Eddie's peccadillos. Frankly, she's leaning toward her auntie's strategy for dealing with unfaithful husbands: poisoning the bastard. Meanwhile, Grace engages in some extremely volatile confrontations, including the public unrepressing of a lot of sordid little affairs, which gives her southern lady friends something to talk about besides their upcoming homemakers' cookbook. Revenge may be a dish best served cold, but Grace is intent on ladling it out piping hot.

Grace's unleashed fury functions as a catalyst not only for her own growth but for that of her mother, her daughter, and even her husband. A fine validation of female anger, this one is exceptionally satisfying for the recently wronged.

▪ *What's Love Got to Do With It* (1989)

Stars: Angela Bassett, Laurence Fishburne
Director: Brian Gibson
Writer: Kate Lanier, based on I, Tina *by Tina Turner and Kurt Loder*

We all know the story by now—rock singer Tina Turner, after years of verbal and physical abuse by her domineering husband, walked out with only her name and the clothes on her back. She began again from scratch, and reached heights of fame, fortune, and artistic success that her ex could never hope to achieve. But knowing the story and experiencing the humiliation right along with Tina makes her triumph all the more sweet—and Angela Bassett and Laurence Fishburne's Oscar-nominated performances make real impact.

Fishburne plays the villainous Ike, who has an eye for talent as well as an eye for the ladies, and parlays his act into a highly successful rock and roll revue. This results in the accumulation of gold records, recording contracts, critical praise, and a locust-like cloud of hangers-on descending on his rec room to snort up whatever narcotic's on the menu for the evening. Ike, however, is too far into his self-created scene to pay attention to his diminishing profit margin, much less his wife's need to express herself freely. But with the help of Buddhism, Tina (Bassett) *namio orenge kyo*'s her way to seeing a world beyond her own little hell, and from there it's only a matter of time and opportunity.

Gruesome, disturbing, and, in the end, exhilarating.

■ ***Women on the Verge of a Nervous Breakdown*** *(1988)*
Stars: Carmen Maura, Fernando Guillén Cuervo, Antonio Banderas, and Julieta Serrano
Director and Writer: Pedro Almodóvar

In this subtitled Spanish-language farce, Carmen Maura plays Pepa, a woman who just discovered that her lover, Ivan (Fernando Guillén), is off for the weekend with another woman. She unleashes a fury that results in a garbage can full of his belongings, a torched bed, and a roomful of sleeping victims of her barbiturate-spiked gazpacho (see, she meant to poison him—just enough to make him sick, to wake him up so to speak—even if she did use downers instead of uppers. This is what happens when you don't plan out your revenge scenario carefully).

As if her own rage weren't enough to keep Pepa in a state of frenzy, she's got to deal with a best friend who's suicidal because her last boyfriend turned out to be a Shiite terrorist, the crazy gun-toting pink Chanel suit–wearing ex-wife of her lover, not to mention a love triangle featuring Ivan's son Carlos (Banderas, looking positively boyish in curls and wire-rimmed glasses). And she's pregnant to boot. Thank goodness the maid's coming in the morning, 'cause somebody's going to have to clean up after this mess.

If your life seems to be spinning out of control post-breakup, try to remember: It's all a comedy. You're going to look back someday and laugh. Really.

Classic Bette Bytes

Bill is thirty-two. He looks thirty-two. He looked thirty-two five years ago, and he'll look thirty-two twenty years from now; I hate men.

★ Bette Davis as Margo Channing in *All About Eve*

The Handy Hunk Chart Key

Hunk Ratings:

All-American Boy 🏈

The Wounded Soldier 🗡

The Passionate Priest ✝

DMCA = *Devil-May-Care Attitude* **FSG** = *Feckless Schoolboy Grin* **RUM** = *Raw Unpredictable Masculinity* **SIN** = *Smoldering, Inscrutable, and Noble* **TSHT** = *That Sexy Homicidal Thing* **TWL** = *That Wounded Look* **UGB** = *Urban, Gritty, and Brooding*

The Handy Hunk Chart

Gary Oldman

DMCA, RUM, TSHT, UGB

Top Drool Pics: *Bram Stoker's Dracula, Chattahoochee, Criminal Law, Immortal Beloved, Murder in the First, Prick Up Your Ears, Romeo Is Bleeding, The Scarlett Letter, Sid and Nancy, State of Grace, Track 29*

✝ We know, Gary Oldman is not your run-of-the-mill hunk. He's not traditionally handsome or even, really, untraditionally handsome. He chooses roles that put him in the most bizarre assemblage of wigs ever set on a man's head and . . . well, he's British. But there is something about his wild-eyed stare, his crooked smile, and his willingness to escalate way past the bounds of naturalistic behavior that really flips our switch. There's something intensely sexy about a guy who's not afraid to look like an idiot on the screen. It's generally refreshing, except for that one performance where he plays a one-eyed, half-cocked Jamaican drug dealer/extraterrestrial. What was that about? Who was that one-eyed man? Where did he come from? We have no idea. So next time you're feeling hemmed in by the limited horizons of a rational universe, watch an Oldman flick and go where no man has gone before. ■

. . . continued

Matt Dillon

DMCA, FSG, TWL, UGB

Top Drool Pics: *Drugstore Cowboy, The Flamingo Kid, Grace of My Heart, Liar's Moon, Little Darlings, Rumblefish, Singles, To Die For*

Matt Dillon began as just another New York–based James Dean knock-off in the obligatory T-shirt and cuffed jeans with a cigarette hanging out of his mouth. Ho hum. But lately, Matt Dillon has traded in his urban tough chrysalis for the butterfly wings of middle-age spread. And as the dumb but lovable palooka, he's really starting to register on the adorability scale. Matt Dillon has grown up. Now, instead of smoldering, he phumphers. Instead of baring his teeth, he bares his soul. He's replaced the junkyard dog within with a lovable but dumb golden retriever. And when that big lovable mutt looks up at us with trust in his eyes, begging for dinner, we go running for the Gravy Train. Woof! ■

James Dean

DMCA, FSG, SIN, TWL, UGB

Top Drool Pics: *East of Eden, Giant, Rebel Without a Cause*

What do you say about an icon who has inspired generations of young actors to roll up their jeans, don T-shirts, and take up smoking as a contact sport? Ever since James Dean first meandered onto the scene and elevated bad behavior to an art form, male actors have been mistaking insouciance as good acting, much to the consternation of casting directors everywhere. But James Dean invented the genre. He was the original boy gone wrong; he was more than an actor, he was an anthem to a lost generation. Dean made adolescent angst into a cinematic genre, and taught us all that sometimes you have to break the rules in order to break new ground. Of course, he also taught us that some rules aren't made to be broken, like the speed limit, for example. . . . ■

▪ ***Misery*** *(1990)*
Stars: Kathy Bates, James Caan, Lauren Bacall
Director: Rob Reiner
Writer: William Goldman, based on the novel by Stephen King

It's not that Annie Wilkes (Kathy Bates) is writer Paul Sheldon's (James Caan) wife or girlfriend or anything, but his fictional character Misery Chastain has sustained Annie through so much in her own life that it's almost as if he's written the series for her. So when he kills off Misery in order to move out of the imprisonment of churning out a commercial fiction series, Annie is livid. Not that Paul would normally let himself be swayed by one fan's disappointment, but ever since he broke his legs in a car accident and woke up to find himself lying in a bed in her isolated mountain home, completely dependent on her, Paul has been paying careful attention to Annie's opinion of his writing.

Paul doesn't have a lot of options here. While his brain works overtime trying to find a way to get the phone without her knowing, Annie is ever present, sweetly prattling away in her turtleneck, jumper, and little silver cross necklace, her limp brown side-parted hair lying flat against her head as she shakes his pee bottle in emphasis while imparting her literary advice. Guess Paul's going to have to make nice, won't he?

You may not be able to cut the phone lines and break his ankles so that he stays immobile until he hears you out, but it's kind of a nice little image for a gal to hold on to, isn't it?

Chapter 9

Someday Has Come and Gone and My Prince Still Hasn't Shown Up: Happily Ever After Movies

We know, you've tried everything: eating poison apples, leaving your glass slippers behind at royal balls, or pricking your finger on a spindle, but Prince Charming just doesn't seem to be getting the hint. When you find yourself going head to head with one of the fundamental archetypes of the collective unconscious and coming up empty-handed, suspend your disbelief a little while longer! Tune in to one of these movies, and pretend that fairy tales really do come true, that utterly perfect relationships can exist, and that one day you will wake up and find yourself living happily ever after.

- ***Moonstruck** (1987)*
  Stars: Cher, Nicolas Cage, Vincent Gardenia, Olympia Dukakis, Danny Aiello
  Director: Norman Jewison
  Writer: John Patrick Shanley

Loretta Castorini gave up on romance long ago, convinced that she is cursed with bad luck: The husband of her youth was hit by a bus, dooming her to a life of spinsterhood. No, it's not 1870, but it might as well be, given Loretta's attitude toward the options left to her (this is what happens when a single gal spends all her time in Little Italy—thing is, you've got to just buy your prosciutto and panettone and then get the hell back uptown to the twentieth century). Not only does Loretta give in to going gray, she has to maternally guide her mama's boy suitor Johnny Cammareri (Aiello) into a proper marriage proposal. She doesn't really love Johnny, of course, but at thirty-seven she feels he's her last chance.

Loretta begins to question her low expectations for herself only when she meets Johnny's angst-ridden younger brother, Ronny (Nicolas Cage), whose passionate heights and depths force Loretta into a more intense, more exquisite experience of life. Meaning, of course, an orgasm. And *La Bohème* at Lincoln Center. And a dye job, a dark matte lipstick, and some really sexy red spiked heels. After these sensory experiences, Loretta realizes that a folliclely challenged wuss is not for her.

See what a makeover can do for a girl's outlook? And Loretta even wins the guy *before* she gets to the beauty parlor. Now that's our kind of movie!

■ ***An Officer and a Gentleman*** *(1982)*
Stars: Richard Gere, Debra Winger
Director: Taylor Hackford
Writer: Douglas Day Stewart

Zack Mayo (Richard Gere) is a navy brat who is following in his father's footsteps. He enrolls as an officer candidate in navy flight school, where the motto is "Get jets" and the mascot is a rotating assortment of local mill girls with bodacious tatas and dreams of becoming an officer's wife with a few jets of her own.

Zack is a prime candidate. He has all the right stuff: resolute jaw, clear, bright eyes, a will of iron, and the cutest little butt that ever parade-marched in a pair of dress whites. Unfortunately, Zack also has a serious attitude problem that runs him afoul of his tough-as-nails drill sergeant, Foley, who decides to whittle Mayo down to size. One other tiny character flaw: Zack's a male chauvinist pig with intimacy issues, who is ambivalent about committing to Paula (Debra Winger), the mill girl of his dreams. While she is an engaging

Faking It: Phony Girl Films That Really Piss Us Off

Crossing Delancey *(1988)*
Stars: Amy Irving, Reizl Bozyk, Peter Riegert, Jeroen Krabbé
Director: Joan Micklin Silver
Writer: Susan Sandler, adapted from her play

Yes, we all have had those hormonal crushes on jerks who write poetry, and we do know better, but poor Amy Irving isn't even allowed to boff the guy (Krabbé) long enough to come to her senses on her own. No, Bubbeh (Bozyk) has to interfere, pressuring her to date the potato-sack-shaped pickle salesman (Riegert). He has no poetry or passion, but he's a nice guy and available, so our gal had better jump on him quick before spinsterhood is inevitable. Nice message.

Even if you're years away from the audible ticking of your biological clock, this movie will overstimulate your panic glands. This is what comes of blind dates set up by Grandma. ■

diversion, protocol dictates that he discard her on the rubbish heap of outgrown toys once OTS is over.

Will Zack toss Paula away like a used candy wrapper, callously abandoning her to her tawdry fate as a loom operator in a sweatshop, or will he swoop like an avenging angel, disentangle her from her prison of polyester basting thread, and ride off with her into the sunset on his gleaming white Harley?

Let's put it this way: Spend two hours watching Richard Gere flexing his biceps and probing his deepest emotions, and it's going to be damn hard not to feel optimistic about the fate of the human race.

■ ***Don Juan DeMarco*** *(1995)*
Stars: Marlon Brando, Johnny Depp, Faye Dunaway
Director and Writer: Jeremy Leven

This movie is sort of like *Equus* meets *Miracle on 34th Street* with a nineties twist. Johnny Depp stars in yet another role that requires eyeliner, contoured cheeks, and a blunt cut as Don Juan DeMarco, a classically beautiful kid from small town U.S.A. who believes that he is the legendary lover of classical literature, Don Juan.

Don Juan DeMarco attempts to live his life according to the principles of courtly love (now there's an impossible dream for you), paying chaste homage to his lost lady faire, the pristine Doña Rosa, whom he has enshrined in the sanctuary of his romantic imagination. Until he finds Rosa, however, every other woman in the world is fair game, and he goes about the country pleasing women wherever he finds them. It's his mission . . . pleasing woman.

Forget Santa Claus. You need a boost after a discouraging life passage? Start believing in Don Juan, a pilgrim of pleasure, who seeks only to give women exactly what they want without having to be asked. To us, that sounds like happily ever after *and* a bag of fries.

Words to Live By

Paris is always a good idea.

★ Audrey Hepburn as Sabrina in *Sabrina*

▪ ***Indiscreet*** *(1958)*
Stars: Cary Grant, Ingrid Bergman, Cecil Parker, Phyllis Calvert
Director: Stanley Donen
Writer: Norman Krasna, based on his play Kind Sir

You know you've stepped into a different era when a flustered Ingrid Bergman is advised by her sister (Phyllis Calvert) to put on a girdle so she'll feel better. In fact, this whole movie has a surreal quality. First, you've got a male love interest (Cary Grant) who is not only suave, sophisticated, and charming, he's got a glamorous, high-paying job, is single and straight, and is able to drink Scotch and sodas morning, noon, and night and never show the slightest hint of inebriation or under-eye puffiness. Then you've got a female love interest (Bergman) who is an actress living in London, who never seems to have a role yet can afford designer matching dress and coat ensembles. Plus, she has a sympathetic sister and brother-in-law (Cecil Parker) nearby and no loser boyfriend in sight. She, too, can drink Scotch and soda morning, noon, and night and still walk straight and have a gorgeous figure, and even more implausibly, she can carry off avocado-and-burnt-orange gowns. *In what universe?*

Of course there are all sorts of cute little twists to keep the couple apart, and an outrageously daring act on her part that shows she's plucky as well as beautiful, and it all ties up in one neat little package requiring no restrictive foundation undergarments.

Watch this, and tell yourself that a half bottle of wine and handful of Godivas won't go straight to your thighs, 'cause at this point you'll believe anything.

■ ***It Happened One Night*** *(1934)*
Stars: Clark Gable, Claudette Colbert
Director: Frank Capra
Writer: Robert Riskin, based on the story "Night Bus" by Samuel Hopkins Adams

She's an heiress engaged to a nobleman, but glamour and fortune aren't enough when what she really wants is love. So she takes a dive off a ship, plunks neatly into the water, swims off to the nearest bus station, and starts a journey to find herself. And lucky Ellie Andrews (Claudette Colbert) doesn't get stuck next to an unshaven psoriasis sufferer with B.O., halitosis, a *Penthouse* in his hand, and a string of pickup lines—noooo, she ends up next to a devilishly handsome and chivalrous gentleman who fends off all the icky boys, provides a manly shoulder to sleep on, sports a sexy grin, and lets loose a string of witticisms that are utterly endearing (Clark Gable).

Of course, it turns out that he's a reporter and she may very well be no more to him than a big scoop, but this and every other wrinkle will certainly be ironed out by the last reel. And the madcap dash-across-a-field ending is as wildly life-affirming as it gets.

■ ***Singin' in the Rain*** *(1952)*
Stars: Gene Kelly, Debbie Reynolds, Donald O'Connor, Jean Hagen
Directors: Gene Kelly, Stanley Donen
Writers: Betty Comden and Adolph Green

A crinkly-eyed Irishman who has a flair for tap-dancing in the rain, a wonderful sense of humor, and a set of tanned and highly defined biceps peeking out from rolled-up sleeves that hint at upper body development worthy of the semi-nude scene that never comes because this is a G-rated 1950s picture, literally drops into Debbie Reynolds's life. Don Lockwood (Gene Kelly) is, of course, a huge movie star with exceptional talent, a minimal ego, and a quick mind. He's wealthy but not ostentatious, ready to fall in love and commit himself to marriage without a whisper about a prenup. Oh, there's an arrogant actress named Lina Lamont (Hagen) trying to steal poor Debbie's man as well as her career, but really Lina's just setting us all up for a dramatic revelation of bright-eyed Debbie's talent that will launch her, comet-like, into stardom and then straight into the arms of her dancing man.

Lots of laughs, a cute little plot involving the movies turning from silent to talkies, and completely gratuitous and totally engaging dance sequences featuring Kelly and O'Connor will whisk away those dark storm clouds above your head in no time.

Christmas in July

It doesn't have to be the holiday season for you to appreciate these Christmas classics, all of which will get you into that cheerful, warm-hearted, pre-January-credit-card-bill spirit.

It's a Wonderful Life (1946)
Stars: Jimmy Stewart, Donna Reed, Henry Travers
Director: Frank Capra
Writers: Frank Capra, Frances Goodrich, Albert Hackett, and Jo Swerling, based on a story by Philip Van Doren Stern

Before guardian angels became overcommercialized with all those cheap lapel pins and Learning Annex courses, there was good old Clarence (Travers), a bumbling angel who saves George Bailey (Stewart) from ending it all after a particularly hellish day. Clarence shows George that without him, quaint little Bedford Falls would be reduced to a depressing hamlet devoid of reasonably

. . . continued

priced housing, the local war hero, and Zuzu's petals, which serve as a poignant if overly sentimental reminder of life's beauty and fragility. Only then can George Bailey appreciate all the love that surrounds him, from his beaming wife to his dotty uncle to everyone in the entire town, who all pitch in at his darkest hour.

Avoid the garish colorized version, do a Donna Reed and whip up some cocoa, and ready yourself for some life affirmation. In fact, why not ring a bell or two to intensify the magical effect?

Miracle on 34th Street *(1947)*
Stars: Maureen O'Hara, Edmund Gwenn, Natalie Wood
Director: George Seaton
Writer: George Seaton, based on a story by Valentine Davies

Doris Walker (Maureen O'Hara) is a disillusioned woman whose dreams of love and wedded bliss have laid a big fat egg. Consequently, she has become a severe and bottom-line-driven "career woman" (another one of those phrases that is always in quotes) who thinks only about her job at Macy's and refuses to believe in intangibles like love and happily ever after. Her daughter, Susan (Natalie Wood), who looks adorable in a constantly rotating assortment of perfectly coordinated coats and caps that foreshadow the Jackie O ensembles of the early sixties, is a precocious version of her mother: She refuses to believe in Santa Claus. Then Doris and Susan run into a man in a red suit and a beard who calls himself Kris Kringle (Edmund Gwenn). Kris insists that he is the real Santa, even though Susan and Doris scoff at him and recognize him for the poor, mentally infirm nursing home refugee that he is. But Kris has a few tricks up his sleeve, and challenges Susan and Doris to invite wonder into their world, and let impossible dreams work magic in their lives.

What could be better when you're feeling the heel of the boot of cynicism stomping its cigarette out on your head than a movie that proves that Santa Claus really does exist? It doesn't have to be Christmas to reinvest in

. . . continued

some of your earliest illusions, like justice prevails, love conquers all, and single moms who work at Macy's will find a bungalow in the burbs under the tree on Christmas morning. The perfect antidote for that lump-of-coal-in-your-stocking blues.

> ⚠ Warning Label: *Remember, he knows when you are sleeping, and he knows when you're awake, and he probably knows your PIN number too.*

Christmas in Connecticut (1945)
Stars: Barbara Stanwyck, Dennis Morgan, Sydney Greenstreet
Director: Peter Godfrey
Writers: Lionel Houser and Adele Commandini, based on a story by Aileen Hamilton

Thanks to a ridiculous PR stunt cooked up by her overzealous publisher, a Martha Stewart–type columnist (Stanwyck) has to scurry to cover up her less-than-idyllic domestic scenario. Seems Elizabeth Lane, "America's Best Cook," isn't really the hostess with the mostess with a husband, chubby baby, and darling farmhouse in Connecticut after all, but a harried single gal in an alley-facing apartment off 46th Street who lives on takeout from downstairs and doesn't even own a window box. In real life, the publisher would be in on the deception, but that wouldn't make for a comedy of errors with a postwar Christmas theme, would it?

Aided by her bland fiancé (who actually owns a farm in Connecticut—how likely is *that?*), a screwy uncle (the cook at the restaurant downstairs), and some conveniently available babies lent by the women next door (so one's a blond boy and the other's a dark-haired girl; big deal, it's a kid, isn't it? Who's gonna notice?), she manages to pull off a ridiculous deception for the benefit of her publisher and a gen-u-ine war hero with a beautiful Irish tenor (Dennis Morgan), and even finds true love just in time to get a New Year's Eve date.

Only in the movies.

The Thin Man Movies, 1934–47

Stars: Myrna Loy, William Powell
Directors and Writers:

The Thin Man: director W. S. Van Dyke, writers Albert Hackett and Frances Goodrich, based on the novel by Dashiell Hammett
After the Thin Man: director W. S. Van Dyke, writers Albert Hackett and Frances Goodrich
Another Thin Man: director W. S. Van Dyke, writers Albert Hackett and Frances Goodrich
Shadow of the Thin Man: director W. S. Van Dyke, writers Irving Brecher and Harry Kurnitz, based on a story by Harry Kurnitz
The Thin Man Goes Home: director Richard Thorpe, writers Dwight Taylor, Harry Kurnitz, and Robert Riskin, based on a story by Harry Kurnitz and Robert Riskin
Song of the Thin Man: director Edward Buzzell, writers Harry Crane, Steve Fisher, James O'Hanlon, and Nat Perrin, based on a story by Stanley Roberts

If you pay very close attention to the six Thin Man movies, you may be able to discern a plot line here and there, but if you don't, no matter. The point, really, is the martini jokes. Well, that and Myrna Loy's hats, which are fabulously silly concoctions that probably look a lot more sensible when you've been tippling martinis all day. Accompanied by their lovable terrier, Asta, and on occasion little Nick Junior as well, the ever sophisticated, ever droll Nick and Nora Charles are fabulously fun as they solve various murders in this series. Start with the first, work your way through, and if the quality starts to slip just a bit with the last few, believe us, you won't notice if you've been keeping up with the Charleses. Just be sure to have plenty of aspirin on hand for tomorrow.

■ ***When a Man Loves a Woman*** *(1994)*
Stars: Meg Ryan, Andy Garcia
Director: Luis Mandoki
Writers: Ronald Bass and Al Franken

Alice Green (Meg Ryan) is rude, crude, and unreliable, making Andy Garcia a wreck whenever he has to leave home in his natty pilot's outfit for a flight, but, of course, he bucks up because all those people are relying on him. And boy, can you rely on him. Observing his wife's unhappiness and erratic behavior, does he go out with the boys to drink and bitch about the old ball and chain? Does he start flirting with that gal at the office? Noooo, he thinks, all she needs is an exotic island vacation to adjust her attitude, and *whoosh*, off she goes, to join him in a smoochfest in a little private pool at some resort. Then, when Alice goes so far as to slap the kid and pass out in the bathroom, her husband not only doesn't desert her but lovingly confronts her with her alcoholism and puts her in rehab while he works, takes care of the home and kids, and reminds her of his undying love for her. Yes, no matter how nasty she gets, he's there to love and support her and look damned fine doing it.

Watch it for Meg Ryan's acclaimed performance if you like, but the real delight to this film is imagining being married to someone who looks like Andy Garcia and doesn't so much as leave a sock on the floor or utter a peep about your wild mood swings. Can someone clone this guy?

Words to Live By

I could never be intimate with someone who wore a pinky ring.

★ Susan Sarandon in *Compromising Positions*

▪ ***When Harry Met Sally . . .*** *(1989)*
Stars: Meg Ryan, Billy Crystal, Carrie Fisher, Bruno Kirby
Director: Rob Reiner
Writer: Nora Ephron

The key elements to a long-term love affair and happily-ever-after marriage are, according to this film, serendipity, character-defining personality quirks, and patience. That, and Meg Ryan. I mean, this girl gets every guy in every film, no matter how annoying she acts. All she needs is her trademark giggle and a big head of layered blond hair. We wish it were that easy.

Anyway, after viewing this romantic comedy it'll be a lot easier to cling to the hope that just around the corner is the man of your dreams. Yes, if you just wait long enough, he'll humble himself before you in public, turn your every character flaw into a shining virtue, and pledge himself to you for eternity. Hmm . . . never worked for us.

Harry and Sally spend eleven years being "just friends," oblivious to the fact that they were made for each other. They even go so far as to fix each other up with their best friends (Carrie Fisher and Bruno Kirby), only to experience a double rejection and end up, as usual, alone on New Year's Eve. But it's only a matter of time before Harry and Sally realize their true love has been there all along.

> ⚠ Warning Label: *If it's been a while since . . . well, you know, approach with caution: you may find yourself whipping up some unrealistic expectations about an unsuspecting old friend.*

■ ***Sleepless in Seattle*** *(1993)*
Stars: Meg Ryan, Tom Hanks, Bill Pullman, Rosie O'Donnell
Director: Nora Ephron
Writers: Nora Ephron, David S. Ward, and Jeff Arch, based on a story by Jeff Arch

Annie Reed (Meg Ryan) is engaged to a good-enough fellow (played by good-enough actor Bill Pullman) who is hopelessly boring and allergic to everything, but appropriately safe husband material for a woman who can't help believing there's some truth to that statistic about being more likely to be killed by a terrorist than married before she's forty. Still, there's a small part of her that dreams of more—the part of her that has spent far too much time watching *An Affair to Remember* and weeping over the tragic outcome of Deborah Kerr's impetuous jaywalking (see *Love Affair,* Chapter 1).

Annie's new habit of listening to late-night talk radio leads her to write to a lonely-hearted widower in Seattle named Sam Baldwin (Hanks), whose adorable son is seeking a new mommy. Egged on by pal Becky (Rosie O'Donnell), Annie invites Sam to fly cross-country, sight unseen, to meet her at the top of the Empire State Building, just like in *An Affair to Remember,* only presumably with less of that pride, fear, and spinal cord damage that kept Deborah Kerr and Cary Grant suffering in silence for the last half of the movie.

Unfortunately, this warmhearted romance is a rather flaccid follow-up to Ephron's classic *When Harry Met Sally. . . .* Still, it's got a few good lines and the ever affable Ryan and Hanks, and how can you ignore this movie when it's the source of the term *chick flick?*

▪ *Pillow Talk* (1959)

Stars: Rock Hudson, Doris Day, Tony Randall
Director: Michael Gordon
Writers: Stanley Shapiro and Maurice Richlin, based on a story by Russell Rouse and Clarence Greene

From the moment those credits roll, with Doris and Rock gaily tossing pink and blue satin pillows in the air while Doris croons "there must be a boy, must be a pillow, must be a pillow talkin' boy for me," you know you're in for one surreal romp. Originally billed as a "sexcapade," *Pillow Talk* is a bizarre little gem of the prefeminist, pre-Pill, pre-Stonewall era. Doris Day is a freckle-nosed goody-goody career gal in a silver helmet wig, the hairs of which wouldn't stir even in a nuclear blast. Her frigidity is the central joke (yeah, like any single woman wouldn't have "bedroom problems" in the pre-Pill, pre-vibrator fifties!). It's up to poor Doris to handle those fellows who are all hands, like that lothario who shares her party line, Brad Allen (Rock Hudson). Oh, she's never met him, but his overheard conversations with girl after girl prove he's just another on-the-make bachelor who can't be trusted. Men! They're such animals!

When Brad finally catches a glimpse of his attractive phone mate, he decides to try her on for size. Affecting a Texas accent, he pretends to be a gentleman out to woo her without compromising her virtue—at least until the sixth date. Trick is, he has to avoid tipping off their mutual acquaintance (Tony Randall) to his scheme. Meanwhile, in his own voice he hints to Doris that maybe her new beau isn't a gentleman after all. Maybe he's one of those sensitive fellas who likes interior decorating and recipe collecting. How's that for an ironic little plot twist? I mean, don't you just wish you were a fly on the wall of Rock Hudson's brain when he delivered those lines? Talk about repression!

Faking It: Phony Gal Films That Really Piss Us Off

My Best Friend's Wedding

Stars: Julia Roberts, Dermot Mulroney, Cameron Diaz, Rupert Everett
Director: P. J. Hogan
Writer: Ronald Bass

That dazzling smile that could illuminate an entire studio's worth of soundstages. That perplexed furrowing of the brow, which shows that she's not just another pretty face but a woman engaged in a powerful internal struggle. That tiny, firm little belly that peeks out above her jeans, proving that she is young, nubile, and worthy of admiration and love from whatever man she chooses. All of this and more are supposed to make up for the fact that in this romantic comedy, Julia Roberts plays a little brat that we wish would go away before we personally slap her one.

The setup is that her character, Jules, is taken aback by the news that her best friend (Dermot Mulroney) is going to get married in four days. She sets out to bust up the wedding, at first because she's just feeling territorial, then because she realizes she loves him. Then we are introduced to the bride-to-be, who is not only devastatingly sweet but the most sympathetic character in the movie (Cameron Diaz). While Dermot Mulroney unleashes his egotistical male rage at his fragile fiancée, demanding she give up her education and her life for him, Julia runs about trying to destroy the happiness of both parties. Then the groom starts making eyes at Julia, finally settles on marrying his doormat of a betrothed, though he won't extend her the courtesy of seriously discussing a compromise between their conflicting needs. And Julia stands by his decision, knowing it will ruin the poor girl's life and end in divorce court.

How romantic. Where's the comedy? When the gay male sidekick (Everett) is the one who gets the girl, ya gotta wonder what's going on out there in La La Land.

Why not put on some pink pajamas, curl up with lots of fluffy pillows, and pour yourself a nice grasshopper, brandy alexander, or pink lady to sip while you enjoy this frothy little piece of Americana?

World-Class Wrecks

I look upon Brad Allen like any other disease. I've had him. I'm over him. I'm immune to him.

★ Doris Day as Jan Morrow in *Pillow Talk*

▪ ***The Ghost and Mrs. Muir*** *(1947)*
Stars: Gene Tierney, Rex Harrison, George Sanders, Natalie Wood
Director: Joseph L. Mankiewicz
Writer: Philip Dunne, based on the novel by R. A. Dick

Defying her stuffy and controlling in-laws, the newly widowed Mrs. Muir (Gene Tierney) decides she needs to start a life of her own for the first time, so taking her little daughter (Natalie Wood) by the hand, she departs from London for the sea. There she finds a charming little cottage that's just the right price, but the local real estate agents discourage her and she soon discovers why: The former owner, Captain Gregg (Rex Harrison), died in the house and now haunts it. Well, the Captain may be determined to spend an eternity walking through the rooms of her new place, but she's the one paying the bills, dammit, so he'd better start respecting her boundaries. First, maniacal laughter is acceptable, but swearing is not. Second, she'll do the decorating and landscaping, thank you very much. And third, he's to restrict his frightening noises and movements to scaring off unwanted visits from the in-laws, but not terrifying her little girl.

These firm boundaries in place, Mrs. Muir soon finds that the salty old Captain has taken a shine to her and even solves her major financial crisis. But when she begins to pine for a flesh-and-blood man, he magnanimously takes his leave and frees her to explore the possibilities of a loving relationship with a man of this world. Let's see: unselfish, fiscally responsible, respectful of her rules and tastes regarding decor, good to the kid, effective bouncer at the door. Death, apparently, does wonders for a man's character.

Chapter 10

I Am Woman, Hear Me Roar: Straining to Hear Your Inner Voice Movies

Who are you? Why are you? Is this all there is? Shouldn't there be something else? Something larger? Shouldn't your life be dedicated to a resonant and noble cause? Perhaps there's a long-neglected country and western singer at the heart of you, waiting for her moment in the spotlight at the Grand Ole Opry. Or perhaps an adenoidal Australian in a shag belting out, Merman-like, her feminist hymns? If you want to get in touch with your inner Helen Reddy, watch one of these I Am Woman, Hear Me Roar movies, and cut loose.

- ***Coal Miner's Daughter*** *(1980)*
  Stars: Sissy Spacek, Tommy Lee Jones, Beverly D'Angelo (as Patsy Cline)
  Director: Michael Apted
  Writer: Thomas Rickman

Back in Butcher's Holler, Kintucky, li'l ol' Loretta Lynn (played by a young Sissy Spacek, whose petite wide-eyed look makes Tommy Lee Jones seem all the more beefy and powerful) was jes' a slip of a thang, and a purty one at that, when a fast-talking, fast-driving, jes' plain ol' *fast* boy named Doolittle (Jones, with a frightening red-blond dye job) took a shinin' to her. Loretta's sexual naiveté gets them off to a rocky start—"I ain't gonna get used to you gettin' on me and sweatin' like an old pig!" she protests on her wedding morning, and wisely deduces that it's hubby's grubby technique that's turning her off. 'Course, that doesn't stop her from poppin' out puppies at the tender age of fifteen, but Doo has bigger plans for his li'l hillbilly gal: She's gonna be singing to more than her babies, if he has anything to say about it. His vision pays off big time, but Doo descends into some pain-in-the-ass *A-Star-Is-Born* behavior that starts turning sinister. Will he straighten out and get hisself back to where he belongs and stand behind his woman?

■ ***Muriel's Wedding*** *(1994)*
Stars: Toni Collette, Rachel Griffiths, Bill Hunter
Director and Writer: P. J. Hogan

Set in Porpoise Spit, Australia (don't you just looove that?), this coming-of-age tale focuses on Muriel, an overweight adolescent malcontent who muddles through her mundane, misfit life by dreaming of a grand wedding, underscored by an ABBA medley.

Muriel has to travel a long and winding road before she realizes her top 40 fantasies. She steals money to go on a tropical vacation and find the Fernando of her dreams. Instead, she meets a zany girlfriend who proves the perfect harmonic counterpoint to her Europop vision, and together they go off in search of their personal orchestration.

Next time you feel like your personal plotline is being underscored by a phlegmatic eighties-style Swedish pop song, rent this one and celebrate the musical mediocrity of life.

■ ***Grace of My Heart*** *(1996)*
Stars: Illeana Douglas, John Turturro, Matt Dillon, Eric Stoltz
Director and Writer: Allison Anders

Loosely based on the life of Carole King, this rite-of-passage tale chronicles the epic journey of Edna Buxton (Illeana Douglas), a hit songwriter and singer in the changalang-adingdong days of New York's pop heyday. Edna lends her heart and her talent to every comer in a pair of peg-legged pants with a guitar in his hands who asks her to write a song for her. She learns the hard way to take possession of herself and claim her own voice.

Classic Kate Quotes

I made Louis take me on Crusade. I dressed my maids as Amazons and we rode bare-breasted halfway to Damascus. Louis had a seizure and I damn near died of windburn . . . but the troops were dazzled.

★ Kate Hepburn as Eleanor of Aquitaine in *The Lion in Winter*

Oh, that's silly. No woman could ever run for President. She'd have to admit she's over thirty-five.

★ As Mary Matthews in *State of the Union*

Don't trust no man farther than a shotgun can hit.

★ As Triggers Hicks in *Spitfire*

Henry's bed is Henry's province, he can people it with sheep for all I care. Which on occasion he has done.

★ As Eleanor of Aquitaine in *The Lion in Winter*

A daughter of a wealthy Philadelphia family, Edna was never able to fill out her debutante ball gown, no matter how many seamstresses her perpetually disapproving mother hired to custom fit her. She wins a trip to New York in a record-company-sponsored singing contest and meets with nothing but discouragement, until an ungainly, mop-topped, sideburned, and bespectacled producer Joel (John Turturro) changes her name to Denise Waverly, replaces her pedigree with a back-alley upbringing, and sits her down at a keyboard in a tiny cupboard on Swing Street. There, Denise starts cranking out the hits. Then, just when things are starting to go her way, just when she's finally getting the opportunity to access her full potential and make all her dreams come true, she falls in love. Don't you hate when that happens? And, of course, she chooses the biggest loser on the block. Some guy called Howard (Eric Stoltz), a chronic malcontent who covers up his lack of character with a verbose devotion to counterculture politics. Howard proves to be the first in a long line of unfaithful, emotionally inaccessible talent vampires who suck Denise dry, until she learns to find a way to possess herself, and own her talent.

This is not just a movie, it's an anthem. It'll make you want to sing it, and sing it loud.

■ ***Desert Bloom*** *(1986)*
Stars: Jon Voight, Annabeth Gish, JoBeth Williams, Ellen Barkin
Director and Writer: Eugene Corr, from a story by Linda Remy and Eugene Corr

"I had a theory that glasses would make me look like Ingrid Bergman. . . . I thought the glasses gave me mystery, and cheekbones." Ahh, the sweet delusions of youth!

Just outside of Las Vegas, Nevada, in the 1950s, awkward teenager Rose Chismore (Annabeth Gish) gets fitted for her first pair of nerd-chic cat's-eye glasses. Now, for the first time, she has a clear view of her family and realizes that part of growing up is understanding that grown-ups are just like children, only far more confused. There's her stepfather, whose pompous posturing and endless lecturing on physics factoids pulled from *Popular Mechanics* magazine are merely a pitiful attempt to cover his feelings of inadequacy (actually, his drunken rages are rooted in post-traumatic stress disorder, but that's an observation she won't make in this pre–talk show, pre-movie-of-the-week era). There's her mother, who is covering up her own inability to control her husband, or provide a stable home life, by putting on a cheery smile, offering motherly homilies like "A girl wrapped up in herself makes a mighty small package," exhorting her sailor-suited daughters to sing hideously off-key Andrews Sisters tunes for Daddy, and tossing tuna and cream of mushroom soup over rice and calling it a home-cooked meal. And there's the only person to have any fun at all in this house—Aunt Star (Barkin), who has an appreciation for tight red dresses, falsies, and quickie divorces (which is why she stays a spell in Nevada with the family). Too bad Rose can't also see through the federal government's insistence that those A-bomb tests out in the desert are perfectly harmless as long as she ducks and covers.

This coming-of-age tale is a good reminder of your own powers of observation, and the importance of acknowledging the truth beneath the lies—particularly when they involve government reassurances.

■ ***The Net*** *(1995)*
Stars: Sandra Bullock, Jeremy Northam, Dennis Miller
Director: Irwin Winkler
Writers: John D. Brancato, Michael Ferris, Irwin Winkler, Rob Cowan, and Richard Beebe; John D. Brancato and Michael Ferris (story)

When a computer geek (Bullock) is seduced by a con man (Northam), her naiveté rings true—after all, a gal whose face-to-face contact is limited to the pizza delivery boy and an Alzheimer's-stricken mother is more easily duped than most. Even the high-tech intrigue here is plausible—unless you're a computer geek, in which case you'll have to overlook some poetic license, or unless you're someone who has actually tried to retrieve a deleted computer file. *In our dreams!* But what we didn't buy for a moment was that a woman approaching thirty who spends all of her time in a chair and lives on Domino's Pizza has the bod of Sandra Bullock and can carry off itty-bitty black bikinis at the beach. Still, despite her total lack of body fat, Bullock is thoroughly likable as a woman-in-jeopardy who tries to rescue herself with minimal help from the only reliable man in her life—the sleazeball therapist who seduced her years ago (Miller). In the process, she finds the courage to venture out of the chat rooms and into the real world, where she discovers her own wit and courage.

■ ***Born Yesterday*** *(1950)*
Stars: Judy Holliday, Broderick Crawford, William Holden
Director: George Cukor
Writer: Albert Mannheimer, based on the play by Garson Kanin

Oh, she's got a voice all right—one that'll peel paint. Screeching in a high-pitched, outer borough, working-class accent, Billie (Judy Holliday) nevertheless goes unheard by her thug boyfriend, Harry Brock (Broderick Crawford), who thinks of her as no more than a plaything. And boy does she dress the part—the woman hangs out in white sparkly lounging pajamas and high heels. But Harry thinks Billie's gum-cracking, gin-playing ways might be a detriment to his wheelings and dealings, even if they do make her the most fascinating dumb blonde ever to grace the screen (which is why you shouldn't consider for a moment watching the Melanie Griffith remake of this movie instead of the original). You see, Harry has just rented a suite in D.C. to do some business, namely, buying himself a congressman with his ill-gotten gains. He figures it might help him get in with the locals if he hires a journalist, Paul Verrall (William Holden), to teach Billie some a' dat classy stuff. Little does Harry realize that the unleashing of a mind, no matter how simple a mind it is, is the unleashing of a spirit.

Them's Fightin' Words

I'll be no man's slave and no man's whore, and if I can't kill them all, by the gods they'll know I've tried.

★ Lana Clarkson as Amathea in *Barbarian Queen*

Don't fuck with me, fellas. This ain't my first time at the rodeo.

★ Faye Dunaway as Joan Crawford in *Mommie Dearest*

My teenage angst bullshit now has a body count.

★ Winona Ryder as Veronica Sawyer in *Heathers*

Lick it, put a stamp on it, and mail it to someone who gives a shit.

★ Kyra Sedgwick as Emma Rae in *Something to Talk About*

I've said it before, and I'll say it again: "No more fucking ABBA!"

★ Terence Stamp as Bernadette in *The Adventures of Priscilla, Queen of the Desert*

Exposed for the first time to what American democracy is meant to be, and to the possibility that even though she has all she wants, maybe that's only because she doesn't really know what she wants, Billie begins to reconsider her own personal pursuit of happiness and learns how to think for herself. And what she thinks of Harry ain't so good. And what she thinks of Paul is, well, you can pretty much guess how that mentor relationship plays out, can't you?

▪ ***Driving Miss Daisy*** *(1989)*
Stars: Jessica Tandy, Morgan Freeman, Dan Ackroyd
Director: Bruce Beresford
Writer: Alfred Uhry

A classic entry in the it's-never-too-late genre, this movie, adapted from the stage play, traces the relationship between Daisy (Jessica Tandy), an elderly Jewish widow living in Atlanta, and her driver of twenty years, Hoke (Morgan Freeman). Initially, their relationship is as bone-dry and inflexible as Miss Daisy herself, who wears an almost perpetual scowl, suspects everybody of dishonorable conduct, and gives new dimension to the term *control freak*. Gradually, however, as these two castaways from life grope their way along the unfamiliar corridor of interracial relationships in the South, tender young sprouts begin to form on Miss Daisy's woody stem. Well into her eighties, Miss Daisy at last finds love and acceptance flowering in her heart, and a new independence with which to begin on a fresh chapter of her long life.

▪ ***I Like It Like That*** *(1994)*
Stars: Lauren Vélez, Jon Seda, Lisa Vidal, Griffin Dunne
Director and Writer: Darnell Martin

It's a little hard to hear your inner voice when the kids are screaming and pounding on the bathroom door, the radio is blasting salsa, and Mrs. Gonzales downstairs is banging on her ceiling so hard that your bathroom tiles are bouncing up from the floor. The only recourse Lisette (Lauren Vélez) has is to sing along and dance passionately with the mop. Yup, five-minute break for a total meltdown and then it's right back to reconstructing her disaster of a life. She's got a loser husband, Chino (Seda), sitting in jail for trying to steal her a tape player (God forbid he actually gets a job to pay for household appliances), she's broke and unemployed, her little boy is shoplifting and falling in with the wrong crowd, and that bitch Magdalena (Lisa Vidal) is just waiting to pounce on Chino once he's back on the street and steal him back from Lisette. So, using her brains, her bod—or at least the bod created with the help of her transvestite brother's falsies—her chutzpah, and her knowledge of Puerto Rican street culture, Lisette wrangles her way into a great job and an office romance. But when her skeevy yuppie boss, Price (Dunne), proves that the South Bronx has no patent on pain-in-the-butt men, Lisette's got to figure out what she really wants for herself.

■ ***Light of Day*** *(1987)*
Stars: Michael J. Fox, Joan Jett, Gena Rowlands
Director and Writer: Paul Schrader

This could've been a totally forgettable story about two siblings (Fox and Jett) torn apart by one's need to rebel and the other's need to settle down and make peace with Mom (Rowlands) but for Joan Jett as the uncompromising rock-and-roller of the family. She's a breath of fresh air in this stagnant Jersey world of limited expectations and watered-down ideals. Okay, so the emotions are overly simplistic and the direction heavyhanded, and there's no way we buy Joan Jett selling out to some phony haircut band (Courtney Love, maybe, but not our Joan). Still, it's inspiring to see the flash of her black eyes and the serpentine curl of her back as she teaches that whitebread, boyish, Canadian sitcommer how to rock and roll. And knowing that in real life Jett still hasn't settled for a day job or given up despite patchy success makes it all the more fun to vicariously enjoy her integrity here.

■ ***sex, lies, and videotape*** *(1989)*
Stars: Andie MacDowell, Peter Gallagher, Laura San Giacomo, James Spader
Director and Writer: Steven Soderbergh

When Ann, a prudish, flowing-skirted suburbanite (MacDowell), finds her sister's earring on the floor of the bedroom she shares with her husband (Gallagher), it's a cue to stop blushing and start owning her sexuality again. Now, there's no need to turn slut like her sister (San Giacomo), but an odd fellow who just blew in from God-knows-where (Spader) teaches her that even an impotent man with the upper body of the Pillsbury Doughboy, can, with the right high-tech equipment, manage to seduce women and reacquaint himself with his sexual response without any exchange of bodily fluids. Of course, his safe-sex method is a little, um, lacking in intimacy. But he does inspire Ann, who is preoccupied with landfills and urban waste disposal, to stop sublimating her libido, don some tight jeans, and set herself in an assertive stance, videocamera in hand. Of course, the subject of her little film, her direction, and especially her distribution are all crucial if it's going to have the desired effect.

A good reminder that expressing one's self artistically can be supremely empowering, but the results might be better off locked in a cabinet, away from snoops.

■ ***Jane Eyre*** *(1983)*
Stars: Zelah Clarke, Timothy Dalton
Director: Julian Amyes
Writer: Alexander Baron, based on the novel by Charlotte Brontë

First her aunt and cousins torture her because they had to take her in after her parents died. Next, the school headmaster says she's bound for hell. Then a tuberculosis epidemic sweeps away her best friend. And finally, just when she thinks her employer Mr. Rochester is about to close the book on her miserable past by marrying her and making her mistress of his estate, those eerie noises emanating from servant Grace Poole's quarters upstairs turn out to be a flesh-and-blood manifestation of a repressed past transgression by Rochester. Talk about skeletons in the closet!

All of which impel Jane, who is as plainspoken as she is plain-faced, to say no to Rochester's proposal and strike out on her own to answer some questions about her own past and identity, which she does with the great help of coincidence and a typical Victorian twist concerning inheritances. Only then will she feel complete and able to consider marriage to a sexy, passionate, dark-eyed man with a flair for erotic sea metaphors.

Viewer's Note: Many versions have been made of this classic about a woman determined to find herself and her destiny, but by far the sexiest is this BBC production in which Timothy Dalton is cast as an implausibly gorgeous Rochester to Zelah Clarke's homely Jane—a refreshing change from the Hollywood mentality, which would've pitted some gorgeous blonde against some over-the-hill leading man who has deteriorated into repulsiveness (remember *As Good As It Gets?*). The other versions may do an okay job with the love story but they all take too many liberties with Jane's story of self-actualization to be truly satisfying. (Avoid the exceptionally bad 1997 A&E remake with Samantha Morton.)

▪ ***Fast Times at Ridgemont High*** *(1982)*
Stars: Sean Penn, Jennifer Jason Leigh, Judge Reinhold, Phoebe Cates
Director: Amy Heckerling
Writer: Cameron Crowe

This is the first of many coming-of-age ensemble stories that Cameron Crowe has become famous for. Everybody finds their voice in this piece, although, to be honest, along the way they hit quite a few clunkers.

Stacy Hamilton (played by Jennifer Jason Leigh before she shed her baby fat) wages an epic odyssey in search of love and winds up alone and pregnant. Her brother (Judge Reinhold) is an ongoing sight gag as he dons one absurd fast-food uniform after the other in his search for commercial success, and finds only bad fashion statements in unbreathable fabrics. Mark Ratner, the class geek, finally gets the date of his dreams and forgets his wallet. Finally, the centerpiece of this movie, Jeff Spicoli (Sean Penn in his defining role as the class clown), a bleached-blond surfer dude with the stupidest expression ever to stare blankly from a silver screen, is engaged in a perpetual search for the next wave, which ultimately beaches him on the shores of entry-level life without any skills.

Such developmental disasters are part and parcel of adolescence, but through the smelting fire of this maturational conflagration, we, along with the characters in this movie, learn to tell the difference between dreams and illusions, and isolate, at last, the right song to match our individual voices. . . .

God help the person who starts humming "Inna Gadda da Vida."

■ ***Moll Flanders*** *(1996)*
Stars: Robin Wright, Morgan Freeman
Director: Pen Densham
Writer: Pen Densham, based on the novel by Daniel Defoe

Not to be confused with *Moll Flanders,* the book by Daniel Defoe. Oh, it's the same source material, but after redheaded Moll leaves Newgate prison as an infant the plot bears little resemblance to Defoe's, and Wright's Moll is far more vulnerable—and contemporary—than Defoe's as well. Even so, you'll cheer on our kindhearted, plucky, ahead-of-her-time heroine as she struggles to survive in nineteenth-century England, where a woman without means was in perpetual danger of starvation and molestation by paying and non-paying customers alike. Thank God for passionate painters seeking model lovers. Watch for gritty lines like "My arsenal was something feral that nature had provided me—a sense of self that these women would never understand, let alone possess." You go, girlfriend.

Viewer's Note: For a version that's more true to the spirit of bad girl Moll and Defoe's plot, not to mention a lot more fun and sexy, try the 1996 *Masterpiece Theatre* version with Alex Kingston (the naughty British doc on *ER* who does obscene things with hard-boiled eggs).

Words to Live By

People on 'ludes should not drive.

★ Sean Penn as Jeff Spicoli in *Fast Times at Ridgemont High*

■ ***The Miracle Woman*** *(1931)*
Stars: Barbara Stanwyck, David Manners, Sam Hardy
Director: Frank Capra
Writer: Jo Swerling, based on the play Bless You Sister *by John Meehan and Robert Riskin; dialogue continuity by Dorothy Howell*

Fiery Florence Fallon, indignant at the hypocrites in her late father's congregation, turns evangelical preacher à la real-life holy roller Aimée Semple Macpherson, on whom this film is based. She preaches the Word in a ringing voice that inspires the downtrodden and even prevents suicide, not to mention rational thought. Spirit may motivate Sister Fallon, but she pays the tabernacle bills by employing modern advertising techniques, circus lions, two-bit actors to play the part of healed lepers and whatnot, and a fresh-faced choir of young people in FF-initialed tennis sweaters to bring in the crowds, which Fallon whips into a tithing frenzy. Oh, she protests weakly at the deception that con man Hardy orchestrates, but it's hard to argue with success when hundreds of adoring fans shout hallelujah at you and you get to wear fabulous angelic gowns and be stunningly backlit. Fallon is determined to have it all: true love (albeit with an adoring blind man who woos her with a creepy ventriloquist act—pickings are slim in this small town) as well as her very own cult of personality. Doesn't every gal deserve that much?

■ ***The Piano*** *(1993)*
Stars: Holly Hunter, Harvey Keitel, Sam Neill, Anna Paquin
Director and Writer: Jane Campion

If you need your symbolism delivered with a two-by-four, this is definitely the one for you. Holly Hunter plays Ada, a nineteenth-century mail-order bride who arrives in New Zealand with a precocious little cartwheeling daughter (Anna Paquin) and a piano that gives voice to her deepest emotions since she is, in fact, mute. Her new husband, Stewart (Sam Neill), is deaf to her pleas and before she can even unpack he sells off the one thing she values most, that piano, to his neighbor, Baines (Harvey Keitel). Why? Because he can. And because he's a greedy, insensitive bastard who wouldn't appreciate a sonata if it bit him in the butt.

Now, Baines knows the value of the piano, and he shrewdly trades the local equivalent of the Brooklyn Bridge for it. Once the instrument is set up in his hut, Baines decides to improve himself with some piano lessons, courtesy of the lady down the road. Soon it is clear that this illiterate and tattooed man, who is capable of integrating with his environment and learning the language of others, may be a manipulator with a kinky sensibility, but he's got a lot more going for him than the allegedly civilized Stewart. Lots of shots of blue mud and Harvey Keitel's nude frontside and backside later, a fateful showdown occurs and Ada discovers her voice at last, literally and figuratively. 'Course, with a naked Harvey Keitel staring at your ankles, you might scream too.

Now if we could just shut up that kid.

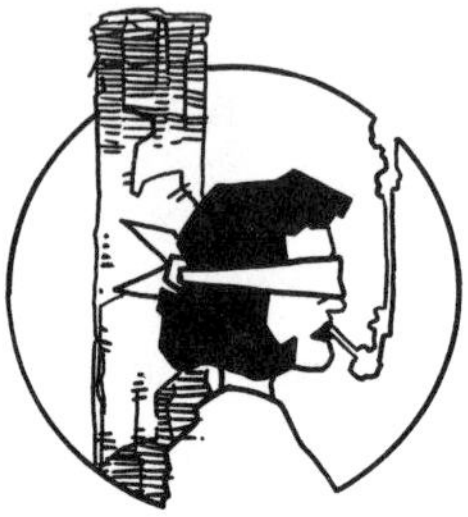

Famous Last Words

I'm not going to be ignored, Dan.

★ Glenn Close as Alex Forrest in *Fatal Attraction*

He even wrote something in my yearbook in French! "Ménage à Trois." I bet that means "You're the most."

★ Christine Taylor as Marcia Brady in *A Very Brady Sequel*

Whoever you are, I have always depended on the kindness of strangers.

★ Vivien Leigh as Blanche DuBois in *A Streetcar Named Desire*

■ ***Anastasia*** *(1956)*
Stars: Ingrid Bergman, Yul Brynner, Helen Hayes
Director: Anatole Litvak
Writers: Guy Bolton and Arthur Laurents, based on the play by Marcelle Maurette

Who is she? Just another crazy homeless woman who is starting to believe the many stories she dreamed up to win over her caretakers at the asylum? Or Anastasia, the lost princess of Russia, the sole survivor of a brutal attack on the royal family, so bruised by her experience that her memories are buried deep within her psyche? Or everyone's favorite Swedish actress with lots of gray and yellow pancake makeup barely disguising that flawless complexion? Talk about one's inheritance—if they could bottle that particular string of Ingrid Bergman's DNA, maybe we'd all have a chance to look like Isabella Rossellini.

Now, if this lost soul is the true Anastasia, con man Prince Bounine (Yul Brynner) stands to make a tidy profit and she's got a nice chunk of change coming to her as an inheritance. But even if she isn't, he need only make sure she puts on a good enough show to convince the real Anastasia's grandmother (Helen Hayes) that she's no charlatan. But is this all just a scam, or is "Anastasia" actually the lost princess?

Face-to-face at last, both women come to realize that without the emotional inheritance of a flesh-and-blood connection to the past, each is missing a vital piece of herself. And lucky for Anastasia, her identity issues aren't going to be complicated by DNA testing, which might well deny her her true inheritance. Anastasia realizes that with or without Romanov blood flowing in her veins, she's a true princess possessed of an ethereal beauty that demands to be set off by one elaborate satin evening gown after another.

▪ *An Angel at My Table* (1990)

Stars: Kerry Fox, Alexia Keogh, Karen Fergusson
Director: Jane Campion
Writer: Laura Jones, based on the autobiographies of Janet Frame

Feeling ugly, dorky, crazy, totally inept at relationships? Here's one that'll inspire you: Based on the true story of award-winning New Zealand writer Janet (Jane) Frame, *An Angel at My Table* is the story of a late bloomer, an artist whose severe lack of social skills and confidence nearly cripples her, but who nevertheless achieves great critical success.

As a child, Jane is the sort one overlooks, which is sort of hard to imagine given that here she resembles a chubby little Ronald McDonald in a striped shirt and plaid skirt. In any case, she shows promise early with her poetry and achieves a working-class dream of being a college teacher. She is too shy to mix with others, too scared even to enter the student union building, perhaps because she not only has not outgrown her fright wig hair but has also developed a case of tooth decay so severe that a dentist could retire on her mouth's work alone. Jane grows more and more isolated until she suffers a complete breakdown. She's diagnosed as schizophrenic, subjected to electroshock therapy, and then, just when she's about to get a lobotomy and lose a significant portion of gray matter, her short collection wins the Hubert Church Award. Will she get a reprieve? Or will surgery be rescheduled for after the author tour?

And you thought you were neurotic! Isn't it a comfort to know that even if you lose your mind, your work may well find an appreciative audience?

■ ***Dancing Lady*** *(1933)*
Stars: Joan Crawford, Clark Gable, Franchot Tone
Director: Robert Z. Leonard
Writers: Allen Rivkin, Zelda Sears, and P. J. Wolfson, based on the novel by James Warner Bellah

Pre–shoulder pad, pre-padded-hanger-demanding Crawford loves hoofing it so much that by gosh she'll even settle for being in burlesque, where she's spotted by a young man with too much money, too little heart, and too little sex appeal to win the girl by the end of the last reel (gee, do you think this part went to Tone or Gable?). Our starry-eyed gal won't part with her virtue, even if the Park Avenue cad does bribe her with a chorus line job. She just knows that her prodigious talent will be noticed by the musical director, brusk yet warmhearted Patch Gallagher (Gable, barely passing as a rough Irishman who appreciates the finer points of Broadway choreography). Gable's lock of black hair bobs teasingly over his forehead as he barks at the young starlet to toughen her up, but of course she passes the test—offscreen as well, which is quite obvious given their zestful performance in that spanking scene.

Viewer's Note: You may be able to convince him to sit through this obvious chick flick with you by reminding him that this is the film debut of The Three Stooges, whose screen time, thankfully, is limited.

Famous First Words

My name is Tina Turner. I have 32 cents in my pocket. If you can give me a room I promise you I will pay you back as soon as I can.

★ Angela Bassett as Tina Turner in *What's Love Got to Do With It*

▪ ***Love Field*** *(1992)*
Stars: Michelle Pfeiffer, Dennis Haysbert, Stephanie McFadden, Brian Kerwin
Director: Jonathan Kaplan
Writer: Donald Roos

It's November 22, 1963, which means that Jackie O–obsessed Texas housewife Lurene Hallett is going to have a very bad day.

The devastating loss of her role model's husband shakes up Lurene so badly that she defies her own husband (Brian Kerwin) and sets off for the President's funeral in her Chanel knockoff, pillbox hat on her bleached-blond head, pink suitcase and matching vanity case in hand.

In the bus depot, she meets a mysterious black man named Paul (Haysbert), who is traveling with a silent little girl (McFadden). The overly gregarious Lurene soon gets herself caught up in their own flight toward freedom. By the time the three of them reach the end of their journey they've changed irrevocably. Most important, Lurene steps out of Jackie's shadow, moves beyond naiveté, forges an identity outside of her husband, and discovers natural pallette hair dyes, which is going to be crucial in the post-Camelot, post–Aqua Net era.

Finding your voice

and realizing you probably should have kept your mouth shut . . .

▪ ***Georgia*** *(1995)*
Stars: Jennifer Jason Leigh, Mare Winningham, Ted Levine
Director: Ulu Grosbard
Writer: Barbara Turner

Sadie Flood (Jennifer Jason Leigh) has had the same dream since she was a child: She wants to be a singer. And seemingly, she's got all the makings of a disturbed, drug-addicted, but soulful and inspired Joplinesque chanteuse. Unfortunately, Sadie can't carry a tune in a bucket.

Her sister Georgia (Mare Winningham), on the other hand, has none of Sadie's driving ambition or complicated spiritual substance. She wants a comfortable life, as a mom and wife, safely removed from the spotlight. Kicker is, Georgia can sing like an angel.

Driven by guilt and a misguided desire to help her sister, Georgia, a singing star, gives Sadie her big moment at a stadium concert. Finally in the spotlight she has craved for so long, Sadie massacres a Van Morrison arrangement in front of forty thousand of her sister's appalled fans. Which just goes to show you, sometimes when you find your voice, you discover that you are tone deaf and it might have been better if you'd just kept your mouth shut.

This is one of those movies that can't help but make you feel good about yourself by comparison.

Chapter 11

I'm Gonna Eat Some Worms: Martyr Syndrome Movies

It's always you, isn't it? You're always there, whenever anybody needs anything. But when you need something . . . well, that's a different story, isn't it? All of a sudden everybody's too busy cutting their toenails or whatever to help you out. But maybe someday they'll turn around and you'll be gone. Maybe you'll join the Red Cross, or dedicate yourself to the preservation of the faith in your native France. Yeah, that's it, you can martyr yourself to the cause, get burned at the stake, and then they won't have you to kick around anymore. That'll show them.

Feeling indignant and self-righteous and ready for a self-pity party because you're involved with an unavailable man (even if you happen to be married to him)? Tired of people mistaking your unique vision for psychosis? Why not just dish up a double scoop of nightcrawlers, hit the play button on one of our Martyr Syndrome movies, and wallow in self-pity, despair, and the ultimate futility of all human endeavor?

▪ ***Waterloo Bridge*** *(1940)*
Stars: Vivien Leigh, Robert Taylor
Director: Mervyn LeRoy
Writer: S. N. Behrman, George Froeschel, and Hans Rameau, based on the play by Robert E. Sherwood

Her first mistake was giving away her good-luck charm to that mustachioed soldier in the trenchcoat. And now look where she is: The boss has given her the boot and she's lost track of her beau before she could say goodbye or even squeeze in a quickie wartime marriage to a fellow she's known for all of twelve hours. And now as she glances over this morning's paper, there's his name on the casualty list (er, that *was* his name, wasn't it?). So does she happen to mention this crucial bit of information to his mother, just off the train from Scotland, when she sits down for a get-acquainted luncheon? No, she merely melts into tears and an apoplexy born of British repression that can only lead her to one thing: soliciting soldiers on Waterloo Bridge even though she has the face and figure of Scarlett O'Hara and an accent worthy of a BBC broadcaster. No other jobs available while all the boys are at the front, eh?

Polish that resumé, honey—you *do* have other career options.

▪ ***Now, Voyager*** *(1942)*
Stars: Bette Davis, Paul Henreid, Gladys Cooper, Claude Rains
Director: Irving Rapper
Writer: Casey Robinson, based on the novel by Olive Higgins Prouty

A mouse of a girl (Davis) with a mother (Cooper) who is destined for her own special circle in hell gets some postbreakdown psychotherapy, meets a handsome stranger, and embarks on a love affair. It should be happily ever after from there (after all, shouldn't successful therapy be some sort of guarantee of happiness?), but with Bette Davis in the lead role there has to be a tragic glitch somewhere. It seems her lover can't leave his wife—a coldhearted bitch who doesn't understand him (an explanation Davis actually buys—that ought to be fodder for several more shrink appointments). Then, for the sake of his children, he suggests they limit their romantic interludes to deeply erotic, teary-eyed exchanges of cigarette smoke.

> ⚠ Warning Label: *This is a great movie to despair to, especially if you're weepy over a married man, but don't indulge if you're trying to give up nicotine.*

▪ ***The Song of Bernadette*** *(1943)*
Stars: Jennifer Jones, Charles Bickford, Vincent Price; Linda Darnell as the Virgin Mary
Director: Henry King
Writer: George Seaton, based on the novel by Franz Werfel

Why is it that your pesky sisters always interrupt in the middle of your holy visions? Then Mom and Dad ground you and even try to ship you off to relatives to get you to stop all this nonsense; the parish priest expects miracles on demand; and the local cops do a Mutt and Jeff routine to get you to cease drawing crowds to the dump, where the pretty lady with the golden roses on her feet, blue girdle, and white robe beams beatifically at you. Look, just because your asthma attacks prevented you from finding the time to memorize the catechism doesn't mean you don't have a straight line to the Holy Mother. They'll be sorry, dammit, when you become a legend of southern France.

▪ ***Household Saints*** *(1993)*
Stars: Lili Taylor, Tracey Ullman, Vincent D'OnoFrio
Director: Nancy Savoca
Writers: Richard Guay and Nancy Savoca, based on the novel by Francine Prose

So your mom doesn't understand your Saint Teresa of Lisieux fixation, which compels you to scrub floors with a toothbrush and fast until your parents relent and allow you to marry Jesus? Mom was never much one for symbolism, religious or secular, anyway, and even your father failed to seduce her with the erotic possibilities of a raw Italian sausage.

In *Household Saints,* Lili Taylor plays the wispy-voiced Teresa Santangelo, an old-fashioned good Catholic girl whose romantic notions drive her mother (Tracey Ullman) and father (Vincent D'OnoFrio) to distraction. A little too enamored of mystery and the examples of the saints, Teresa is often found lying prostrate on hardwood floors, writing essays on Why Communism Is Anti-Christ, or filling her notebook with details of her struggles to be worthy of Jesus' love. But her misty-eyed embrace of the monotony of daily toil à la The Little Flower appeals to a college boy named Leonard Villanova, who proposes that serving one's husband is a dandy substitute for serving the Church. Leonard launches Teresa on the Villanova life plan, which involves dropping this convent nonsense and starting in on his ironing, and in wide-eyed appreciation she sets to work.

Oh, they scoff at your dedication now, but when you quietly slip away, leaving behind the scent of roses, they won't laugh. Yes, they'll be sorry when you become a legend of Little Italy.

■ ***That Hamilton Woman*** *(1941)*
Stars: Vivien Leigh, Laurence Olivier
Director: Alexander Korda
Writers: Walter Reisch and R. C. Sherriff

Naive young Emma Hart thought she'd put her past as a veil dancer from Liverpool behind her (not exactly a plausible backstory for a woman with a face like Vivien Leigh, but so be it) and she fairly floats into the British ambassador's home in Naples that bright afternoon in the late eighteenth century, bubbling over with excitement at the prospect of marrying his nephew Charles. But the ambassador kindly relieves her of that particular delusion. In fact, he informs her, she is just another lovely item packed in amongst a whole shipment of objets d'art his nephew has sent him in repayment of a debt.

Emma is heartbroken and humiliated—but not for long. Eventually, she gets used to the elaborate meals served by footmen, the opulent gowns, the royal lifestyle, and even marries the old art collector. Then, one day as she is planning a dinner party, her husband informs her that the French ambassador will not be able to attend, being that his country has just declared war on England. Don't you just hate it when that happens? Luckily, the finely sculptured Horatio Nelson, captain of the British fleet, is available to fill in, and thus begins a habit of Emma's securing troops for Nelson's use and providing him with other essential services that cause a lot of gossiping amongst the nobility. But then the war ends and the lovers must deal with their respective spouses. Proudly, Emma refuses to give up her lover or take his financial support, which, given the time and place, doesn't exactly leave her a lot of economic options beyond veil dancing. The British scorn her, even though she saved their skin on several occasions; her husband threatens to cut her off; and Lord Nelson may cut a fine figure in a uniform, but when it comes to standing up to his wife he's a total wuss. Well, that's just fine. She'll manage somehow.

Uh huh.

Next time you're feeling unappreciated, find yourself a cheap bottle of Bordeaux, put this one in the VCR, and wallow in the inevitability of a brilliant woman's despair and degradation. They'll be sorry when you're a legend in all of England.

■ ***All This and Heaven Too*** *(1940)*
Stars: Bette Davis, Charles Boyer, Barbara O'Neil
Director: Anatole Litvak
Writer: Casey Robinson, based on the novel by Rachel Field

In this martyr classic, Bette Davis portrays a French teacher in a girls' school who is tormented by her gossipy pupils until she fesses up about her scandalous past. Oh yes, she admits, there were intense gazes and inappropriate exchanges of metaphors (which is about as much as Napoleonic-era lovers can get away with when there's a bevy of spying servants surrounding them). But poor Mlle Deluzy-Desportes (Davis) denied herself even a stolen kiss or embrace from her would-be illicit lover, the Duc (Boyer). Instead, the demurely coiffed, beatific governess was a paragon of virtue, thereby able to respectfully but firmly deny any wrongdoing to her histrionic and jealous employer, the Duchesse (played by an overly Pan-Caked O'Neil, in quite a departure from her role as the ethereally poised Mrs. O'Hara in *GWTW*). Though madamoiselle is the only true mother figure to the Duc and Duchesse's adorable urchin offspring, and she is the Duc's only chance for romance, still she asks herself, what of honor? What of integrity? What about the future of the French government?

Screw 'em, we say. Consequences of catastrophic proportions just make a passionate affair all that more delicious, don't they? But since this is the mid-nineteenth century, Mademoiselle will have to be a good girl, holding her head high as she is relegated to a life of correcting verb conjugations.

And those naughty girls will be sorry, now that you're a legend of post-Napoleonic France.

▪ ***Camille Claudel*** *(1988)*
Stars: Isabelle Adjani, Gérard Depardieu
Director: Bruno Nuytten
Writers: Marilyn Goldin, Bruno Nuytten, and Reine-Marie Paris

Based on a true story, this movie recounts the tragic life of Camille Claudel (Isabelle Adjani) , the talented sister of the writer Paul Claudel, who was not only a beautiful woman but also a supremely talented sculptress. She gets an opportunity to work as Auguste Rodin's assistant, and very shortly thereafter becomes his lover. But Rodin proves to be as selfish a mentor as he is a lover. He uses her talent and her charms, and then tosses her on the discard heap, along with his marble chips, when he's mined what he wanted from her raw materials.

Next time you're feeling underappreciated, watch this movie and remember that if you aren't a nineteenth-century sculptress who braves society's disapproval to express herself as an artist, and then, after a lifetime spent suffering for her art, has somebody else sign their name to her Pietà, then you're definitely a few steps ahead of the game.

⚠ Warning Label: *Walk softly but carry a* big *chisel.*

The Handy Hunk Chart Key

Hunk Ratings:
All-American Boy 🏈
The Passionate Priest ✝

ASD = *Aristocratic, Suave, and Debonair* **BE** = *Bedroom Eyes,* **EGL** = *Exotic Good Looks* **EMT** = *Eyes Moist with Tears* **FSG** = *Feckless Schoolboy Grin* **PBE** = *Piercing Blue Eyes* **RGH** = *Really Good Hair* **RUM** = *Raw Unpredictable Masculinity* **SIN** = *Smoldering, Inscrutable, and Noble* **TSHT** = *That Sexy Homicidal Thing* **TWL** = *That Wounded Look*

The Handy Hunk Chart

Leonardo DiCaprio

FSG, PBE, RGH, TWL

Top Drool Pics: *The Basketball Diaries, Man in the Iron Mask, Marvin's Room, Romeo & Juliet, Titanic, Total Eclipse*

A leading man in the flyweight division, Leonardo DiCaprio, like many a golden boy before him, is emblematic of the doomed beauty of youth. He is luminescent, pale yellow in the first light of manhood's morning. He winks, he twinkles, and he nods. Which, from what we hear, really works wonders with the prepubescent set. Leonardo, though, unlike many a golden boy before him, is quite a good actor. He's uncannily convincing as Gilbert's mildly retarded brother in *What's Eating Gilbert Grape,* and seemed primed to mature into one of America's finest young actors. And then James Cameron got ahold of him, and he exploded onto the big screen with all of the force of a twenty-thousand-kilo hull into an iceberg in the middle of the North Atlantic. Total devastation. No survivors.

Ship of dreams . . . indeed. ■

Liam Neeson

BE, EMT, RUM, SIN

Top Drool Pics: *Ethan Frome, The Good Mother, Michael Collins, Nell, Rob Roy, Satisfaction, Suspect*

✝ Liam Neeson is great at playing those big lugs with the hearts of gold who just never seem to get an even shake. But they never complain. They're like mountains, towering in the distance, taking all of the abuse that mankind can hurl at them and never once breaking their vow of silence. Totally hot

. . . *continued*

stuff. And he's got that Irish thing working for him too. You know, the puppy dog eyes, that wonky smile, the lilt in his speech, the original guilt? There's nothing sexier than a guy willing to flagellate himself for love. And boy, can this man fill out an Emerald Isle sweater. Manly, yes, but we like it too. ▪

Ralph Fiennes

ASD, EGL, PBE, RGH, SIN, TSHT

Top Drool Pics: *Emily Brontë's Wuthering Heights, The English Patient, Quiz Show, Strange Days*

✝ Ralph, that tortured, priestly rogue; that blue-eyed, broken-winged scion of the landed gentry whose delicate soul and gentle spirit mask a rushing stream of molten intensity. While it is unfortunate that Ralph has no chin; he does have those cheeks carved into impossible angles by years of bitter isolation, and that irresistible hint of the homicidal in his gait that renders him irresistible to most of us modern masochists. And despite a similar lack of endowment in the caboose area, he does look fetching in a frock coat. Our hope is that he keeps right on doing roles that bring out the dark side of even the most sunlit heroes, featuring lots of double-breasted, full-skirted outerwear, and big leather riding boots. Giddyup! ▪

▪ ***Queen Margot*** *(1994)*
Stars: Isabelle Adjani, Vincent Perez, Daniel Auteuil
Director: Patrice Chéreau
Writers: Danièle Thompson and Patrice Chéreau, based on the novel by Alexandre Dumas

Isabelle Adjani (aren't there any other leading ladies in France?) stars as Margot de Valois, the devoted sister of the child king Charles XI, who is married off to Henri of Navarre by her Machiavellian mother, Catherine de Medici, in an attempt to make peace between the Protestants and the Catholics. The marriage alone is a personal sacrifice demanding canonization, because while Henri of Navarre is a prince, he is definitely *not* charming.

Margot runs into a handsome stranger, La Mole, in an alley, during some massacre or another staged by her power-mad mother and her various oedipally identified male offspring, and falls instantly in love. . . . And no wonder, because the stranger, La Mole (Vincent Perez), looks like a sixteenth-century interpretation of a Calvin Klein underwear ad. Unfortunately, he's Protestant, she's Catholic, and their religious differences, coupled with her mother's boundary issues, make for a very stormy relationship track. People drop like flies in this movie.

Regardless of the ambient carnage, this is a painfully beautiful love story, mostly because Vincent Perez is so beautiful, he'll make your joints ache. Two hours spent looking at his lithe, naked torso will make you feel a whole lot better about your own border disputes.

■ ***The French Lieutenant's Woman*** *(1981)*
Stars: Meryl Streep, Jeremy Irons
Director: Karel Reisz
Writer: Harold Pinter, based on the novel by John Fowles

We all remember the image. That mysterious lady in the hood, poised at the end of a rampart, the Lyme Regis winds whipping the Channel to a froth as she gazes forlornly into the horizon, waiting for the return of her beloved French Lieutenant.

And of course we knew, even before she turned around, that it was going to be Meryl Streep. Who else could manage that air of silent suffering, that incredibly static plotline, and the regional dialect? It's funny because, no matter how many times we watch this movie, that's all we can remember. That long pull-back of the woman they call Tragedy, the French Lieutenant's whore, gazing into the distance. And actually, there's a very detailed plotline in motion. They jump back and forth in time, there's a play within a play, an extramarital affair, but none of it registers, much like when you ask for help washing the dishes, because you're so focused on her agony.

Next time you're feeling depressed about the uselessness of it all, watch this movie, heck, watch it twice, and then try to tell somebody what it was about. You'll feel a lot better about your own unrecognized plotline.

■ ***Romeo & Juliet*** *(1996)*
Stars: Leonardo DiCaprio, Claire Danes
Director: Baz Luhrmann
Writers: Baz Luhrmann and Craig Pearce, based on the play by William Shakespeare

This is the MTV version of Shakespeare's timeless tale of two star-crossed lovers from opposing families, whose controversial love brings them to ruin at the hands of their feuding kinsmen. Juliet (Claire Danes) is your typical teenage budding rose, fairly bursting at the seams to savor love's first fruit. Romeo (Leonardo DiCaprio) is a hopeless romantic who vows that the sun rises and sets in his lady's eyes, and cannot live for longer than twenty minutes at a time without indulging in her ambrosial presence. Romeo is a devoted pilgrim, a priest of love, willing to lay down his life and his hope of salvation for just five moments alongside the goddess of his idolatry. We don't know about you, but this sounds like our kind of guy!

But wouldn't you know it, he's a Montague. Which would be all right except for the fact that Juliet is a Capulet. The Montagues and the Capulets are the Elizabethan version of the Hatfields and McCoys, whose generations of malignant squabbling poison the lives of their children, leaving them to face the sins of their fathers and challenge their own fragile mortality in a tomb amongst a brace of their moldering kinsmen.

> ⚠ Warning Label: *Don't watch this if you're experiencing difficulties with your in-laws. All may be punished.*

■ ***Breaking the Waves*** *(1996)*
Stars: Emily Watson, Jean-Marc Barr, Stellan Skarsgård
Director and Writer: Lars Von Trier

This is the ultimate Martyr Syndrome movie, because it is basically a metaphor for female self-sacrifice expressed to the point of perversion, set in a backward, religiously oppressive community in some unpronounceable village in Scotland. A naive young woman, Bess McNeill, who is a bit "tetched" in the head, falls in love with Jan, a strapping Scandi-

Ten Burning Questions to Contemplate

In that endless self-analysis mode? Caught up in a shame spiral? Wondering what it's all about, Alfie? Here are some questions that'll keep you stuck in the midst of an obsessional thinking mode:

1. I've no regrets. I've been everywhere and done everything. I've eaten caviar at Cannes, sausage rolls at the dogs. I've played baccarat at Biarritz and darts with the rural dean. What is there left for me but marriage?
   Margaret Lockwood as Iris Henderson in *The Lady Vanishes*
2. Where shall I go? What shall I do?
   Vivien Leigh as Scarlett O'Hara in *Gone With the Wind*
3. Who forgives God?
   Mimi Rogers as Sharon in *The Rapture*
4. Does the word "duh" mean anything to you?
   Kristy Swanson as Buffy in *Buffy the Vampire Slayer*
5. Is there something wrong with me?
   Vivien Leigh as Blanche DuBois in *A Streetcar Named Desire*
6. Heather, why are you such a mega-bitch?
   Winona Ryder as Veronica Sawyer in *Heathers*
7. Why do women insist on loving men for what they want them to be instead of what they are?
   Melvyn Douglas as Brice Chamberlain in *The Sea of Grass*
8. Sydney, how does it feel to be almost brutally butchered?
   A reporter to Sydney (Neve Campbell) in *Scream*
9. Have you ever met a man of good character where women are concerned?
   Rex Harrison as Professor Henry Higgins in *My Fair Lady*
10. If I don't feel sorry for myself, who will?
    Virginia Field as Kitty in *Waterloo Bridge*

navian oil rigger. They marry and Bess's life is transformed into one long, inbred rural Scottish interpretation of a seventies-style love song.

When Jan becomes crippled in an accident and can no longer make love to Bess, he asks her to go out and make love to other men and bring him home the lurid details, so that he can enjoy a vicarious sexual experience with her. Bess indulges him, pushing her sexual exploits to the point of degradation, all the while believing that her actions are a prescription from God to cure Jan, and of course the villagers, being the sensitive, well-educated lot that they are, respond to her distress by stoning her in the village square.

When you feel like you're doing all the work in your relationship, watch this movie and remind yourself that you're not being dumped on, you're being visited by God, who will give you the ability to relieve your partner of his psychic suffering. There now, don't you feel better about everything already?

■ ***Washington Square*** *(1997)*
Stars: Jennifer Jason Lee, Ben Chaplin, Maggie Smith, Albert Finney
Director: Agnieszka Holland
Writer: Carol Doyle, based on the novel by Henry James

She is a woman utterly without guile . . . and without poise, beauty, social skills, grace, talent, pride, charm, or self-possession. She's a woman with far too much money and far too little taste in ball gowns, which leads her to show up at parties looking like nothing so much as an upholstered chaise lounge from a nineteenth-century bordello. And for all that her aunt Lavinia (Maggie Smith) tries to create the illusion that her niece has a full dance card, no one believes that Catherine (Jennifer Jason Leigh) is juggling the attentions of several suitors, least of all her passive aggressive father (Albert Finney) who, unbeknownst to his daughter, blames her for her mother's death. But while Catherine may be a fool and even a laughingstock, hanging her head each time her father unleashes another one of his sarcastic little attacks on her, once she catches the attention of a young gentleman (Ben Chaplin) who flatters her shamelessly, she begins to blossom. Bravely, she challenges her father's dismissal of her suitor as a gold digger, and challenges her beloved to prove his affections have no price tag. She is, after all, worthy of love, so why wouldn't he love her for herself?

We won't give away the ending except to say this story will remind you that if you believe misery and loneliness can be much tempered by stubborn pride, you'll love this movie, and if you really want to wallow in self-pity, the original version with Olivia de Havilland and Montgomery Clift will be even more satisfying (particularly since Jennifer Jason Lee's displays of discomfort and awkwardness feel really nineties, and Ben Chaplin's no better than Montgomery Clift was at creating a plausibly nineteenth-century suitor).

■ ***Brief Encounter*** *(1945)*
Stars: Celia Johnson, Trevor Howard
Director: David Lean
Writers: Anthony Havelock-Allan, David Lean, Ronald Neame, and Noël Coward, based on the play Still Life *by Noël Coward*

Laura Jesson is just sitting there in the Milford Junction train station refreshment room, minding her own business and trying to forget about her mundane life, which is punctuated by the weekend highlights of the Sunday *Times* crossword and the children's endless pleas to be taken to the pantomime. In flies a speck of dust, which conveniently settles in her eye, and a warmhearted GP rushes over to rescue her from certain blindness. Well, maybe it isn't all that dramatic, but compared to life in the suburbs of Britain post–WW II, it has the makings of a sweeping romantic story. Swiftly, they are caught up in the current of a burning love that makes even detailed discussions of lung diseases afflicting coal miners endlessly fascinating (don't you love hormones?). Unfortunately, repression, faithfulness, duty, and honor raise their ugly heads, forcing Laura (Celia Johnson) and Alec (Trevor Howard) to endure bittersweet agonies as they ponder whether to part ways or run off together in a fit of passion. And just when they're about to cut loose, some crashing boor always seems to show up.

Wonderfully agonizing.

■ ***Anna Karenina*** *(1935)*
Stars: Greta Garbo, Fredric March, Basil Rathbone, Freddie Bartholomew
Director: Clarence Brown
Writers: S. N. Behrman, Clemence Dane, and Salka Viertel, based on the novel by Leo Tolstoy

Anna (Greta Garbo) would give up everything for him (Fredric March)—financial security, social position, even the right to visit her son—at least until she can convince her self-righteous husband (Basil Rathbone) that punishing little Sergei (Freddie Bartholomew) because he's angry at her is inhumane. And in return, her lover is willing to give up his career for her—well, at least until the next opportunity to run onto a battlefield and drive a really big sword through some poor sod, then celebrate afterward with a few dozen shots of vodka. After all, a fellow can't spend all his time on the Riviera, leisurely enjoying the sunsets and basking in the glow of his beloved's devotion. Where's the glory in that?

Unfortunately, all that sissy girly stuff like love and tranquillity is kinda right up Anna Karenina's alley, which makes her situation, in the end, rather tragic. Yes, she's found out the hard way that there's a reason for all that hypocritical secrecy about tête-à-têtes after she flouts convention, puts love above honor and duty, and trusts men to treat passion and devotion as worthy of self-sacrifice. Well, if her choice has doomed her to misery, by God she's going to make a statement worthy of a classic Russian novel.

Definitely go for the Garbo version rather than the Vivien Leigh one, not only because it lays out Anna's emotions more clearly but because in the end it rubs his nose in it—far more satisfying when you're in a worm-eating blue funk.

Chapter 12

Nobody Understands Me Like You Do, Girlfriend: Girl's Night Movies

Come on, admit it. Men aren't any fun anyway. It's way more of a hoot to be hanging out with your best girlfriend, doing facials, feasting on popcorn and good white wine, and gossiping about the idiotic thing your date did at the office party last weekend. What a moron! Forget about him. Forget about all of them. Invite your best girlfriend over, crack open the box of blackhead strips and some microwave popcorn, watch one of these Girl's Night movies, and celebrate the sisterhood!

- ***Romy and Michele's High School Reunion*** *(1997)*
  Stars: Mira Sorvino, Lisa Kudrow, Alan Cumming, Julia Campbell, Janeane Garofalo
  Director: David Mirkin
  Writer: Robin Schiff

When roommates and best friends Romy White (Mira Sorvino) and Michele Weinberger (Lisa Kudrow) realize that their tenth high school reunion is fast approaching, they're positively giggly at the thought of going back and finding out whatever happened to . . . until they realize that what happened to *them* was less a tale of two iconoclasts who blossomed under the bright sun at Venice Beach than the story of two ditzes deluding themselves with that California dreamin'. You see, aside from their remarkable ability to accessorize and their talent at finding brightly colored spandex and garish patent leather separates inappropriate for all occasions, their postgrad resumés are, well, pretty damn pathetic. Which is why, before they set off for their reunion, they pad their CVs with the claim that they invented Post-it notes, a fiction inspired by their cranky and neurotic fellow classmate (Janeane Garofalo), who invented another dandy paper product: fast-burning cigarette paper for "twice the taste in half the time for the gal on the go."

This one's a hilarious romp about best friends who love you enough to overlook the fact that you have a big *L* for loser branded on your forehead. Watch it with an old high school buddy and afterward, even you might find the inner strength to crack your yearbook.

■ ***Soul Food*** *(1998)*
Stars: Vanessa Williams, Vivica A. Fox, Nia Long, Michael Beach, Mekhi Phifer, Brandon Hammond, Jeffrey D. Sams, Gina Ravera, Irma P. Hall
Director and Writer: George Tillman, Jr.

Just how long does it take for a warm, loving family to disintegrate into a roiling stew of overly spiced accusations once the family matriarch takes a leave of absence? As quickly as you can wolf down them chitlins, apparently. Even a fine spread of southern cooking can't restore the ritual Sunday night dinner gathering without Mama (Irma P. Hall) there to play Jimmy Carter to the warring factions. Oh, everyone's got a valid point, but they're too busy backstabbing, calling some hoodlums to rough up an errant in-law, and engaging in Jerry Springeresque affairs to remember that we must accept our families as they are, not as we wish them to be. *Final Thought for the Day:* We must all learn to leave the past behind us, embrace the family rituals that have warmed our hearts over the years, and refrain from acting like a ho' when you *know* he's *my* man.

With a little luck, this may melt a cold war between frosty sisters. Invite the group for a viewing in a mutually-agreed-upon neutral zone, and be sure to wear a whistle around your neck.

■ ***Fried Green Tomatoes*** *(1991)*
Stars: Mary Stuart Masterson, Mary-Louise Parker, Kathy Bates, Jessica Tandy
Director: Jon Avnet
Writers: Fannie Flagg and Carol Sobieski, based on Flagg's novel Fried Green Tomatoes at the Whistle Stop Café

Kathy Bates stars as Evelyn Couch (as in "big as a"), who is experiencing a marital slump. She just can't get her husband to look up from his B&M beans and notice her, despite the fact that she's tried everything to catch his eye, including wrapping herself up in a Saran Wrap cocktail dress. Guess it comes as no surprise that this Ziploc fashion statement does not put any freshness back in her marriage.

While visiting her carping shut-in of a mother-in-law in the local nursing home, she runs into a kind old woman (Jessica Tandy) who, over the course of the next few months, tells Evelyn the story of Idgie (Mary-Louise Parker), an irrepressible, unmanageable woodland sprite of a person, whose free spirit and brave heart changed the lives of everyone around her.

The story inspires Evelyn to challenge herself and change her life. She eschews the B&M beans for sushi and sprouts, and begins bouncing for hours on a trampoline in a spandex exercise suit and a terry cloth headband.

Evelyn starts making other changes too. She starts talking back to her husband, making herself a priority, and gradually reclaims herself.

This movie is a sweet reminder of how well women do when there aren't any men around to make a mess of things. Nobody fights, everybody is in touch with their feelings and up front about expressing them. It's, like, a female functional paradise at the Whistle Stop Café.

■ ***Career Girls*** *(1997)*
Stars: Katrin Cartlidge, Lynda Steadman
Director: Mike Leigh
Writers: Mike Leigh and the cast

You can't remember what it was about, can you? There's just the vague, uncomfortable memory of nasty little barbs as you each separated out your books, pretended to give a damn about who got the extra ceramic cup and saucer, and slammed your possessions into cardboard boxes. And now, as you look back, what comes to you is how she insisted on cutting the onions because you couldn't do it without crying, or the time she tried desperately to deflect your boyfriend's advances toward her, or your secret manipulative plan to dump your third-wheel roommate so you two could get your own flat.

Now that their Human League records have been long since misplaced and their twentysomething dermatalogical problems are behind them, these two best friends get together for a weekend. Only then do they realize how much they meant to each other, and Annie (Lynda Steadman) and Hannah (Katrin Cartlidge) rediscover their mutual admiration, loyalty, and appreciation.

Watch it with an old friend, and leave plenty of time afterward for reminiscing and hauling out those godawful records you actually used to think were profound.

World-Class Wrecks

He's a real gentleman. I'll bet he takes the dishes out of the sink before he pees in it.

★ Shirley MacLaine as Ouiser Boudreaux in *Steel Magnolias*

▪ ***Waiting to Exhale*** (1995)

Stars: Angela Bassett, Whitney Houston, Lela Rochon, Loretta Devine

Director: Forest Whitaker

Writers: Tom Bass and Terry McMillan, based on the Terry McMillan novel

Did you ever notice that all of the good ones are taken? Then again, maybe it's just that there are no good ones. Well, at least it seems that way when you consider the various liars,

Faking It: Phony Gal Films That Really Piss Us Off

The Women **(1939)**

"A little motherly advice—don't trust in your girlfriends."

With lines like these, you know *The Women* is *not* a girl-bonding film. Of course, Julia Roberts will be starring in a remake of this 1939 classic about a group of bitchy, shallow New York women with too much time and money on their hands—she sure has a penchant for picking offensive premises (see *Pretty Woman* and *My Best Friend's Wedding*). Don't be tempted by the strong female cast (Joan Crawford, Norma Shearer, Joan Fontaine, etc.), the famed "woman's director" (George Cukor), or the female stage and screenplay writers (Clare Booth Luce and Anita Loos, respectively), all of whose talents are wasted on this nasty little film. Of course, if your idea of a real woman is Ru Paul, you'll appreciate this bitchfest and the Paulette Goddard/Rosalind Russell catfight. Otherwise, do you really need to watch a movie that depicts female friendship as inherently shallow, defined by jealousy, cruelty, and backstabbing?

We'll forgive fashion fanatics who rent this on a discount night and fast-forward to the goofy Technicolor fashion sequence, which features a lot of high-quirk couture and some of the perkiest chapeaux this side of Myrna Loy (see *The Thin Man* series). Otherwise, it's a must-miss. ■

manipulators, sad sacks, and snakes these four girlfriends have to sort through. Not even one worth burying in the back of a little black book when everything's tallied up. There's the guy who dumps his wife for a younger woman and starts secretly sheltering all their money, the guy who dumps Whitney Houston but thinks she should still sleep with him after he's married another, the guy who tries to rape Thelma in the parking lot—oops, wrong movie. Anyway, you get the idea: lots of despicable men, gals bonding over bottles of wine and tears and laughter, and a hilariously incendiary woman-scorned rampage of fury featuring Angela Bassett. And just when you've about given up on men entirely, the girl with the biggest booty ends up with the one great fellow (Gregory Hines). Now that calls for a toast!

■ ***Little Women*** *(1994)*

Stars: Winona Ryder, Susan Sarandon, Trini Alvarado, Claire Danes, Kirsten Dunst, Samantha Mathis, Mary Wickes, Christian Bale
Director: Gillian Armstrong
Writer: Robin Swicord, based on the novel by Louisa May Alcott

You'd think a Victorian-era story about the love between four sisters and their mother would be hopelessly outdated, with so many references to a heavenly respite for the frail Beth and the unabashed declarations of affection between siblings; but this movie draws you into a simple world that seems far more civilized than our own. Then again, it takes place within the home of the March family rather than on the streets of Civil War–era America, where women were still children in the eyes of the law. Amazing how women have the ability create a haven of humanity no matter what the current social and political atmosphere, isn't it?

Sarandon plays Marmee, the matriarch filled with wisdom and understanding who teaches her daughters not to be swayed by the shifting winds that blow outside their door. Ryder is the indomitable Jo, who learns how to maintain her tomboyishness even as she becomes a nurturing woman. Meanwhile, her sisters fearlessly address their character flaws in an attempt to become the best women they can be. If all this sounds treacly, don't worry—there are no cheap emotions to be found here. This one's best shared with your own sister-figures, whoever they may be.

Warning Label: *"Critics' choices" aside, skip the early versions, which inevitably feature cloying direction and hyperactive Jo's who are too old for the part (though, just for fun, keep an eye out for the 1970s version featuring the cult-TV cast of Susan Dey as Jo, Eve Plumb as the doomed Beth, and William Shatner as the professor—too bizarre!).*

■ ***Personal Best*** *(1982)*
Stars: Mariel Hemingway, Patrice Donnelly, Scott Glenn
Director and Writer: Robert Towne

Athletes and lesbians—take these two subjects and a lesser writer could've churned out a cliché-ridden script with lots of female names for essentially male characters. But Towne is better than that. Instead, this is a story about how women find creative and loving ways to maintain friendships when they're in competition with each other. The track coach (Glenn), who wants to wrangle the best performances out of his female team, just doesn't get it. He tries to psychologically manipulate his complementary star athletes—the one with the killer instinct but limited talent (Donnelly, a real-life Olympic star) and the one with the tremendous potential and too-nice demeanor (Hemingway)—and resents the way their petty personal problems and issues—like, say, mutual love, loyalty, and respect—keep complicating matters. Winning, isn't that all that counts? Chicks!

When both friends have to compete for a place on the Olympic pentathlon team, they've got to get past their jealousy, fear, and love to achieve their personal best, which in femme-speak means everyone wins.

Words to Live By

You see, the way it works is, the train moves, not the station!

★ Jon Lovitz as Capadino in *A League of Their Own*

■ ***Thelma & Louise*** *(1991)*
Stars: Susan Sarandon, Geena Davis, Harvey Keitel, Brad Pitt
Director: Ridley Scott
Writer: Callie Khouri

Women We Wish We Could Go for a Beer With

Carrie Fisher: Especially if we're in the mood to commiserate . . . or need to bum a Dunhill.

Sandra Bullock: But listen, babe, we'll do the driving, okay?

Angelina Jolie: Because if we hung out with her, we'd be cool by osmosis, and if any creeps started to bother us, she'd deck 'em.

Una Merkel: Who? Look, Una's not just a vowel-endowed crossword puzzle favorite (along with Oona Chaplin, Ona Munson, and Yoko Ono), she was bad girl Jean Harlow's sidekick, egging her on to more outrageous, trashier behavior. A gal who doesn't need a glass with her Rolling Rock—or an opener, for that matter.

Janeane Garofalo: She's gotta know a great dive bar with an awesome jukebox, where you can smoke.

Joan Cusack: Because she's the gal pal extraordinaire and makes our worst fashion mistakes look stylish by comparison.

Emma Thompson: We'd like to hang out and soak up her dry wit—and we're buying, in appreciation of her rescuing Jane Austen from the library and making her hip in Hollywood.

Rosie Perez: We'd never get a word in edgewise, but we'd be laughing too hard to care.

Myrna Loy: Though, of course, with Myrna we'd drink cosmopolitans instead . . . and perhaps muse about whodunnit.

Drew Barrymore: She'd be drinking n/a beer, but she'd provide plenty of bubbles. ▪

Women Who Drive Us to Drink

Madonna: For treating movies like long-form music videos starring Madonna.

Courtney Love: For mutating into an unspeakably dull, Versace-wearing nonentity.

Demi Moore: For role after role in which she acts even less skillfully than she did as Jackie Templeton on *General Hospital,* and for proving that there are only two reasons she is the highest-paid actress in Hollywood.

Liv Tyler: For being all that we loathe about traditional ingenues—all teenage beauty, no womanly substance.

Sandra Dee: Oh, if only we could lock her in a room with Courtney Love.

Juliette Lewis: Do not come to our window. Do not stand in the light of our moon. And stop taking yourself so seriously! ■

Okay, we know, this is supposed to be a Girl's Night movie, but can we just talk for one second about Brad Pitt as the mischievous drifter, with his shirt off and that blow dryer in his hand? And that Stetson cocked on his head, crooked as his smile? And that hungry twinkle in his eye? And that cute little southern accent. And he was so limber in those days . . . practically acrobatic. Okay, nuff said.

Thelma (Geena Davis) is married to this guy named Darryl who is probably the most obnoxious man ever to wear a leisure suit and sell used cars. Thelma teams up with her friend Louise (Susan Sarandon) to go on a fishing trip, but their quick weekend getaway turns into a race for their lives when Thelma and Louise finally let their hair down and run afoul of the law.

Next girl's night at your house, pop this movie in and let the bobby pins fly!

■ ***Mystic Pizza*** *(1988)*
Stars: Julia Roberts, Annabeth Gish, Lili Taylor
Director: Donald Petrie
Writers: Perry Howze, Randy Howze, Alfred Uhry, and Amy Holden Jones (also story)

The plot gets convoluted in this movie, but it isn't really important. What makes this movie a girl's night favorite are the enduring images of sisterhood.

Two sisters—Daisy (Julia Roberts) and Kat (Annabeth Gish), and a dear friend, Jojo (Lili Taylor)—go through their life's passages together, working in a pizza parlor in Mystic, Connecticut. And that's really what this movie is about. They laugh, they cry, they sell slices, they trade shifts, they fall in love, they stumble, they get up again. They fight, they make up. They drive around in trucks singing Motown together off key. You get the idea. . . . Press play and celebrate the sisterhood.

Words to Live By

You shoot off a guy's head with his pants down, believe me, Texas ain't the place you want to get caught.

★ Susan Sarandon as Louise Sawyer in *Thelma & Louise*

■ ***Boys on the Side*** *(1995)*
Stars: Whoopi Goldberg, Mary-Louise Parker, Drew Barrymore, Matthew McConaughey
Director: Herbert Ross
Writer: Don Roos

This is another movie about girls driving around in cars and singing along with the radio at the top of their lungs as life stretches before them like an open highway. Sure there

Faking It: Phony Gal Films That Really Piss Us Off

Spice World *(1997)*
Stars: Melanie Brown (Scary Spice), Victoria Adams (Posh Spice), Melanie Chisholm (Sporty Spice), Emma Bunton (Baby Spice), Geri Halliwell (Ginger Spice)
Director: Bob Spiers
Writers: Kim Fuller and Jamie Curtis

Let's see: They steal the concept from *A Hard Day's Night*, the surreal group apartment from *Help!*, the crazy British officer from *Magical Mystery Tour*, the tag ending from *Yellow Submarine*—too bad they didn't steal the breakup from *Let It Be*. While this pop music quintet from England professes they just wanna have fun (concept lifted from Cyndi Lauper) and inspire girls everywhere (concept lifted from the Riot Grrrls), their utter inability to come up with an original idea (concept lifted from the Monkees) makes them just another prepackaged commodity that preys upon preteen pocket money. "I don't get it. Why is it people stereotype us all the time?" whines Sporty Spice. Sheesh, at least the Go-Gos had last names, not to mention a working knowledge of their instruments. Look, if you can't discourage your favorite prepubescent from indulging in this derivative merchandising vehicle of the moment, remind her that it's just not the same ever since they lost . . . Cinnamon Spice? Basil Spice? Poultry Seasoning? Whatever.

are a few plot twists—Robin (Mary-Louise Parker) has AIDS, and Jane (Whoopi Goldberg) is a lesbian, and Holly (Drew Barrymore) is on the run from an abusive, drug-dealing boyfriend.

But basically it's about the driving, and the singing, and the laughing and the crying and about Drew Barrymore, spiritually liberated at last, dancing a free interpretative celebration of herself in bare feet with daisies in her hair. Really good for a girl's-night-with-a-solstice theme. Watch this movie, weave some flowers in each other's hair, shake off your shoes, and dance along with Drew to the song of yourself.

World-Class Wrecks

Well, goodbye. Thanks for calling. If you ever need a pallbearer, remember I'm at your service.

★ Ginger Rogers as Jean Maitland in *Stage Door*

■ ***Stage Door*** *(1937)*
Stars: Katharine Hepburn, Ginger Rogers, Adolphe Menjou, Gail Patrick, Eve Arden, Lucille Ball, Andrea Leeds
Director: Gregory La Cava
Writers: Morrie Ryskind and Anthony Veiller, based on the play by Edna Ferber and George S. Kaufman

If you've got to be unemployed, wouldn't it be some consolation to hang out in the lobby of your boarding house with your fellow would-be stage stars, topping each other's wisecracks, playing the ukulele, and teasing each other about beaux? (As opposed to real-life roommates, who use up your groceries, trash the bathroom, and sleep with your boyfriend.) Eve Arden, Lucille Ball, Gail Patrick, and Ginger Rogers play cynical young actresses who keep the jokes running and constantly rib Terry Randall, the self-possessed society girl (Hepburn—who else?) who joins their crew. Trained in the classics, Terry is not only aware of the fact that Mr. Shakespeare is dead but is still convinced that hard work, determination, and honing one's craft will pay off. When shy girl Kaye (Andrea Leeds), down to her last dime, loses out on a big break, the girls learn a heartfelt lesson about the power of the theater to move hearts. Guess there has to be *some* plot structure and a moral to what is essentially a party movie about witty gals hanging out together.

■ ***Steel Magnolias*** *(1989)*
Stars: Sally Field, Julia Roberts, Dolly Parton, Olympia Dukakis, Shirley MacLaine, Daryl Hannah, Tom Skerritt
Director: Herbert Ross
Writer: Robert Harling, based on his stage play

Truvy's Beauty Parlor is the congregating point for the neighborhood women, where they share tears, fears, laughter, and love while having their hair teased to heretofore unattainable heights. Ah yes, the South in the eighties, when Big Hair reigned triumphant.

It's the day of wedding of Shelby (Julia Roberts), a grand affair requiring an armadillo-shaped groom's cake, decorations in the complementary colors of blush and bashful (pink and darker pink, for you Yankees), and the all-out efforts of Shelby's father (Tom Skerritt) to frighten the starlings out of the trees lest Shelby find unwanted off-white accents on her and her bridesmaids' dresses. It's an occasion for tears, fears, laughter, and love. The women bond. Next, there's the matter of diabetic Shelby's dangerous pregnancy. It's an occasion for tears, fears, laughter, and love. The women bond. Then Shelby gets a kidney transplant, which provides not only an occasion for tears, fears, laughter, and love, but an opportunity for the women to bond. Annelle (Daryl Hannah) finds the Lord, Truv opens a new branch of her business, Ouiser gets a beau, Shelby has her baby: tears, fears, laughter, bond, bond, bond.

Okay, so it's a soap opera, but it's a soap opera with some great lines and some gut-wrenching moments to share Kleenex over. Invite the gals, do some girly beauty stuff, and bond, bond, bond.

Character-Defining Moments

I'm not crazy. I've just been in a very bad mood for forty years.

★ Shirley MacLaine as Ouiser Boudreaux in *Steel Magnolias*

Words to Live By

The only thing that separates us from the animals is our ability to accessorize.

★ Olympia Dukakis as Clairee Belcher in *Steel Magnolias*

■ ***Julia*** *(1977)*
Stars: Jane Fonda, Vanessa Redgrave, Jason Robards
Director: Fred Zinnemann
Writer: Alvin Sargent, based on the memoirs of Lillian Hellman

This movie recounts Lillian's (Jane Fonda) lifelong friendship with the extraordinary Julia (Vanessa Redgrave). When we first meet Lillian, she is in the midst of enjoying the fame that comes with her first smash hit on Broadway as well as her passionate romance with the terribly sexy but taciturn Dashiell Hammett.

Lillian is called by her childhood friend Julia, who has eschewed her privileged lifestyle to right the wrongs of the world. She asks Lillian to smuggle money through Nazi Germany to benefit the anti-fascist cause that Julia has devoted her life to. As Lillian allows Julia to lead her far out of her comfort zone, she comes to understand the influence that her friend has had upon her life, and to appreciate the pure beauty of Julia.

This movie is an homage to the magical transformative powers of friendship. Watch it with someone who's been a seminal influence in your life, and salute your solidarity.

■ ***The Color Purple*** *(1985)*
Stars: Whoopi Goldberg, Danny Glover, Margaret Avery, Adolph Caesar, Oprah Winfrey
Director: Steven Spielberg
Writer: Menno Meyjes, based on the novel by Alice Walker

The dogwood is in bloom, the fields are golden, and yet for all the pastoral visions of the South that director Steven Spielberg was intent on capturing, this film won't have you and your girlfriends sipping mint juleps and calmly swaying a palmetto fan, although you may end up swinging it at the head of the nearest male.

From the moment Celie appears on the screen, glowing with excitement and the bloom of youth, it's clear she's just a kid—a pregnant kid. Her rapture is cut short when her father greets her with the pronouncement "Celie, you've got the ugliest smile this side of creation." Yep, the credits have barely ended and already the men are acting like jerks.

Celie's father's act of unbridled hostility toward the daughter he impregnated is just the beginning of a long list of cruelties inflicted upon the hapless Celie and all the women around her, by men who probably have some deep-rooted psychological problems that would explain their need to slap, rape, verbally abuse, and humiliate every female in this film. Even the indomitable Oprah gets slapped down, though of course she rises again phoenix-like at the end (after all, she is *Oprah*—you didn't think she was gonna take this crap, did you?).

Afraid your girlfriend party will turn into a grim scene if you rent this one? Don't worry—the powerful messages about female loyalty, love, perseverance, and friendship that are interspersed among this male ugliness will have you and your friends bounced emotionally from heaven to hell and back, with some humorous and sentimental side trips along the way. Get ready for a major bonding and cathartic experience.

Words to Live By

You get what you settle for.

★ Susan Sarandon as Louise Sawyer in *Thelma & Louise*

▪ *A League of Their Own* (1992)

Stars: Geena Davis, Lori Petty, Rosie O'Donnell, Madonna; Tom Hanks as the manager
Director: Penny Marshall
Writers: Lowell Ganz and Babaloo Mandel, based on a story by Kelly Candaele and Kim Wilson

Like their Rosie the Riveter sisters, the women who played in the all-female baseball league during WW II got the job only because the boys were at the front, and were expected to go back to babymaking and cookie baking once the war was over. After all, who would want to watch women play pro sports?

This fictional account of those pre–Title IX women's experiences discovering the comradeship and glory of playing pro ball is entertaining but at times shamefully over-the-top (the scene with the bumbling telegram boy will make you want to slap Penny Marshall), and Lori Petty's endless whining and pouting ought to have been reined in. Still, Davis, O'Donnell, and even Madonna will win you over. By the time those Georgia Peaches have their reunion at the Baseball Hall of Fame, you'll be tearfully vowing to sign up for an organized sports team right away. Then again, maybe you'll just do the guy-thing and channel surf to see if there's an NWBL game on. Either way, give yourself permission to luxuriate in feminine empowerment.

Character-Defining Moments

DORIS (Rosie O'Donnell): ***Mae, that dress is too tight.***
MAE (Madonna): ***I don't plan on wearing it that long.***

★ from *A League of Their Own*

▪ ***The Turning Point*** *(1977)*
Stars: Anne Bancroft, Shirley MacLaine
Director: Herbert Ross
Writer: Arthur Laurents

This is a movie about the special bond that exists between women, which is able to transcend time, regret, personal differences, and, yes, even middle age.

Deedee (Shirley MacLaine in her pre-astral years) and Emma (Anne Bancroft, who, thankfully, has neither pre- nor post-astral years . . . she's Italian, you know) were prima ballerinas together back in their glory days. Deedee opts out of professional dancing for life as a wife and mom. Emma went on to become a star but now is teetering on the verge of hasbeendom. They meet again when Deedee's young daughter stands at the brink of adolescence, and a bright new career as a prima ballerina.

Obviously, this raises a few issues between these two old friends, who are each simultaneously envious and contemptuous of the other's choices. The film culminates in a great knockdown drag out (literally) with Lincoln Center in the background, but the true victor is the love that endures between them, no matter how divergent the roads they have traveled.

Special Bonus: Hermit's Night

Denise Calls Up *(1996)*
Stars: Tim Daly, Caroleen Feeney, Dan Gunther, Dana Wheeler-Nicholson, Liev Schreiber, Aida Turturro, Alanna Ubach
Director and Writer: Hal Salwen

You say you tried to get everyone together for a girl's night, but with everyone's busy schedule you never got beyond the planning stage? Don't feel bad—you're perfectly set up to rent *Denise Calls Up*, a fun look at a group of friends who are so dependent on modern technology for communication that nothing—conception, birth, sex, death—is experienced face-to-face. Couples meet, have sex, feel smothered, break up and don't recognize each other on the street, and a conference call lets everyone share in the happy event of Denise's labor—even Dad coaches her via cell phone.

If you don't get together with your pals after this cautionary tale, you never will. ■

Chapter 13

When Women Were Women and Men Were Nervous: Men Behaving Well Movies

It wasn't always like this, you know. There was a time, a better time, when men would come to call, and would kiss a woman's hand and lay down their crisply pressed morning coats beneath a woman's feet lest she muddy her slippers in the wet, fertile soil of the spring thaw delta. There was a time, long ago, when men were actually a little afraid of us. Not petrified, mind you, but just cautious enough to make them behave like gentlemen. If you've got a case of the modern "let's go Dutch" malaise, try one of our Men Behaving Well movies and watch these film goddesses rule.

- ***Titanic*** *(1997)*
  Stars: Leonardo DiCaprio, Kate Winslet, Kathy Bates, Billy Zane, Frances Fisher
  Director and Writer: James Cameron

Okay, look, we know, it's a ship of dreams, an emblem of man's tragic hubris, a floating metaphor for the decline of Western civilization, the loss of a great love, or the inevitable death of one's vision. But for God's sake, people, *it's just a boat*! Actually, it's just a lame James Cameron script with an inflated production budget and a super-sophisticated version of Adobe Page-Maker.

Anyway, Kate Winslet is regal as Rose in her pushup Edwardian finery and her unlaced appetite for life, and she puts in a performance that's measured and substantive. Kathy Bates is thoroughly enjoyable as the Unsinkable Molly Brown. And then there's Leonardo DiCaprio as Jack Dawson, who is very cute, if you're into eighty-pound, pubescent male waifs glowing with the first flush of superstardom and copious quantities of bronzing powder number 10. At the apex of Jack's apotheosis, DiCaprio stands at the prow of the doomed ship, his arms outstretched like a figurehead; challenging the briny deep, he cries out, "I'm king of the world," and we're thinking, "King of the world? One stiff updraft, buddy, and you're going up over that mast like a feather in a Santa Ana."

But despite the adolescent rendering of Jack Dawson, he's really our kind of guy. His motto is self-sacrifice and he gives his all, surrendering even his life so that his heart might live on. And before he descends into the watery depths, mermaid-like, looking his last at the face of his beloved, like a lotus flower taking its final glimpse of the sun, he implores Rose to "live, promise me you'll live." And we're thinking, what's with hogging the whole hunk of scenery for yourself, Rose? Couldn't you share a little of that raft with Jack? Or, like, trade off, or let him lie on top of you or something? That might stave off hypothermia for a while. Did Jack really have to die, so that Rose might live? No one will ever know, but ya gotta admit it was really nice of him to offer.

■ *A Room with a View* (1986)

Stars: Helena Bonham Carter, Maggie Smith, Julian Sands, Daniel Day-Lewis
Director: James Ivory
Writer: Ruth Prawer Jhabvala, based on the novel by E. M. Forster

This is one of those visually rich Merchant-Ivory contributions to the "uptight Brit goes to Italy, gets sensually reawakened, and then can no longer endure life back in stultifying England" genre. Lucy Honeychurch (Helena Bonham Carter), an uptight British girl, goes on a trip to Italy prior to her official engagement to Cecil, an uptight British gentleman, and is sensually reawakened by the visual and visceral feast that is southern Italy. While in the piazza one day, she witnesses a murder and swoons. She is caught, before her pristine white gown can kiss the pavement, by George Emerson, a formerly uptight British man who has already been sensually reawakened by a previous trip abroad, and his eccentric father, whose quirky behavior has relegated his son and himself to the margins of polite English society. George and Lucy fall in love, but Lucy is frightened of such strong emotion and makes a hasty decision to marry the stultifying Cecil. George never pressures Lucy about her decision; he leaves her to make up her own mind about her situation, never stages a scene, makes unreasonable demands or witholds his affection. George is the man who behaves extremely well, and because this story was written in the Edwardian period when the good boy rather than the bad boy was revered, you can guess which guy gets to taste the honey in Lucy's church.

▪ ***Sense and Sensibility*** *(1995)*
Stars: Emma Thompson, Kate Winslet, Alan Rickman, Hugh Grant, Kristin Scott Thomas
Director: Ang Lee
Writer: Emma Thompson, based on the novel by Jane Austen

Thompson plays Elinor Dashwood, an uptight British woman in need of being reawakened by feasts of visual and visceral sensation. Her sister Marianne (Kate Winslet) is perpetually swept away by such feasts, particularly when they take the form of a sideburned gentleman on a horse who appears suddenly in the rain to rescue her from certain death—oh well, at the very least a bad chill. You know how it is when you're swept away by feasts of visual and visceral sensation.

Turned out of their home after their father's death by their half brother and his shrewish snob of a wife (Kristin Scott Thomas), the impoverished sisters Dashwood spend their days in a little cottage hoping for the best they can achieve: a good marriage to a kind, wealthy gentleman. Unfortunately, the repressed Elinor learns that her beloved (Hugh Grant) is secretly engaged to another, while the passionate Marianne is beleaguered by an ever present, ever-ready-to-serve pest of a nice-guy gentleman caller who just won't take a hint (Alan Rickman). Of course, both gentlemen defy reality and turn out to be equal parts ardor and faithfulness (and, of course, they have beautiful estates with rolling green hills as well), so both women end up with an appropriately well-rounded, perfect specimen of masculine behavior and a wedding in a darling little country church.

Viewer's Note: If you're in the mood for happily-ever-after-romance and patient chivalry, don't miss this pinnacle of the big-budget costume comedies of manners.

Words to Live By

Bad table manners, my dear Gigi, have broken up more households than infidelity.

★ Isabel Jeans as Aunt Alicia in *Gigi*

■ *The Remains of the Day* (1993)

Stars: Emma Thompson, Anthony Hopkins
Director: James Ivory
Writer: Ruth Prawer Jhabvala, based on the novel by Kazuro Ishiguro

Well, it's a Merchant-Ivory movie about British people, starring Emma Thompson and Anthony Hopkins. . . . Want to guess the theme? Bingo! An uptight British butler is sensually awakened by the arrival of a housekeeper who brings with her a feast of visual and visceral sensation. Okay, maybe the feast is not quite visceral, but she does push the envelope by doing things like dusting at inappropriate moments, and missing the baseboards, and making very personal remarks to the butler himself, who is unaccustomed to displays of emotion. Of course, they wind up falling in love, but it takes the entire movie for the housekeeper to polish away the butler's patina and reach the pure gold. And all the while he behaves so well, it's almost irritating. In fact, it is extremely irritating. In fact, it isn't until he starts behaving badly that he can really be said to be behaving well, which is confusing, but the English are famous for that sort of conundrum.

Next time you're feeling like a housekeeper, and wishing that your head butler would do some work around the house for a change, watch this movie and remember to be careful what you pray for . . . because sometimes your prayers are answered.

▪ ***Howards End*** (1992)
Stars: Emma Thompson, Helena Bonham Carter, Anthony Hopkins, Vanessa Redgrave, James Wilby, Samuel West
Director: James Ivory
Writer: Ruth Prawer Jhabvala, based on the novel by E. M. Forster

Wealthy Ruth Wilcox (Vanessa Redgrave) takes a shine to the charming, intelligent, young middle-class woman across the street, Margaret Schlegel (Emma Thompson), and scribbles an addendum to her will, bequeathing her estate, Howards End, to her newfound friend. But since this act of impetuous generosity born of love and devotion would contradict British class restrictions, and really annoy the poop out of the rest of the family, patriarch and widower Henry Wilcox (Anthony Hopkins) decides to ignore his dead wife's request. Very bad move, karmically speaking, because, as he will learn the hard way, being a gentleman requires more than a clipped accent and the right amount of household staff.

While Margaret is in denial about the wealthy man's ugly nature and oblivious to her stolen inheritance, her sister Helen (Helena Bonham Carter) senses the stench of corruption around Henry Wilcox like so much Limburger cheese—you've been around enough to know it's supposed to be a delicacy, but that honest and forthright part of yourself can't help thinking, "This stuff isn't an acquired taste, it's just a chunk of moldy dairy product that'll contaminate everything around it and wreak havoc on my gastrointestinal tract." Still, it takes tremendous tragedy, upheaval, and—God forbid—emotional scenes in public before Wilcox gets his comeuppance and the Schlegel family get their proper due.

Words To Live By

All you need to start an asylum is an empty room and the right kind of people.

★ from *My Man Godfrey*

Hoopskirt Dreams: Dresses-to-Die-for Movies

Not that we don't have an appreciation for sci-fi costumes and historically accurate if bland clothing, but some movies outfit women in such amazing gowns, ensembles, and accessories that they can inspire even the least fashion conscious. Here are some to check out:

The Age of Innocence (1993)

True, we have to remember that the fabulous fashions in *The Age of Innocence* could only exist because a tiny elite group of obscenely wealthy capitalists were exploiting the poor and subjecting small children to short, miserable lives in coal mines and textile factories. But if you're going to be a capitalist pig with no social conscience, you couldn't look much better than the characters in this movie. When hoopskirts went out, the bustled-in-back look came in, with sweeping trains and plenty of luxurious fabrics bundled up at the butt (a good thing, since those multiple-course meals must've done a number on the ladies' rears and thighs). Best of show: Winona Ryder's beautiful shimmering white gown. (Costumes by Gabriella Pescucci) ■

An American in Paris (1951)

Gene Kelly's choreography is beautiful enough, but the dresses here, especially in the long dream sequence, are each more dazzling than the next. There are the Toulouse-Lautrec can-can girl outfits lifted straight from his Moulin Rouge poster, the roomful of black and white carnival outfits (check out the double fur boa), and our favorite—the red valentine heart gowns of the chorus girls. If only our dream sequences were so well costumed! (Costumes by Orry-Kelly, Walter Plunkett, Irene Sharaff) ■

. . . continued

Anastasia (1956)

Whatever her birthright, she was born for these outfits: the simple white satin number with the mini–shoulder cape and that royal robe and gown in white with gold and red trim. And having a mourning dress like Grandma's, with the sequins and billowing ostrich plumes, would just about make up for losing one's entire family to a squad of assassins. (Costumes by René Hubert) ▪

Romy and Michele's High School Reunion (1997)

They may be from some nowheresville in Arizona, but Romy and Michele's Valley Girl couture puts them on the map. For evening wear, there are those minidresses in a variety of loud colors with lots of shine: tinsel-y turquoise with fringe, metallic orange, metallic blue with matching baby blue cuffs and collar. And for workout wear, how about a lavender patent leather miniskirt, flowered spandex top, and turquoise boxing gloves to liven up that kickboxing class? If only we all had those southern California bodies ten years post–high school so we could carry off crazy fashions like these. (Costumes by Mona May) ▪

Bringing Up Baby (1938)

Katharine Hepburn's usual sensible but stylish streetwear is still inspiring to working women everywhere, but her rich girl costumes in this film are delightfully silly, from a polka dot pantsuit to a shimmering lamé evening gown (we're betting on gold—you've got to use your imagination in this b&w era). Best of all, it's got this gossamer hood thing with a squiggly ribbon as edging that makes it seem to float in the air around her face like some sort of futuristic halo. (Gowns by Howard Greer) ▪

. . . continued

Gone With the Wind (1939)

Even Barbie has taken to donning the indomitable Miss O'Hara's costumes, which range from the infamous green velvet dress made from draperies (check out the gold bell cord), the low-cut green sprigged muslin "afternoon dress" that she defiantly wears to the morning barbecue, the sultry red gown with sequins and dyed ostrich feathers that Rhett makes her wear to Ashley's party to "look her part" as the seductress (Vivien Leigh's cleavage secret: duct tape), and the charming blue waist-length jacket and frilly white dress combo she wears on that fateful trip to the lumber office. (Costumes by Walter Plunkett) ■

The Wings of the Dove (1997)

Bad girl Kate's scheming ways and attention to detail obviously extend to accessorizing. She and her pals drape themselves in fabulous hand-painted silk, velvet, and embroidered art nouveau gowns that marry black with rich peacock blues and greens. They also don Orient-inspired robes and overcoats that create that post-Victorian diamond profile. And those accessories! Drop necklaces, plumed headbands, cigarette holders, turbans, elbow-length black gloves, impossibly large-brimmed hats . . . And in these mouthwatering dresses and that darling little matador costume for carnival, Helena Bonham Carter looks the most stunning of all, a role model to girls everywhere who have unmanageable curls and a total lack of tanning ability. (Costumes by Sandy Powell) ■

Pillow Talk (1959)

What Jan Morrow (Doris Day) lacks in sex appeal she sure makes up for in fashion sense. Yes, she may be an interior designer, but it's her exterior that lights up the screen: There's that green spaghetti-strap gown with

. . . continued

the turquoise necklace, bracelet, and earrings—remember matching jewelry combos? There's the emerald day dress with that outrageous hat that looks like a pile of seaweed and yet somehow works; that humongous black mink cap that looks like a marmot parked on her head; the red-orange coat with the leopard skin pillbox hat and muff—and all of it set off by that glossy bubblegum-pink lipstick and silver-white wig. If shopping sprees are merely a substitute for sex, frigidity never looked so good. (Costumes by Jean Louis; jewelry by Laykin et Cie) ■

Angels and Insects (1995)

The shimmering hoopskirted frocks in this movie represent deceptive and transient beauty, but you'll want to freeze frame on these dazzling creations: golden stripes on an emerald-colored skirt and basque, a royal blue ball gown with fuchsia crisscross detail, a deep purple taffeta riding habit, a black-and-yellow bumblebee-inspired getup with an appropriately netted hat, and a gossamer white gown that reflects back even the dimmest of ambient light. Sinister, shminister. Where does this gal shop? (Costumes by Paul Brown) ■

My Fair Lady (1964)

Not only does Eliza Doolittle's elocution improve, her fashion sense takes a huge leap forward after meeting Professor Henry Higgins. In the Ascot Park scene, where black against white contrasts and geometrical patterns are the rage (much like that carnival scene in *An American in Paris*), she wears that unforgettable white mermaid dress with little black-and-white-striped ribboned accents that match the huge bow on her wagon-wheel-wide hat. And her meeting-the-Queen-of-Transylvania outfit, with its simple Grecian lines, shoulder-to-fingertip gloves, and elaborate jewel collar, is the perfect excuse for yet another Audrey Hepburn tiara. (Costumes by Cecil Beaton) ■

. . . continued

Born Yesterday (1950)

Judy Holliday's Billie may be a dumb blonde, but she's a fashion genius. When playing the part of her thug boyfriend's boy toy, she dons black-sequined skintight sheaths, an asymmetrical diamond drop necklace suggestive of a side-tied scarf, and double draped low-cut necklines. Her idea of a housecoat is white sparkly lounging pajamas with turned-out black collar and cuffs, spike heels, chunky jeweled bracelet, and black cigarette holder. And when she explores the D.C. monuments, even her nerd glasses (the better to read the Bill of Rights with) don't detract from her smart little suits. Who else would have the chutzpah to visit the Capitol building while wearing a white bustier and long black gloves? (Costumes by Jean Louis) ■

Annie Hall (1977)

Ralph Lauren may have been the costume designer in this Woody Allen flick, but we suspect Diane Keaton had major influence on the choices here—camel-colored trousers, crisp white shirts and turtlenecks, plenty of vests and ties and jaunty black men's hats with round brims, and big semidark sunglasses. If you're too young to remember the short-lived Annie Hall look, check this one out—you may consider reviving it. (Costumes by Ralph Lauren) ■

Death on the Nile (1978)

Whodunnit? In this Agatha Christie film, set in the 1920s, the bigger question is, where do I get clothes like this? As they cruise down the Nile the ladies on the ship model wonderfully crisp summer wear in cool colors with simple lines. There's also some lesbian chic menswear worn by Maggie

. . . continued

Smith, and some overblown and outrageous black-and-gold art nouveau–era getups on the tippling Angela Lansbury. But it's the slinky evening gowns that'll wow you—cut to the navel and backless, like the one in shimmering silvery blue. Definitely worth murdering for. (Costumes by Anthony Powell) ■

Hot weather does keep one in a continual state of inelegance.

★ Lady Russell in *Persuasion*

No Man of Her Own (1932)

Like so many of those classic romantic comedies from the thirties and forties, *No Man of Her Own* has the hidden delight of costuming that makes the most of the limitations of black and white—lots of sparkle and shine, contrast, and unusual lines. Carole Lombard gets to prance around in silk lounging pajamas (which she packs for a weekend in a country cabin—don't you just love the *idea* of lounging pajamas?), a naughty little lace-trimmed tap panties-and-bra set, a white silk robe with layer upon layer of light-grabbing folds, and a simple-line black floor-length gown with sleeve ruffles that have inexplicably been moved to her elbows (where, oddly enough, they actually work). When the inside of a gal's closet looks like this, you don't ask too many questions about her fellow's choice of career. (Costumes by Travis Banton) ■

. . . continued

Clueless (1995)

If there's one thing Valley Girl Cher and her friends are not clueless about, it's how to look smashing. Cher has a huge closet filled with plaid miniskirt and blazer combos in primary colors, simple monochromatic designer minidresses ("Who says that's a dress?" demands her father when spotting her in a skimpy little white number. "Calvin Klein!" she insists), and all the right accessories—thigh-high black cotton stockings, berets, big hats with huge fake flowers, mini-backpacks, and adorable little party purses that couldn't fit a pocket comb. In fact, she needs a computer program and a Polaroid camera to help her keep her outfits perfectly coordinated. Of course, anyone over seventeen and outside L.A. would look positively ridiculous in these getups, but they're great fun to look at. (Costumes by Mona May) ■

■ ***Emma*** *(1996)*
Stars: Gwyneth Paltrow, Jeremy Northam; or Kate Beckinsale, Mark Strong
Director: Douglas McGrath (Paltrow version); Diarmuid Lawrence (Beckinsale version, produced by A&E)
Writers: Douglas McGrath (Paltrow version); Andrew Davies (Beckinsale version); based on the novel by Jane Austen

Emma is a chit—a charming but shallow butterfly that alights here and there, never stopping for long, assuming her luck and her fortune will never run out and that she'll never find herself pinned up stiffly inside some frame hung on the wall of a museum of bimbos of the early nineteenth century. Oblivious to the annoying and even destructive effects of her immature and self-important behavior, she laughs at the gentle but firm scoldings of the most eligible bachelor in town, who is, after all, just a friend.

Now, only in a great romantic classic by Jane Austen would that nice guy best friend cut a dashing figure in his flap-fly breeches, have scads of real estate holdings and impeccable manners and taste, *and* hang around long enough for a flighty heroine to come to her senses, do a complete inventory of her faults, pay her penance, and ripen into full emotional womanhood. Meanwhile, we can sit back and enjoy Emma's self-absorbed romps, knowing that when she's ready he'll be there, carriage awaiting.

Viewer's Note: It's a toss-up as to which of these versions is better; we say, consider your deepest feelings about Gwyneth Paltrow—lovely and talented victim of heartless ex-beau Brad Pitt? or impossibly gorgeous and thin rich girl who deserves a fall already, dammit?—and then go for the appropriate version.

■ ***Angels and Insects*** *(1995)*
Stars: Mark Rylance, Kristin Scott Thomas, Patsy Kensit, Jeremy Kemp
Director: Philip Haas
Writers: Belinda Haas and Philip Hass, based on the novella Morpho Eugenia *by A. S. Byatt*

Butterfly collector William Adamson (Rylance) is taken with a rare specimen called *Morpho Eugenia,* the male of which is a beautiful shimmering blue while the female is a drab, dull brown, which Darwin would interpret as an example of a compensation device necessary to attract one who can bring forth life despite its lack of beauty. And perhaps if this kindhearted, soft-spoken gentleman were a bit more adept with poetry and metaphor and less absorbed in the natural sciences, he'd figure out that he ought to pursue the sensible brunette in the simple gray and black frocks (Scott Thomas) instead of the neurotic blonde in stunning blue confections (Kensit). I mean, the blonde's name is Eugenia, for God's sake. How thickheaded can you get?

Then again, if he caught on any more quickly to the secrets of the Alabaster family—which all the servants and even the local insect populations have figured out (men, of course, being less attuned to emotional subtleties than bugs)—we'd be deprived of a parade of scrumptious gowns as well as a fascinating morality tale, and one that uses blondes to symbolize shallowness and brunettes to represent goodness, morality, honesty, and a host of other human virtues. This one'll convince you that real gentlemen are only momentarily distracted by the short-lived beauty of butterflies and will eventually wise up. It'll also convince you to forgo the peroxide and have faith that your obscure references to classic poets and your socialist leanings will net you a choice specimen.

Worst Pickup Lines

Gosh you're cute. Wanna buy a monkey?

★ David Letterman as Old Salt in *Cabin Boy*

You're a groovy boy. I'd like to strap you on sometime.

★ Edy Williams as Ashley St. Ives in *Beyond the Valley of the Dolls*

I'm highly attracted to you. Why, when I look at you I feel wee tadpoles jumping in my spine.

★ Dodie Heath as Meg Brockie in *Brigadoon*

You know, you're beginning to fascinate me, and I resent that in any man.

★ Alice Brady as Aunt Hortense in *The Gay Divorcee*

What do you do with all the hearts you break?

★ Clark Gable to Carole Lombard in *No Man of Her Own* (P.S. It works)

■ ***Mrs. Brown*** *(1997)*
Stars: Judi Dench, Billy Connolly, Antony Sher, Geoffrey Palmer
Director: John Madden
Writer: Jeremy Brock

The heartbroken Queen Victoria, having lost her beloved Prince Albert to typhoid in 1861, spent the rest of her seventy-five-year reign in widow's weeds, thereby ensuring that several generations would not only feel compelled to cling to restrictive mourning rituals but hyperventilate at the sight of a piano limb. But maybe, this film posits, Victoria wasn't as repressed as the public assumed. Maybe she was able to find a beautiful and enduring love once again, even if the days of passion and orgasm were behind her. Well, you can't have everything.

In this fictional love story based on fact, John Brown (Billy Connolly), an old friend of Albert's, is a consummate gentleman despite his hard-drinking Scottish ways, but once introduced to the royal household as a servant he deliberately oversteps his place. He's willing to risk offending the queen (Judi Dench) because he has a compelling need to bring her back to life from her unfettered morbidity. Despite the disapproval of the queen's allies, who find him overbearing and overprotective of their monarch, he loves Victoria too much to pay them any mind. Mr. Brown forces the queen to face her pain and literally puts her back in the saddle so that she might be able to resume her duties and yet also delight in brisk rides on horseback across the Scottish Highlands, thus breathing life back into her black crepe existence.

Chock full of kilts, heather, and chivalry, *Mrs. Brown* is an ode to the beauty of courtly love.

> ⚠ Warning Label: *Don't take your hands off the remote. The Victorian locutions uttered in an impenetrable Highland brogue are virtually incomprehensible without rewinding often.*

■ ***My Man Godfrey*** *(1936)*
Stars: William Powell, Carole Lombard, Gail Patrick, Alice Brady
Director: Gregory La Cava
Writers: Morrie Ryskind and Eric Hatch, based on the novel by Eric Hatch

Godfrey (William Powell) is a forgotten man, living in the city dump next to the East River. One night he is discovered by a disgustingly rich Park Avenue partygoer named Cornelia Bullock (Gail Patrick), who wants to claim him like so much flotsam for a treasure hunt. Appalled, Godfrey pushes Cornelia into a pile of ashes, then allows Cornelia's sister Irene (Lombard) to haul him in to the judges and win the contest. Why? Because she is deserving of his chivalry. You see, unlike her sister, Irene may be ridiculous, but she's *lovably* ridiculous, prone to schoolgirl crushes, histrionic spells whenever her whims aren't catered to, and horseback rides up the front steps of her Fifth Avenue home. Though Godfrey senses he's merely a replacement for Irene's late Pomeranian, he nevertheless agrees to keep her company by working as a butler for the ridiculous Bullocks, even if it does make him a lapdog in a monkey suit. Moreover, he maintains his patient dignity as he tolerates Irene's positively silly advances and ministers hangover remedies to the entire eccentric brood.

Of course, Godfrey turns out to have a secret that makes him worthy of a society girl, and far more respectable than the Bullocks can ever hope to be, and naturally he uses his influence to benefit all the forgotten men. Whatta guy! And to think that he could be found at the dump. Sort of brightens your outlook about the singles scene, doesn't it?

■ ***The Age of Innocence*** *(1993)*
Stars: Daniel Day-Lewis, Michelle Pfeiffer, Winona Ryder
Director: Martin Scorsese
Writers: Jay Cocks and Martin Scorsese, based on the novel by Edith Wharton

As Edith Wharton loved to point out, New York society in the 1870s was slavishly devoted to conspicuous consumption—an endless feast of sumptuous food, ornate furnishings, overly passionate entertainments, and fabulously opulent clothing (images of which Scorsese piles on here with shot after shot of obscenely fussy accessories, dinner courses, and accoutrements). Such luxuries, however, produced as well a severe famine of meaningful conversation, as Newland Archer (Day-Lewis) knows all too well. While those around him babble on about the minutiae of their startlingly dull lives, he's gearing up to seal his inescapably pallid fate with a marriage to a particularly gorgeous and empty-headed ornament, May Welland (Winona Ryder). But a meeting with his new in-law, the lovely and iconoclastic Countess Olenska (Michelle Pfeiffer), wakes him up like a winter gale cutting across the stagnant swamp of his existence. Being a gentleman, of course, he gives no indication of his transferred affections, not even to himself, until he can't stand it anymore and prostrates himself to kiss the toe of her slipper. Poor Newland has to settle for the ultimate in safe sex—appropriate and subtle acts of kindness to his beloved to ensure her acceptance in society despite her intoxicating perfume of nonconformity. This does not exactly satisfy the yearnings of his heart or libido, although it sure makes for a sensual buildup. Forget naked bodies rolling in slo-mo; you'll be turned on by wrist-kissing by the time he finally gets the Countess alone.

But when Newland does get the chance to go beyond mere flirtation, will he honor true love or social convention? Will he find the courage to speak his piece and make his move? And most important, won't he ever get a soft-focus, golden-lighted nude scene so we can check out Daniel Day-Lewis's butt?

▪ *Pride and Prejudice* (1995)

Stars: Colin Firth, Jennifer Ehle
Director: Simon Langton
Writer: Andrew Davies, based on the novel by Jane Austen

In an era where family and breeding are major factors in one's future romantic prospects, Elizabeth Bennet's got a lot to overcome: Her mother is a shrill and vulgar busybody, her father a curmudgeon, and her sisters include a hopelessly untalented singer who insists on inflicting her off-key warbling on trapped party guests and another who is dimwitted and boy crazy. Worse, Elizabeth's dowry is practically nonexistent and she lives in the countryside, miles from the well-heeled gentlemen. Yes, the pickings are paltry until that visitor from London, Mr. Darcy (Firth), shows up. Unfortunately, he proves to be sullen, rude, and conceited, which is a real shame because he's got two carriages, six liveried servants, and £10,000 a year.

Lucky for Elizabeth, and even luckier for her gold-digging mother, her prejudice against the prideful Mr. Darcy is lifted when he eventually turns out not to be a cad after all. Why, he even humbles himself to Elizabeth, albeit not until after she has, in essence at least, smacked him upside the head for being an arrogant jerk. It may take a little work, but his true gentlemanly spots soon show.

Don't you wish all fixer-uppers could be so easily renovated?

Viewer's Note: The 1940 version is worth watching if you're a fan of the vivacious Greer Garson, or if you want to gaze at Laurence Olivier's perfect cheekbones, adorable cleft, and flashing black eyes. Unfortunately, its overly precious direction and musical score, along with its dopey Hollywoodesque costuming (especially dopey given that the ladies wear hoopskirts instead of Regency-era Empire waists), make it far less satisfying than the newer versions. What's the point of a Jane Austen adaptation if you can't drool over beautiful gowns, rolling green fields, and the opulent interiors of English estates?

■ ***The Purple Rose of Cairo*** *(1985)*
Stars: Mia Farrow, Jeff Daniels, Danny Aiello
Director and Writer: Woody Allen

In a small American town during the Depression, a fragile young woman (Mia Farrow) waits tables in a cheap diner, lives in a squalid apartment with an abusive lug (Danny Aiello), and finds escape only at the local picture show, where ladies and gents endlessly trade witticisms over martinis and cigarettes and congregate in art deco drawing rooms and New York nightclubs where the orchestra plays all night and the champagne flows freely. If only she could climb up on that screen and be wooed by a real gentleman . . . and then, in a surreal twist, the leading man of the latest screwball offering (Jeff Daniels) climbs down and falls madly in love with this ordinary girl. Somehow they'll carve out a life for themselves, he promises her optimistically, which is going to be tricky given that his money is only prop currency. Still, can a girl find true happiness with a man who is, well, fictional? And how will the plotline advance if he doesn't get back into that drawing room? And how can she possibly join them for champagne cocktails at the club when she doesn't own a single body-clinging bias-cut satin number?

This oddball and sweet little film asks all the quirky questions you don't when you're caught up fantasizing over some screen idol or envying those sophisticated society types that only exist onscreen.

■ ***The African Queen*** *(1951)*
Stars: Katharine Hepburn, Humphrey Bogart
Director: John Huston
Writers: James Agee and John Huston, based on the novel by C. S. Forester

He doesn't exactly look like a gentleman, what with his perpetually unshaven and sweaty appearance, his cigar smoking and gin drinking, and his gastrointestinal problems. Still, Charlie Allnut (Bogart), the captain of the rickety little mail boat, is always extremely polite to Miss Rose (Hepburn), helping her to bury her brother and escape the oncoming

German army. In return, she sees to it that he sobers up, shaves, and minimizes his tobacco usage. Her missionary zeal and dubious, not to mention dangerous, plan to get out of German East Africa and bomb a ship on England's behalf while they're at it may annoy him temporarily, but he shapes up in no time and makes every attempt to live up to Rose's proclamation that "Nature, Mr. Allnut, is what we are put in this world to rise above." And rise above it they do, finding true love amongst the leeches and tsetse flies, as the hedonistic Allnut learns to serve a cause far greater than himself—namely, a woman's whims.

Frankly, we like that in a man.

▪ ***Persuasion*** *(1995)*
Stars: Amanda Root, Ciarán Hinds
Director: Roger Michell
Writer: Nick Dear, based on the novel by Jane Austen

Anne Elliot (Amanda Root) plays sounding board to all her in-laws, graciously suffers a narcissistic hypochondriac sister, tolerates a pompous father and sister who are only interested in social position, stays behind in the countryside waiting for the tenants to show up while everyone else gets to go to town and have a good time, visits infirm widows out of a sense of kindness and obligation, and silently watches as her marriage-minded flighty sisters-in-law buzz about her former beau, whom she gave up eight years ago only out of duty to her family. In the modern era, a hopeless codependent like Anne would attract only con artists, but in a Jane Austen story, a gal like this is destined to marry a wealthy gentleman who adores her. Of course, there has to be a series of plot twists confusing you as to the identity of the particular wealthy gentleman she'll choose (because gals in Jane Austen stories *always* have a choice of wealthy gentlemen).

This one may be a little light on the aesthetics—pale colors, splotchy skin, and bad-hair days abound—but the delayed gratification and chivalry are in full force.

Chapter 14

When Men Were Men and Women Were Wicked: Women Behaving Badly Movies

Are you tired of behaving yourself? Sick of playing Doris Day in a Jean-Claude Van Damme world? Trade the pillow talk for the don't-mess-with-me walk and unleash your killer instincts. These Women Behaving Badly movies will inspire you to put on your red dress, dye your hair platinum, and psychologically torture whichever man has the temerity to cross your path. Remember, good girls finish last, so take no prisoners.

- ***What Ever Happened to Baby Jane?*** *(1962)*
  Stars: Bette Davis, Joan Crawford, Victor Buono
  Director: Robert Aldrich
  Writer: Lukas Heller, based on the novel by Henry Farrell

Bette Davis stars as Baby Jane, an aged (and we do mean *aged*) former (and we do mean *former*) child star. As her career fades, almost with her prepubescence, she must watch her sister Blanche's (Joan Crawford) star rise. This, of course, makes for lots of classic Bette Davis–style mugging. You've got the visual haven't you? Eyes and brows cast heavenward, corners of her mouth bowed down in a perpetual grimace, and of course, the eternally smoldering cigarette, and that hair. Then, as a result of a mysterious car accident, Blanche is paralyzed and placed in Baby's Jane's hands for care. And then Baby Jane gets down with her bad self. She locks her sister in a room, and slowly and methodically disembowels her physically and emotionally. It culminates in a moment of ignominious public acclaim on a beach, under the glaring spotlight of reality, which rivals Nora Desmond's famous "I'm ready for my close-up" moment in *Sunset Boulevard.* And the best part is getting a gander at Bette Davis, in a baby-doll dress, a huge bow in her head, and that ravaged, garishly painted face peering myopically into the spotlight, in search of a redemption that will arrive too late. Classic bad Bette. Plus, what could be better than watching two of Hollywood's most lovable bitches on wheels go at each other full throttle?

Classic Bette Bytes

BLANCHE: ***You wouldn't be able to do these awful things to me if I weren't still in this chair.***

JANE: ***But ya* aah*, Blanche, ya* aah *in that chair!***

★ Bette Davis as Jane in *What Ever Happened to Baby Jane?*

- ***The Scarlet Letter*** *(1995)*

  Stars: Demi Moore, Gary Oldman, Robert Duvall

  Director: Roland Joffé

  Writer: Douglas Day Stewart, very loosely based on the novel by Nathaniel Hawthorne

Hester Prynne (Demi Moore) really wasn't bad. She was just . . . alternative. Granted, she gives birth to an illegitimate child in Puritan New England, which definitely makes a statement. But everybody gets so huffy about everything. Seventeenth-century Puritans definitely had a tendency to overreact. Okay, so Hester did the minister (Gary Oldman), but he's sexy, for God's sake, all laced up like he is, in all that black leather and liturgy, dying to just burst free. But of course then everybody wants to know who the father of the baby is, because people in sexually restrictive societies are passionate gossips, and Hester, who is getting laid on a regular basis, has no need to indulge in sublimated sexuality masquerading as justice. So when she won't tell, they start to torture her, which is yet another sublimated sexual enactment of their own twisted inner workings. But through it all, Hester never budges. Hester is a woman who knows her own mind. She's willing to die for what she believes, and come to think of it, even by today's standards, those are the makings of a very, very bad girl!

> Warning Label: *Okay, we know that Demi Moore's Hester has a morality that's far more L.A. 1990s than New England 1600s, which we admit is pretty grating, but the rolling-in-the-silo sex scenes temper our objections to this bastardization of Hawthorne's words.*

■ ***Mame*** *(1974)*
Stars: Lucille Ball, Bea Arthur, Robert Preston, Bruce Davison
Director: Gene Saks
Writer: Paul Zindel, based on the novel Auntie Mame *by Patrick Dennis*

Mame (Lucille Ball) is retro-bad. She's cigarette-holder-wielding, martini-mixing, bauble-earringed, and rolling-in-bucks bad. She's New York circa 1961 naughty, which was an era that raised misbehaving to the level of high art. When, after the death of her brother, she becomes guardian to her young nephew Patrick (Bruce Davison), she toys with the idea of cultivating a less scandalous lifestyle. The totally cool thing about this movie is, Mame refuses to reform herself and still maintains a perfectly functional and nurturing relationship with her young charge. Even economic hardship can't touch her. When the wolf comes knocking at the door, she finds herself a dashing southern millionaire (Robert Preston), marries him, and imports her New York naughtiness south of the

Mason-Dixon line and makes all the Georgia Peaches blush. Watch this movie when you're feeling irrepressible.

Words to Live By

If your laws don't include me, well then, they don't apply to me either.

★ Anita Crown in *Bad Girls*

▪ ***The Crucible*** *(1996)*
Stars: Daniel Day-Lewis, Winona Ryder, Paul Scofield, Joan Allen
Director: Nicholas Hytner
Writer: Arthur Miller, based on his play

Abigail Williams (Winona Ryder) is very very very bad. She's bad in the way that only sixteen-year-old girls can be bad. She's passionate, self-involved, prone to hysteria, iron-willed, and oblivious to her own evil. When she falls in love with a married man, John Proctor (Daniel Day-Lewis), all hell breaks loose, literally. She harnesses the hysteria of an entire bevy of teenage Puritan beauties, who are also very very bad, and the whole lot of them begin accusing the whole colony of witchcraft. Which leads to the execution of other very bad girls, like Elizabeth Proctor, John's wife, who is bad because she has refused to forgive her husband for having an affair with the sixteen-year-old baby-sitter. In fact, in this film, every single woman is bad, despite the fact that it is a film about the Salem witch trials, which involved a bunch of white men burning women at the stake for witchcraft. Funny how that works . . . isn't it? Watch this one and cast your own Wiccan spell to counteract the patriarchy, which can turn heroines into demonical villainesses, particularly when they sleep with married playwrights and refuse to go away afterward.

■ *Red-Headed Woman* (1932)

Stars: Jean Harlow, Chester Morris, Una Merkel, Lewis Stone
Director: Jack Conway
Writer: Anita Loos, based on a novel by Katherine Brush

They're babies, really. A little leg, a little cleavage, and they'll fork over anything you want, which, for our pert, redheaded, underwear-disdaining, satin-encased heroine Harlow is a good deal of cash, a smashing house in the right neighborhood, and a to-die-for dinner party guest list. Just how many men can this homewrecker and shameless low-class hussy seduce and discard before she's run out of town? Lots, we hope.

Jean Harlow is at her bad-girl finest in this movie scripted especially for her. Keep a scorecard as the world's most lovable homewrecker, egged on by her gum-cracking ill-grammared sidekick, Una Merkel, leaves in her wake plenty of shattered reputations and emptied bank accounts before moving on to the next town full of suckers.

> ⚠ Warning Label: *If a little rough foreplay strikes you as appalling and female promiscuity outrages you, this isn't the one for you.*

■ *The Lady Eve* (1941)

Stars: Henry Fonda, Barbara Stanwyck
Director: Preston Sturges
Writer: Preston Sturges, based on a story by Monckton Hoffe

Fresh from a year exploring the Amazon, heir to a brewing fortune, *über*-dork Fonda ("Snakes are my life") is an easy mark for a con woman. Unlike your average eyelash-batting, handkerchief-dropping gold diggers, Stanwyck is a pro—who else could finagle a gift of roses out of a fellow when they're aboard ship? Hell, even the *Titanic* didn't have a florist! Cardshark Daddy reminds her to remain true to her motto—"They say a moonlit deck is a woman's business office"—but of course she falls for the obtuse sap, only to have her cover blown. How does a gal nab a rich fella without having to betray her bad-ass self? A doubly clever second con, of course. Calculating and clever enough to make Madonna look like Joan Fontaine, Stanwyck will remind you that honesty is usually the least strategically advantageous policy.

Words to Live By

You're not very bright, are you? I like that in a man.

★ Matty Walker in *Body Heat*

■ ***Gone With the Wind*** *(1939)*
Stars: Vivien Leigh, Clark Gable, Olivia de Havilland, Leslie Howard
Director: Victor Fleming
Writer: Sidney Howard, based on the novel by Margaret Mitchell

Would that we could all be Scarlett O'Hara: astonishingly beautiful, pursued by the dashing Rhett Butler and beloved by the ever-loyal best friend Melanie, a supremely successful businesswoman with a mansion in the city and a positively palatial weekend home—and an unrepentant bitch when need be. When Scarlett shakes her fist at the heavens and vows never to be hungry again, you, too, will be ready to rise up, draw on your resources (even if they are limited to a pretty face, chutzpah, and some green velvet portiers), and kick some serious Yankee butt. So the man she loves is emotionally unavailable, she's plagued by flashes of guilt and nightmares about running through fog, and Rhett is growing impatient with her need to take twelve years or so to self-actuate. We know it'll all work out for our Scarlett. She'll simply *will* it to be.

Don't let the four-hour length scare you: you'll be caught up in the sweeping vistas, enchanting costumes, and the sight of Captain Butler waltzing divinely with everyone's favorite southern belle.

> ⚠ Wince Alert: *Be prepared for real eyeball-rolling 1930s racial stereotypes and southern revisionist history.*

■ ***Beyond the Forest*** *(1949)*
Stars: Bette Davis, Joseph Cotten
Director: King Vidor
Writer: Lenore J. Coffee, based on the novel by Stuart Engstrand

We admit it—Davis is just a bit over-the-top here, but who cares? Who wouldn't reach the pinnacle of hysteria living in Loyalton, Wisconsin, where the sawmill spews hot flames and thick smoke all night long so that you have to keep your shades drawn if you're to get any rest from this inferno-like reminder that "Life in Loyalton is like sitting in a funeral parlor, waiting for the funeral to begin. No, not sitting—lying in a coffin and waiting for them to carry you out. . . . You gotta drink?" Yes, the only pastime here is shootin' critters from trees and getting it on with whichever playboy blows into the local lodge for the weekend.

What a dump, indeed.

Rosa Moline may be uppity, she may be cruel and selfish, okay, maybe she's downright evil and will, like the scorpion in a mad fury, sting herself to eternal death, for evil is headstrong (don't you just hate self-righteous narrators?). But surely she deserves a chance to get the hell out on the first train to Chicago and order up a dry martini through room service. And if she may have to murder some old coot to do it? Well, *you* try going without a decent nightlife for years on end.

Pop it in, fix yourself a dry one, and remember, you *are* Rosa Moline.

> ⚠ Wince Alert: *Rosa's "Injun" maid is not only an embarrassing stereotype, but her "blackface" looks like something out of the nineteenth century.*

Classic Bette Bytes

DIXIE: *You know, that son of ours is really something.*
EDDIE: *Oh, yeah, what happened?*
DIXIE: *He comes to me and says, "Mommy, is kissing dirty?"*
EDDIE: *What did you tell him?*
DIXIE: *I said, "Sweetheart, sex between two people can be a beautiful thing. But sex between four people . . . fantastic!"*

★ Bette Midler and James Caan in *For the Boys*

■ ***La Femme Nikita*** *(1990)*—Remade in 1993 as *Point of No Return* with Bridget Fonda
Stars: Anne Parillaud, Jean-Hugues Anglade
Director and Writer: Luc Besson

You know, there's just no point in trying to remake a French film about a bad girl. No American, much less the sweet-faced, perfectly coiffed Bridget Fonda, can possibly carry off cold-blooded murders with the style of a lipsticked, Doc Martened, hedonistic hoyden with major attitude like a scrawny French chick can. Which is why you ought to pass up the watered-down *Point of No Return* and head straight for the stylish, gritty original. Anne Parillaud plays Nikita, whose more endearing qualities are throwing tantrums, dancing maniacally, stabbing men who annoy her, shooting cops in the head, and listening to Nina Simone. Hey, what's not to like?

Of course, the government isn't too keen on letting Nikita run loose, which is why they fake her death and offer her a choice: become a political assassin, or park yourself in row 8, plot 13, which is where everyone thinks she is anyway. Well, what the hell—it's a job, and she is a pretty good shot. But the constant demands—a bombing here, a sniper shooting there—do get to be a drag after a while. What's a bad girl to do?

■ ***Harriet Craig*** *(1950)*
Stars: Joan Crawford, Wendell Corey, K. T. Stevens
Director: Vincent Sherman
Writers: Anne Froelich and James Gunn, based on the Pulitzer prize–winning play Craig's Wife *by George Kelly*

She doesn't mean to be evil incarnate, really she doesn't. It's just there's this backstory thing about her father deserting her and her mother when she was just fourteen, which, if you have any sympathy whatsoever, really ought to make you forgive her for systematically destroying all chances of happiness for the ones who love her most and trust her implicitly.

Oh, right. Go ahead and pick on her. Poor Harriet Craig only means well when she lies to her husband (Wendell Corey) about her sterility (he really doesn't need to be bothered with screaming brats, after all, even if he does think they're cute). Or when she lies to his employer about his embezzling tendencies so that he won't have to take that long-term assignment overseas. Or when she tells her niece (K. T. Stevens) that her beau just wants to get in her pants—she just wants to be sure the poor girl won't have to end up married. Or when she screeches at Grandma Walton for breaking a teacup. All right, Ellen Corbett's not Grandma Walton yet—it's only 1950—but even so. How mean can you get?

The foibles of control freak Harriet Craig will leave you gasping. Watch it with him, then see if he isn't a little more forgiving at that time of the month.

Words To Live By

No man's born ready for marriage. He has to be trained.

★ Joan Crawford as *Harriet Craig*

■ ***China Seas*** *(1935)*
Stars: Clark Gable, Jean Harlow, Wallace Beery, Rosalind Russell
Director: Tay Garnett
Writers: Jules Furthman and James Kevin McGuinness, based on the novel by Crosbie Garstin

Stuck with the bullish Wallace Beery as her shipmate, Harlow, dipped as usual in a liquid satin gown on as many occasions as a screenwriter could possibly invent, is determined to throw him off for the beefy Gable, whose chest and shoulders are fairly bursting out of that all-white captain's jacket. Oh, there's some society dame distracting him, and he puts on a good show of wanting to go respectable and all. But deep down, he knows he deserves a glamorous and curvaceous platinum blonde like China Doll, who can knock back the hard stuff and play King Puff Puff Puff for hours on end, leaving Beery in his cups under the table. It's only a matter of time and a thin plot before she nails him, just as she did in *Red Dust*. Flaunt it, honey.

⚠ Warning Label: *The racist depiction of the Chinese workers hits a low in a cheesy accident sequence—aiiiiieeee! indeed.*

▪ ***Gia*** *(1998)*
Stars: Angelina Jolie, Mercedes Ruehl, Elizabeth Mitchell
Director: Michael Cristofer
Writers: Jay McInerney and Michael Cristofer, based on the book by Stephen Fried

You remember her, don't you? Hard to forget the gal with those big eyes, that insouciant gait, that thick-lipped smile, and that penchant for carving her name in your desk with a switchblade. No bubble-headed supermodel was Gia Carangi, the model of the moment in the late seventies and early eighties. Her rock and roll attitude resulted in photographs whose raw energy leapt off the page, making her a highly commercial commodity. Unfortunately, the superficial, drug-happy culture of the disco era consumed Gia like so much propane in the combustible tank of the modeling industry, leaving her to a gruesome death by AIDS. Played with intensity by Angelina Jolie, Gia is both infuriating and charismatic, deeply vulnerable and totally narcissistic, and completely compelling despite her nasty habits of robbing her loved ones for drug money, nodding off backstage when the heroin kicks in, and lying sweetly about how wonderful it is to be clean when she's just had a toot in the ladies' room. Mom (Mercedes Ruehl), watches helplessly, loving her and yet unwilling to get sucked into the black hole of her daughter's needs, while Gia's ever-suffering lover (Elizabeth Mitchell) stands by dumbfounded, watching Gia's self-absorbed yet fascinating self-destruction.

Now, had Gia picked up a bass and started writing songs, she would have left a back catalogue that would inspire rock and roll girls everywhere. Instead, she is virtually forgotten by an industry that still finds heroin chic cheeky and still sucks the life's blood from wide-eyed heartland girls who are caught up in the glitter. Be pissed . . . be very pissed. And watch it with a teenage girl who thinks she wants to try the runway life.

World-Class Wrecks

Your "look" is not spring. Your "look" is more like nuclear fucking winter.

★ an agent to supermodel *Gia*

■ ***Red Dust*** *(1932)*

Stars: Jean Harlow, Clark Gable, Mary Astor, Gene Raymond
Director: Victor Fleming
Writer: John Lee Mahin, from the play by Wilson Collison

An Indochine tropical forest, a huge barrel full of rainwater (perfect for an afternoon bath), and Clark Gable in a pith helmet, short sleeves, and a layer of manly perspiration—hey, what more does a gal need for a rollicking good time? Working girl—and we mean that in the euphemistic sense—Jean Harlow is quite available for freebies with her favorite rubber plantation overseer (after all, a fellow who can demonstrate the properties of latex is always a safe bet for a worry-free tête-à-tête). Unfortunately, in blows some society dame (Astor) having a full-fledged marital crisis. All right, a malaria-stricken Gene Raymond can't compete with the lusty Gable and the thrill of an illicit affair, but why can't that finger-waved brunette travel a little farther downstream and leave this fine specimen of manhood where he belongs—with Vantine, a platinum blonde with a heart of gold? Well, she'll simply have to be resourceful, won't she? And there is that pistol on the dressing table . . .

> ⚠ Warning Label: *Skip the remake,* Mogambo. *As if Ava Gardner could live up to Jean Harlow's rain barrel skinny dip. Better ignore the cartoony minor characters—you can just guess how they depicted the Asian natives back in 1932.*

■ ***Jezebel*** *(1938)*
Stars: Bette Davis, Henry Fonda
Director: William Wyler
Writers: Robert Buckner, Abem Finkel, John Huston, and Cements Ripley, based on the play by Owen Davis

Oh, what a burden it is to be a vivacious deb with a flair for provocative couture in the antebellum South! The high-spirited Miss Julie (Davis) finds that a fashion faux pas threatens to destroy her relationship, her social standing, and her entire future. Hey, if Scarlett O'Hara got away with showing her bosom before twelve o'clock in that green-flowered afternoon dress she wore to the Twelve Oaks barbecue, why is everyone so uptight about a gal wearing red to an evening affair? We say let Henry Fonda seethe, indulge in a shopping spree and a good cry, then start scoping for the local Rhett, but our gal Bette is determined to make amends for her Jezebel-like ways.

■ ***She Done Him Wrong*** *(1933)*
Stars: Mae West, Cary Grant, Owen Moore, Gilbert Rowland
Director: Lowell Sherman
Writers: Harvey Thew, John Bright, and Mae West, based on the play Diamond Lil *by Mae West*

The skeleton of a plot here isn't the point—suffice it to say Mae West is a bad girl with a heart of gold (and an arm and neck full of diamonds) who just wants to belt out classic honky-tonk ballads in a Bowery saloon, but she finds herself mixed up in murder, the white slave trade, and an undercover FBI investigation. All of which are really quite distracting but provide key setups for Mae West's snappy comebacks, eyeball rolling, and vampish delivery of double entendres. She suggestively encourages several men to "come up sometime and see me," the most engaging of whom is an extremely young Cary Grant, and she eventually nails him—mm, mm.

Unacquainted with the concept of low maintenance, West shows up in scene after scene with her dangerous curves encased in skintight dresses with swooshy little trains, silk flower and feather accents, outrageously oversize hats, silly little parasols, and rhinestones everywhere, proving that the waif look ain't got nothin' on a full-figured gal with an attitude.

> ⚠ Warning Label: *Poor Louise Beavers is wasted in a role as a maid whose raison d'être is to fuss over her mistress's pretty thangs. Sho' nuff annoying, but that's 1933 for you.*

World-Class Wrecks

BARFLY GAL: ***You know, ever since I sang that song it's been haunting me.***

PIANO PLAYER: ***It should haunt you. You murdered it.***

★ from *She Done Him Wrong*

▪ ***Wings of the Dove*** *(1997)*
Stars: Helena Bonham Carter, Linus Roache, Alison Elliott
Director: Iain Softley
Writers: Hossein Amini and Iain Softley, based on the novel by Henry James

Really, it's just a matter of practicality, that's all. Two-birds-with-one-stone kind of thing: See to it that her best friend (Alison Elliott as Milly) experiences the heights of ecstasy and sensual experience before she departs from this world, and see to it that her own impoverished fiancé (Linus Roache as Merton) makes a tidy little fortune so that he can marry. Okay, so there are a few complications, like the fact that Milly isn't content with moonlit gondola rides in Venice or daring climbs up church scaffolding to reach breathtaking views of that ancient city. The girl wants to get laid. By Merton.

Now, Kate (Helena Bonham Carter) is quite secure in her lover's affections—after all, he's one of those socialist journalists who rages at the plight of the working class, which is always a clear-cut indication that he's incapable of betrayal. . . .

Uh huh.

Anyway, she cooks up a plan for Merton to seduce Milly and secure the situation with the will before the girl drops dead. Then Merton and she will marry and live off Milly's fortune, which, after all, she won't be needing anyway once she's in a coffin at the bottom of the canals. But, of course, the best-laid plans can go awry. Still, it's hard to scold a bad girl who is as fiercely determined as Kate, even if she is a cold-blooded mercenary.

The Handy Hunk Chart Key

Hunk Ratings:

All-American Boy 🏈

Steamy Latin Lover (mask)

BE = *Bedroom Eyes* **BND** = *Boy Next Door* **DMCA** = *Devil-May-Care Attitude* **FSG** = *Feckless Schoolboy Grin* **PBE** = *Piercing Blue Eyes* **RGH** = *Really Good Hair* **RUM** = *Raw Unpredictable Masculinity* **SIN** = *Smoldering, Inscrutable, and Noble*

The Handy Hunk Chart

Antonio Banderas — BE, RGH, RUM, SIN

Top Drool Pics: *Desperado, House of the Spirits, Mambo Kings, The Mask of Zorro, Never Talk to Strangers, Outrage* (check the bath scene!), *Women on the Verge of a Nervous Breakdown*

They say he's only five feet four, but that's only on one plane of reality. In the dimension where sexual fantasies take place he is, of course, a towering presence. Blessed with rich black hair—boyish in the Almodóvar years, wild and lion-like in the American thriller years—and eyes dark enough to dive into, Antonio embodies the fiery passion of the Latin lover. While he may be a bit weak in the chin, such a little flaw in a magnificent sculpture of a man serves only to make him all the more desirable. And as he flares his nostrils, tosses his ebony mane, and paws the ground, one can't help but think of racing across the desert whilst perched upon him.

Tom Cruise — BND, DMCA, FSG, PBE

Top Drool Pics: *All the Right Moves, Cocktail, The Color of Money, Endless Love, A Few Good Men, Interview With the Vampire, Rain Man, Risky Business, Taps, Top Gun*

As with his female counterpart Julia Roberts, Tom Cruise has an Ultra Brite smile and knows how to use it. Because baby, he's workin' it. Just as Brad Pitt movies are about his hair, and Julia Roberts movies are about her giggle, Tom Cruise movies are about that world-class grin. In *Rain Man*

. . . continued

he smiles sardonically in sunglasses. In *Risky Business* he smiles winningly in underwear. In *Born on the Fourth of July* he smiles wryly in a wheelchair. We don't know what he did in *Far and Away* because nobody saw it, but we imagine his Irish eyes were smiling, and in *The Firm* he smiled knowingly in a suit and proved that even a spineless yuppie husband who can be seduced by the first bikini'd babe to cross his path will be forgiven if he just turns on that toothy beacon. ■

Chapter 15

My Heart Belongs to Daddy: Father-Issue Movies

When is the last time somebody called you princess and meant it as a compliment? There's nobody quite like Dad, is there? Nobody like him in the world. And we're all, on some level, looking for a guy just like the guy who married dear old Mom, aren't we? Some call this sentimental, others call it a repetition compulsion, but whatever your intergenerational issues, if you're in need of a father's love, try out one of our Father-Issue movies, and remember when . . .

- ***Father of the Bride*** *(1950)*
  Stars: Spencer Tracy, Elizabeth Taylor, Joan Bennett, Don Taylor
  Director: Vincente Minnelli
  Writers: Frances Goodrich and Albert Hackett, based on the novel by Edward Streeter

First of all, forget the Steven Martin version and go straight for the original, which is pure gold. Spencer Tracy is absolutely adorable as Stanley Banks, the sober judge who turns into a lump of jelly when his daughter Kay (Elizabeth Taylor) announces her intention to marry Buckley Dunstan (Don Taylor.) Although Stanley's wife, Ellie (Joan Bennett), is constantly by his side, trying to soothe his ruffled poppa bird feathers, he nevertheless bumbles and bulldozes his way through this delicate rite of passage. He even fails as a bartender at the engagement party, which, by the way, is a classic moment of physical comedy. Despite being emotionally all thumbs, Stanley gets full marks for courage in the line of duty. He pays for the wedding, only gets ugly occasionally, and keeps the martinis flowing. What a dad!

▪ ***On Golden Pond*** *(1981)*
Stars: Henry Fonda, Katharine Hepburn, Jane Fonda
Director: Mark Rydell
Writer: Ernest Thompson

One of America's favorite father figures, Henry Fonda (who must have been a slightly more complex patriarch in real life, given Jane's romantic attachment style) plays aging patriarch Norman Thayer, a retired professor who has been giving his daughter a hard time since forever. You know the deal, aging disciplinarian, never been satisfied, suddenly starts losing his marbles and then you have to deal with actually starting to feel love for the guy when you would have just preferred to go on resenting him for the rest of his life? And to make matters worse, Chelsea (Jane Fonda) has an enabling mom, Ethel (Katharine Hepburn), a complex second marriage, and a stepson to deal with all at the same time. Talk about the whole ball of wax! Nevertheless, in this father–daughter fairy tale, love, like the loon, returns to Golden Pond and finds a peaceful place to nest.

▪ ***Nell*** *(1994)*
Stars: Liam Neeson, Jodie Foster, Natasha Richardson
Director: Michael Apted
Writers: William Nicholson and Mark Handley, based on the play Idioglossia *by Mark Handley*

Jodie Foster stars as Nell, a sauvage naif from the remote backwoods of South Carolina, never having met anyone except her mother, and as a consequence of being raised with absolutely no male influence, has grown up without the powers of speech or rational thinking. Fortunately for Nell, kindly country doctor Jerome Lovell arrives on the scene to provide her with the male role model she needs to set her free from her interior prison, and teach her proper sentence structure. Of course, he also exposes her to a world that can never have a true place for her, and subjects her to the scrutiny of countless scientists who treat her like a specimen, but that's a small price to pay for a father's love, isn't it?

■ ***A Tree Grows in Brooklyn*** *(1945)*
Stars: Dorothy McGuire, James Dunn, Peggy Ann Garner
Director: Elia Kazan
Writers: Frank Davis and Tess Slesinger, based on the novel by Betty Smith

Ironing Papa's shirts while he dreams aloud about better days and the pretty presents he'll buy his little prima donna will make a girl feel like she's the only one for Daddy—especially if her stoic mother (McGuire) is off scrubbing floors somewhere. Who needs a realist for a parent when you've got twinkly eyed Johnny Nolan (Dunn) for a papa, a man who is willing to do just about anything to make his little girl's cup runneth over? Apparently Francie Nolan (Garner) does, since pre–WW I Brooklyn offered no government-sponsored social programs or church basement AA meetings, both of which might've gone a long way toward making up for the shortcomings of a happy-go-lucky singing Irish waiter who's better at dreaming than providing for his wife and kids.

Bittersweet, and sure to inspire a special memory of your own of being Daddy's little princess.

■ ***Educating Rita*** *(1983)*
Stars: Michael Caine, Julie Walters
Director: Lewis Gilbert
Writer: Willy Russell

By his own admission, he's always four parts pissed (the British "pissed," that is), and his favorite possession is a bottle of whiskey hidden in his office behind a copy of *The Lost Weekend.* Yes, he's just your lovable drunken professor type, full of acerbic observations on the utter futility of all human endeavor—which is easy for him to say, since he's got tenure and only has to give a reasonable impression of sobriety for one graduate seminar and 120 minutes of office hours once a week. And then she walks in, a twenty-six-year-old hairdresser who wants to reinvent herself with a new, glamorous name and a liberal arts education, starting with having him tutor her. But why me? he asks. "Because you're a crazy mad piss artist who wants to throw his students through the window . . . I *like* you."

Touched by her acceptance and enthusiasm, and recognizing her genius for getting to the heart of the matter (a skill no doubt acquired through her careful analysis of Harold Robbins novels), Frank (Michael Caine) agrees. As Rita (Julie Walters) blossoms intellectually Frank begins to fall for her, but while she knows he's raised her out of a life of working-class drudgery and expanded her mind, she also realizes that unless he can put his cynicism aside he will just continue to grow mental mold—and we all know a mildewed prof is no erotic turn-on. So, much as Rita cares for Frank, she will have to grow beyond him and her own sophomoric thinking and graduate to being able to tell the difference between inspired and derivative.

A great reminder that it's best to sublimate a crush on a mentor into writing a smashing A+ blue book essay that will please Daddy rather than indulge in an affair with someone who can't forget his own superiority and will always treat you like a child in need of a Mike Bradyesque lecture.

■ ***Rebecca*** *(1940)*
Stars: Laurence Olivier, Joan Fontaine
Director: Alfred Hitchcock
Writers: Joan Harrison, Michael Hogan, Philip MacDonald, and Robert E. Sherwood, based on the novel by Daphne du Maurier

A young girl with self-esteem so low that she doesn't even reveal her name in 132 minutes onscreen marries Maxim de Winter, an older man, in a whirlwind romance, thereby rescuing herself from enslavement as a paid companion to a wretched old woman who smashes out cigarettes in jars of cold cream. The girl is relieved to be free but misinterprets Maxim's elusive, wintery demeanor at every turn and obsesses about Rebecca, his seemingly perfect dead wife. While, of course, she can't live up to her mental image of the sophisticated Rebecca, her marriage is doomed if she won't break her promise to paternalistic

Maxim to "never be thirty years old and wear pearls." Assisting her in her relentless self-flagellation and paranoia is the spooky, unblinking housekeeper (Dame Judith Anderson), who floats like a black harpy down the halls and fetishizes her ex-boss's lingerie. Hitchcock uses shadows, murder, Freudian psychology, and phallic flames to illustrate the fruitlessness of trying to be Daddy's good little girl when you're supposed to be knocking boots with Olivier in his sensual prime.

■ ***Eat Drink Man Woman*** *(1994)*
Stars: Sihung Lung, Chien-Lien Wu, Kuei-Mei Yang, Yu-Wen Wang
Director: Ang Lee
Writer: Ang Lee, James Schamus, and Hui-Ling Wang

Dad's a gourmet cook in Taiwan, whose wildly elaborate dishes involve stuffing frogs and slamming chopsticks down the throat of a sturgeon (well, at least the stir-fry looks tasty). His culinary skills go unappreciated, however, because his three daughters are too busy trying to cook up some romance in their own lives to appreciate sixteen-course dinners every Sunday. Dad seems destined for a lonely old age, appreciated only by the lucky little girl next door, whose lunchpail he packs with fare worthy of the emperor (and you thought Twinkies could buy friends amongst the kindergarten set). Which unlucky daughter will get stuck taking care of aging Papa, who is a lovable curmudgeon but is, unfortunately, beginning to oversalt? Pray that Dad has a secret boiling on some back burner that will free up his daughters to live their own lives and make their own damned bean curd pancakes.

Viewer's Note: Check out director Ang Lee's other squabbling sisters flick: *Sense and Sensibility*.

■ ***To Sir, With Love*** *(1967)*
Stars: Sidney Poitier, Judy Geeson, Lulu
Director: James Clavell
Writers: E. R. Braithwaite and James Clavell, based on the novel by E. R. Braithwaite

Yes, he was a special teacher, wasn't he? Tall, dark, handsome, hand-carved with dignity and grace, who changed before your very eyes from giggle-inspiring anomaly to father figure. Oh, how you sought to elicit that slow and easy smile, and melted with pleasure

Prepubescent Power Pics: Getting in Touch with Your Inner Grrrrl

You don't have to be a kid to enjoy these movies featuring powerful, confident, and self-determined heroines. In fact, some of them are best appreciated from an adult perspective. So borrow a ten-year-old or revert to the preteen within, and remember what life was like before "self-doubt" was in your vocabulary.

FairyTale: A True Story *(1997)*
Stars: Florence Hoath, Elizabeth Earl, Peter O'Toole, Harvey Keitel
Director: Charles Sturridge
Writer: Ernie Contreras, based on a story by Ernie Contreras, Tom McLoughlin, and Albert Ash

In this empowering, aesthetically beautiful film, two Victorian-era little girls photograph fairies and refuse to divulge the secrets of their art despite intense pressure from a bevy of journalists led by Sir Arthur Conan Doyle. A girl's got to have some secrets after all, even if she is only seven years old. ■

Now and Then *(1995)*
Stars: Christina Ricci, Thora Birch, Gaby Hoffman, Ashleigh Aston Moore, Demi Moore, Melanie Griffith, Rosie O'Donnell, Rita Wilson
Director: Lesli Linka Glatter
Writer: I. Marlene King

Lucky for us, most of this movie is in flashback, since the adult versions of the four friends are a study in weak acting (Demi Moore as a neurotic New York writer is especially painful to watch—Jennifer Jason Leigh she

. . . continued

ain't). The plot isn't much to speak of—summertime shenanigans about sums it up— but the emotions of girlhood friendship and longings ring true, and if you're hovering around age thirty-five, the authentic period detail will have you hounding flea markets to get back your groovy shawl, banana bike, and J5 records. ■

National Velvet *(1944)*
Stars: Elizabeth Taylor, Mickey Rooney, Donald Crisp, Anne Revere, Angela Lansbury
Director: Clarence Brown
Writers: Helen Deutsch and Theodore Reeves, based on the novel by Enid Bagnold

You could adjust your TV set to the violet eyes of teenage Liz Taylor in this movie, which are wide with excitement in just about every scene, that is, every time she sees, thinks of, dreams about, or rides a horse. Even if you aren't horsey, her passion and her unflagging determination—to win that unruly gelding, to ride him, and to have him win England's Grand National—will bring you back to the days when you were too young to believe that some things are just impossible. ■

Paper Moon *(1973)*
Stars: Ryan O'Neal, Tatum O'Neal, Madeline Kahn
Director: Peter Bogdanovich
Writer: Alvin Sargent, based on the novel by Joe David Brown

Normally, we detest nepotism, but it sure works here. Tatum O'Neal was never more authentic than when she portrayed Addie Pray, an orphan taken underwing by a con man (Ryan O'Neal) in the Depression. Addie is preternaturally ethical, mature, and street smart, smoking cigarettes and hiding bootlegging profits from the coppers. Too bad O'Neal peaked with

. . . *continued*

this performance—Tatum and Ryan, that is. (P.S. If you blinked, you might have missed Jodie Foster cast as Addie in the short-lived TV series back in the 1970s.) ■

A Little Princess *(1995)*
Stars: Liesel Matthews, Eleanor Bron, Liam Cunningham, Vanessa Lee Chester, Rusty Schwimmer
Director: Alfonso Cuarón
Writers: Richard LaGravenese and Elizabeth Chandler, based on the novel by Frances Hodgson Burnett

An orphaned little girl discovers that a powerful sense of self carries her through her darkest hour in this adaptation of Frances Hodgson Burnett's novel.

Shirley Temple first brought Sarah Crewe to life onscreen and did a fine job with it, but the new version is much better not only because of its visually stunning production, but also because this Sarah's written to be far more obstinate and creative—a forthright feminist blessed with a supremely functional father–daughter relationship that is certain to lead her to a fulfilling and successful career in the Victorian equivalent of the Fortune 500. With unshakable confidence in her princesshood and her internal goodness (mark of a true royal), Sarah will inspire women of all ages to demand their due as True Princesses. ■

The Secret Garden *(1993)*
Stars: Kate Maberly, Heydon Prowse, Andrew Knott, Maggie Smith
Director: Agnieszka Holland
Writer: Caroline Thompson, based on the novel by Frances Hodgson Burnett

During the Victorian era, an orphaned little girl is shipped off to her uncle's place in England, where, with a scowl on her face, she demands to be

. . . continued

waited on hand and foot. Left with plenty of unstructured time and little supervision, little Mary Lennox wanders about and discovers the secrets of the house. In the end she brings the house, its secret garden, her uncle, and herself, back to life, healing the wounds of their traumatic pasts. Talk about girl power!

Skip the 1983 BBC version—the kid who plays Mary whines all her lines until you're ready to bury her in that damn garden. ■

The Wizard of Oz *(1939)*
Stars: Judy Garland, Ray Bolger, Bert Lahr, Jack Haley, Margaret Hamilton, Frank Morgan, Billie Burke
Director: Victor Fleming
Writers: Noel Langley, Florence Ryerson, and Edgar Allan Woolf, based on the novel by L. Frank Baum

It's not that she was dying to go back to sepia-toned Kansas—you know, to her mundane life on a farm in the middle of nowhere, doomed to be forever donning pinafores and counting chicks. As Glinda the Good (Burke) knew, Dorothy's (Garland's) true heart's desire was to make peace with her authentic inner self, to achieve an inner grace that is crucial for a girl seeking to break out of the confines of her limited existence, a grounding that will allow her to explore worlds beyond the rainbow. Whatever, dude. It's a really cool flick, especially if you see it a million times and can sing along with all the trippy lyrics.

Anne of Green Gables *(1985)*
Stars: Megan Follows, Colleen Dewhurst, Richard Farnsworth
Director: Kevin Sullivan
Writers: Kevin Sullivan and Joe Wiesenfeld, based on the novel by Lucy Maud Montgomery

. . . continued

An orphaned girl—hey, wait a minute. What's with all this orphan stuff? Can't a prepubescent self-actualize without having one or both of her parental figures killed off? Apparently not.

Anyway, Anne (Megan Followes), an orphaned girl, is taken in by Marilla Cuthbert (Dewhurst) and her husband (Richard Farnsworth), and despite the drop-jawed reactions of the less spirited people around her, maintains her powerful sense of self, her rich imagination, her poetic sensibility. She goes on to win over everyone on Prince Edward Island without having to compromise her strong personality or become one of those cloyingly cute children's heroines that cause diabetes in anyone over the age of eight. (The sequel, *Anne of Avonlea,* in which Anne becomes a schoolteacher, actually manages to be as entertaining as the original.) ▪

Manny & Lo *(1996)*
Stars: Scarlett Johansson, Aleksa Palladino, Mary Kay Place
Director and Writer: Lisa Krueger

Eleven-year-old Manny (Scarlett Johansson) is an engaging kind of kid, but her teenage sister Lo (Aleksa Palladino) is a talk show producer's dream: sullen, pregnant, drinkin' and smokin', shoplifting, and kidnapping store clerks at gunpoint. Okay, she's not exactly a role model for impressionable preteens, but this story of two lost-in-the-cracks-of-social-services girls desperately seeking a stable mother figure (Mary Kay Place, who else?) has a warm message about family underneath all that black humor. And the sight of Mary Kay Place trying to look dignified as she shuffles along, a bicycle chain around her ankles, is priceless. Definitely not for the kiddies, though—you'll spend the whole night trying to explain the R-rated themes. ▪

. . . continued

Ever After *(1998)*
Stars: Drew Barrymore, Anjelica Huston, Dougray Scott
Director: Andy Tennant
Writers: Susannah Grant, Andy Tennant, and Rick Parks

In this feminist revision of the Cinderella story, Cinderella (Drew Barrymore) is a plucky girl who not only fights for the rights of the downtrodden and protects her extended family from external threats but is bookish as well (a rare combination in the stereotypical world of girl heroines). Her evil stepmother (Huston) is a pitiable victim of sexist conditioning and limited roles for women, and the Prince (Scott) learns to give up his elitist notions in order to be worthy of a poor servant with a noble heart. Though we usually hate late-twentieth-century morality imposed upon the classics, this one really is an improvement on the original. ■

when he addressed you as Miss! Only for him would you leave behind your girlish ways of telling tales and biting nails. No more "sluttish behavior unbecoming of young ladies" for you! And now, as you prepare to test your still moist, fragile wings and flutter forth into the world, you must say goodbye to your best friend. Indeed, how *do* you thank someone who has taken you from crayons to perfume? Alas, there is left for you only a spin in the high school gym and then it must be farewell, forever, as he walks off into the sunset of a position somewhere across the ocean, never again to be seen but always held in your heart. And in your secret dreams, late at night under the pink canopy of your bed, he holds you in his arms and you fall into a kiss.

Be sure to stock up on soda pop and Luvs Baby Soft before indulging in this pre-orgasmic, Electra-complex-inspired euphoria.

■ ***Music Box*** *(1989)*
Stars: Jessica Lange, Armin Mueller-Stahl, Frederic Forrest, Donald Moffat, Lukas Haas
Director: Costa-Gavras
Writer: Joe Eszterhas

How much do you really know about Dad anyway? If, say, the FBI were to investigate his past and spy on his everyday activities, would they find out things you don't know? And if they did, would you really want to know about them? Like who he's having sex with? Definitely one for the "no" column. That he lied on his immigration application? Ahh, there's a plausible explanation. Gotta be. That he was a Nazi war criminal? Yup, definitely something a gal doesn't want to know about dear old Dad. Unless, of course, it's true. Which it can't be. Or so believes Annie Talbot (Jessica Lange), daughter of Hungarian immigrant Michael J. Lazslo (Armin Mueller-Stahl). After all, she knows her gentle old papa, and the man she knows can't possibly be "the Beast." So lawyer Annie takes on the task of defending her father against those who insist he's a war criminal, convinced the Communists in Hungary have cooked up the evidence, and it's a damn plausible explanation. But as events unfold and secrets surface, Annie has to deal with her doubts about the man behind the face he's presented to her all these years, because unless she believes him implicitly, how can she possibly defend him against others? And is it possible that he's a monster hiding behind her faith in him?

Talk about dealing with loyalty issues. This dad and daughter combo will make your own paternal conflicts pale by comparison.

■ ***The Bodyguard*** *(1992)*
Stars: Whitney Houston, Kevin Costner, Gary Kemp
Director: Mick Jackson
Writer: Lawrence Kasden

Rachel Marron (Whitney Houston) is a top singing star whose signature power ballads thrill audiences while only skimming the surface of emotion, thereby belying her gospel roots (okay, the screenwriter chose to leave out that particular observation, but Whitney Houston manages to play to type here anyway). Rachel is blissfully unconcerned that her guard dog naps on the job and the security man is lax about passwords and blind spots, but that's because her overprotective manager is hiding the truth from her—that she's being stalked. The only man who can truly look out for Rachel is Frank Farmer (Kevin Costner), former bodyguard to President Reagan, who unfortunately took an extremely ill-timed personal day and is suffering a massive guilt complex, resulting in a woefully underdeveloped sense of humor and a frighteningly severe hairstyle.

Shirley Temple, The Little Girl Who Could

No, she was not just a rag-curled moppet with a dimple, a sweet little voice, a penchant for tap dancing, and an excessively cute demeanor. When it came to Hollywood, little Shirley kicked some serious butt. She was, for some years, the highest-paid actress in Hollywood. She single-handledly saved the Fox studio from bankruptcy during the Depression, keeping thousands employed, even though she was so young that she had to sign her first contracts with an X because she hadn't learned how to write yet. She broke the color barrier as the first white woman to touch a black man onscreen, tapping away as she held the hand of Bill "Bojangles" Robinson. And she went on to be a UN ambassador when she grew up.

All that's important to keep in mind during the most maudlin and overly precious moments in her films. She couldn't help those overly coy scripts or heavyhanded direction. Focus on the inner Shirley. Watch her handle those lines like a pro, even when she couldn't read 'em yet. Watch her dominate those scenes, drawing the focus away from seasoned actors, shamelessly stealing the limelight. Watch her give her all in the crying scenes, giggle wildly as she lets loose her mischievous self, tap-dance her little heart out, and pout indignantly at the injustices inflicted upon her pint-sized self. And remember, just because someone's got a headful of blond curls and dimpled chubby cheeks doesn't mean she isn't a force to be reckoned with. ▪

Frank is grimly determined to shield Rachel from every conceivable danger and few inconceivable ones as well. But despite her protestations about needing space and independence, she doesn't fight him when he tucks her into those white cotton sheets, surrounds her with dollies, and gazes out stoically at the raging thunderstorm. Frank is so dedicated to Rachel's needs that he doesn't even allow himself the comfort of a furnished apartment, just a few planks and a phallic sword, which leads to some interesting foreplay before he insists on backing off to keep things professional—for her sake, of course. Dedicated Frank will not let his feelings for her interfere with his deep-rooted need to protect her, and no matter how much Rachel fights him, lies to him, or tries to run away, he will be there to take a bullet for her if necessary.

Yes, she pays him well.

If you've got a Costner fixation, you'll especially adore him in this daddy-figure role. Snuggle up and pretend you can afford his fee.

▪ ***Contact*** *(1997)*
Stars: Jodie Foster, Matthew McConaughey
Director: Robert Zemeckis
Writers: James V. Hart and Michael Goldenberg, based on the book by Carl Sagan and the story by Carl Sagan and Ann Druyen

With her beloved daddy gone and the government funding yanked out from under her, Dr. Eleanor Arroway (Jodie Foster) is nevertheless fiercely determined to make her dream come true. She *will* reach beyond the stars! This is her destiny, damn it—to communicate with sentient beings from other galaxies, to seek out new life and new civilizations, to boldly go where no woman has gone before. . . . Lucky for her, the space program today doesn't relegate women to micro-miniskirted uniforms and auxiliary positions on the bridge, although naturally it still takes a woman to figure out what the heck those aliens are trying to say.

When Ellie deciphers aliens' audio signals and hieroglyphics that come to her on a giant radio, she's a sure bet for a position on the spaceship bound for their world—that is, if she can convince ethicist and ex-priest Palmer Joss (McConaughey), who not coincidentally used to be called "Father," that she deserves it. After a saboteur, who embraces a fear-based patriarchal dogma (one that can only result in isolationism and disconnection from the great unconscious stream of the universe) indulges in a violent act that shatters the dreams of a world united in this pacifistic mission to connect, Ellie gets her big chance. Oh, she won't be kicking alien butt—that's Will Smith's gig. No, she drops egglike from the fallopian tube of the alien-designed structure, and thus engendered by a masculine force, she is able to give birth to herself and reconnect with the father she lost.

Look, it's conceptual, okay? Try to keep that in mind when you start nodding off during the lagging plot.

■ ***Table for Five*** *(1983)*
Stars: Jon Voight, Richard Crenna, Marie Christine Barrault, Millie Perkins, Roxana Zal, Robby Kiger, Son Hoang Bui
Director: Robert Lieberman
Writer: David Seltzer

An errant father (Jon Voight) positively beams at the prospect of righting all his wrongs in one grandiose gesture, having put himself in hock to take his three kids (Kiger, Zal, and Bui) on an ocean cruise to Egypt and Greece. His long-suffering ex-wife, Kathleen (Millie Perkins), would just as soon he'd take them to Six Flags, and frankly, the kids would probably prefer it, too, but that's just not his style. So Kathleen and her current husband, the ever reliable Mitchell (Richard Crenna), cross their fingers as Jim (Voight) embarks on the ship of fools, where he ditches the kids so he can flirt with a babe (Barrault) in too tight pants (the kind that give you yeast infections, his too worldly daughter notes) and decides he can fix his son's debilitating learning disability in a few weeks. Of course, it's only a matter of days before he realizes that daddyhood isn't all fun and games, and just when he comes to realize he's better at playing visiting uncle than responsible parent, he faces the prospect of having to be the grown-up whether he likes it or not.

Seltzer's script captures all the complex emotions of kids who've had to deal with an absentee father, and Roxana Zal does an amazing job of portraying a prematurely mature little girl who has yet to learn to trust Dad to play parent. This one'll kick you in the gut with its surprise plot twist and searingly accurate portrayal of filial acceptance—make sure you've got a big box of tissues handy.

Chapter 16

The Girl Can't Help It: Cult Films Ya Gotta Love

Why is it every time someone says "cult film" everyone thinks of martial arts movies, or badly dubbed Japanese monster flicks, or those budget fifties sci-fi things with screaming blondes, or bullet-breasted women from other planets enslaving men for their own sexual purposes? This stuff made us yawn when we were twelve and baby-sitting on a Saturday night. Why should we pay $3.50 to rent it now?

That doesn't mean there aren't cult films that a gal can't love—and watch again and again and again. It's just that unlike most "cult" films, our cult films have a deep message under that bizarre plotline. They deal with real emotional issues (albeit in a surreal or camp sort of way). They inspire us, they move us, they shake us to the very core of our identity and help us to explore our subconscious drives even as we consciously work toward categorizing our everyday experience and infusing it with meaning.

All right, maybe they're just the product of a weird acquired taste, but you gotta admit—that kick boxing crap the would-be Tarantinos go for ain't got nothin' on these.

■ ***Heathers*** *(1989)*

Stars: Winona Ryder, Christian Slater, Shannen Doherty, Lisanne Falk, Kim Walker
Director: Michael Lehmann
Writer: Daniel Waters

It's true. Life is hard. But high school is harder. You remember, don't you? Let your mind's eye wander to the Max Factor face of your bygone Marcia, or Buffy, or Heather. Visualize your personal mega-bitch. She was blond, wasn't she? Of course she was. With flashing violet eyes, and maybe even a pair of dimples shaped like crescent moons just above the upcurls of her cherry-red mouth. And that scarlet ribbon, which struggled to harness her cascading rivulets of liquid golden curls. And when she was good, she was so very, very good, but when she was bad, Heather could have evoked homicidal fantasies in a Franciscan friar at Eastertime.

Live out your fantasies watching this semi-surreal psychological thriller/coming-of-age film, about the revenge of the plain Jane (Winona Ryder) visited upon the heads of two Heathers (Shannen Doherty, Lisanne Falk). The dialogue is sparkling, and the angst is razor sharp. And that moment when Heather drinks the bowl cleaner and pitches headlong through a glass table clutching her delicate white-as-Carrara marble throat? The sublimity of deliverance and the restoration of divine right reason will be visited upon you, fellow Heather-haters! We guarantee it.

Oh, but just one thing, don't you think it's time that Christian Slater started paying Jack Nicholson for the use of that roguish Panhandle twang and deadpan delivery? Christian is cute and alternative-looking and all, but close your eyes and you'll swear you're watching *Carnal Knowledge.*

■ ***Welcome to the Dollhouse*** *(1996)*

Stars: Heather Matarazzo, Brendan Sexton, Jr., Daria Kalinina, Matthew Faber, Eric Mabius
Director and Writer: Todd Solondz

Let's face it, shall we? Let's finally come clean. We were all geeks. Just like poor Dawn a.k.a. "Wienerdog" Wiener (Heather Matarazzo) in this quirky coming-of-age cult movie.

We all wore bad fads, stretch fabrics that did not suit our budding figures, and those Woolworth's ponytail holders with the brightly colored plastic balls on either end. We all endured the ridicule of our peers and the inaccessibility of our elders. And we all fell in love with some alternative idiot, whose largely hormonally driven declaration of masculinity seemed like the courage of conviction. And none of us noticed that he couldn't even carry a tune.

The fashion statements alone in this movie will bring you to your knees, making you worship the kind forces of nature that have brought you past that excruciating period they call puberty and murmur a prayer of thanksgiving for having arrived in the promised land of postadolescence. Here, you don't have to wear a belly blouse or a pair of stretch pants unless you really, really want to, and you can make your own decisions about how you express your identity . . . or can you?

Watch this one and celebrate the nerd within. She's still there, you know. And she always will be. So give her her moment in the sun.

World-Class Wrecks

Searching for a boy in high school is like searching for meaning in a Pauly Shore movie.

★ Alicia Silverstone as Cher in *Clueless*

Look, it's been swell, but the swelling's gone down.

★ Lori Petty as Tank Girl in *Tank Girl*

▪ ***The Brady Bunch Movie*** *(1995)*

Stars: Shelley Long, Gary Cole, Michael McKean, Henriette Mantel, Christine Taylor, Jennifer Elise Cox

Director: Betty Thomas

Writers: Laurice Elehwany, Rick Copp, and Bonnie and Terry Turner, based on the TV show created by Sherwood Schwartz

All right, it may be a seventies thing, but we swear there's a universality to Jan Brady's struggle for a voice amidst the noise of a precocious little lisping sister in pigtails, a perfect cheerleader of an older sis, and three brothers who are constantly causing a hoopla what with composing rock songs about little ponies running or with tossing a football around with Joe Namath out on the AstroTurf in the backyard. Yes, festering underneath that facade of a perfectly harmonious, perfectly symmetrical blended family was the sore of a dream deferred—a dream of a day in the sun, a dream in which Jan was the star of the show instead of just the neurotic middle child.

Brady fanatics will catch plenty of in-jokes and cameos, but even the uninitiated can appreciate Jan's archetypal struggle to be free from the restraints of familial expectations, free to soar on her banana bike past faceless suburban California ranch houses, and outward toward a horizon of hope that someday she too will be recognized as something more than just another seventies fashion victim.

> ⚠ Warning Label: *Ignore the ignoramuses who said the sequel was better than this one. True Bradyphiles know that while the Bradys may have been wide-eyed and goopy, they weren't morons like those pod people in* A Very Brady Sequel. *We know that's hard to believe given their appalling taste in fashions, hairdos, and home furnishings, but that's how we call it.*

■ ***Buffy the Vampire Slayer*** *(1992)*
Stars: Kristy Swanson, Donald Sutherland, Paul Reubens, Rutger Hauer
Director: Fran Rubel Kuzui
Writer: Joss Whedon

Buffy (Kristy Swanson) is this, like, really blond, really well-toned cheerleader who can also do many many backflips in a row from a standing position. One day, mid-backflip, she is visited by some guy in a hat and cape (Donald Sutherland), who tells her that she is actually the chosen one, the vampire slayer, who has lived through many lives that bear one common thread: she snuffs Nosferatus. So Buffy goes through a Rockyesque training period, sharpens up her stake, and goes in search of life's meaning through the metaphor of her persona as the vampire slayer. And, of course, as a reward for her selfless mission to uphold the principles of democracy and proper dietary pursuits, she not only wins the admiration of her peers and reclaims her ancient power, but she gets Pike (Luke Perry) to boot! Now if that's not an argument for going head to head with the forces of the night, and discharging your karmic debts, we don't know what is.

Words to Live By

Look, if you want to torture me, spank me, lick me, do it. But if this poetry shit continues just shoot me now please.

★ Lori Petty as Tank Girl in *Tank Girl*

▪ ***Carrie*** *(1976)*

Stars: Sissy Spacek, Piper Laurie, Amy Irving, William Katt, John Travolta, Betty Buckley

Director: Brian De Palma

Writer: Lawrence D. Cohen, based on the novel by Stephen King

Everyone thinks of this as *the* classic Stephen King horror film, but we say it's the definitive menstruation movie, a cinematic metaphor for the incendiary capacity of a woman's sexuality. Carrie White (Sissy Spacek), a shy, underdeveloped, friendless young girl who has been kept in the closet of her mother's (Piper Laurie) psychosis since birth, gets her period in class one day. Amused by her horror, her classmates ridicule her and even toss sanitary napkins at her (how's that for the ultimate high school nerd's nightmare?), thereby setting in motion a rite of passage that culminates in a prom conflagration complete with pig's blood and charred teenage flesh. Absolute carnage . . . a Bacchanalian rampage.

The next time you're in the mood to rend some flesh, rent this one and run mad through the hills of the ancient Rome in your mind, fueled by the explosive potential of your burgeoning sexual power.

> ⚠ Warning Label: *When running mad through the hills of the ancient Rome in your mind, fueled by the explosive potential of your burgeoning sexual power, it's wise not to do so near an open flame.*

■ ***Clueless*** *(1995)*

Stars: Alicia Silverstone, Stacey Dash, Brittany Murphy, Paul Rudd, Dan Hedaya

Director and Writer: Amy Heckerling, very *loosely based on the novel* Emma *by Jane Austen*

In this Valley version of Jane Austen's *Emma,* Cher (Alicia Silverstone), a dippy but exceptionally well accessorized high school student in Beverly Hills, must grow past her materialistic, self-absorbed adolescence and achieve a reasoned and compassionate womanhood. Yeah, in what universe? Watching this movie is sort of like getting a bird's-eye view of what was lurking beneath the implacable surface waters of the privileged set: Deep down, they were as clueless as we were.

Sure they got everything they ever wanted served to them on a silver platter, but did they really enjoy the feast? Yes, actually, they did, and you will too.

■ ***Flashdance*** *(1983)*

Stars: Jennifer Beals, Michael Nouri, Lilia Skala

Director: Adrian Lyne

Writers: Joe Eszterhas and Thomas Hedley, Jr.

In this loss-of-virginity fable, Alex Owens (Jennifer Beals), a tomboyish steelworker who dreams of being a dancer, finally realizes her dream and becomes a prima ballerina with the Pittsburgh ballet. Hello? Is that a high concept or what? Welding and dancing as a metaphor for the spectrum of symbolic possibility embraced by the expression of the female libido? It's almost too Freudian to get your head around, isn't it? Arcs, and welding wands and ballet bars, and that bulldog of hers. What was that about? The layers of phallic metaphor in this seemingly fluidless narrative will leave you squishy. What a feeling, indeed.

Words to Live By

So like, right now for example. The Haitians need to come to America. But some people are all, "What about the strain on our resources?" Well it's like when I had this garden party for my father's birthday. I put R.S.V.P. cause it was a sitdown dinner. But some people came that like did not R.S.V.P. I was totally buggin'. I had to haul ass to the kitchen, redistribute the food, and squish in extra place settings. But by the end of the day it was, like, the more the merrier. And so if the government could just get to the kitchen and rearrange some things we could certainly party with the Haitians. And in conclusion may I please remind you it does not say R.S.V.P. on the Statue of Liberty! Thank you very much.

★ Alicia Silverstone as Cher in *Clueless*

■ ***Scream*** *(1996) and* ***Scream 2*** *(1997)*
Stars: Neve Campbell, Courteney Cox, David Arquette, Liev Schreiber, Skeet Ulrich (Scream), Rose McGowen (Scream), Drew Barrymore (Scream) Laurie Metcalf (Scream 2), Jamie Kennedy (Scream 2), Elise Neal (Scream 2), Jerry O'Connell (Scream 2), Timothy Olyphant (Scream 2), Jada Pinkett (Scream 2)
Director: Wes Craven
Writer: Kevin Williamson (Scream 2)

Wes Craven's *Scream* and *Scream 2* are self-aware, intelligent, and exceptionally witty horror flicks. On the other hand, if you're not big on closeups of knives piercing through someone's head and red blood splattering all over pink-sweatered gals, these might not be your cup of tea (hey, if you watched thirty hours of TV a week for your entire childhood like the teenagers these films are aimed at, those gruesome stabbings would seem really cool to you too). In both movies, Neve Campbell stars as the ever self-possessed Sid, whose mother was murdered years ago and who is now being stalked by a prank caller who loves to quiz his murder victims about their horror movie knowledge and tease them about his seeming ability to be in all places at all times. In *Scream*, smart girl Sid and her cronies (e.g., Barney Fife–like Deputy Dwight "Dewey" Riley, played by David Arquette), and a few enemies too (such as the obnoxious reporter Gale Weathers, played by Courteney Cox) outwit the killer while bloody body after bloody body turns up just inches away from them. It all seems so implausible until you find out the killer's secret. Well, actually, it's still implausible then, but it *is* clever. Ditto *Scream 2*, which actually manages to one-up its predecessor (and even includes a film class discussion on the inferiority of film sequels and the rules for horror sequels, like an improved body count, as well as some well-placed criticism of the original—how come no one 69'd that caller's ass?—not to mention the highfalutin' references to Greek choruses). What's more, all those bodies get slashed to the sounds of happenin' bands like Nick Cave & The Bad Seeds, Collective Soul, and Foo Fighters. If you like a good scare as well as a good laugh and aren't squeamish about intense brutality, you'll love these. If you're less desensitized to violence, you're better off sticking to black-and-white Hitchcock and his chocolate-syrup-drizzled-over-shower-drains bloody effects—or at least the old hands-over-the-eyes trick.

The Handy Hunk Chart Key

Hunk Ratings:

Knight in Shining Armor (flag)

A Man's Man (barbell)

***ASD** = Aristocratic, Suave, and Debonair, **BE** = Bedroom Eyes **LVV** = Liquid Velvet Voice **RGH** = Really Good Hair **RUM** = Raw Unpredictable Masculinity **SIN** = Smoldering, Inscrutable, and Noble*

The Handy Hunk Chart

Cary Grant

ASD, BE, LVV

Top Drool Pics: *An Affair to Remember, Bringing Up Baby, Charade, His Girl Friday, Holiday, Indiscreet, Penny Serenade, That Touch of Mink, To Catch a Thief,* and, well, any other movie he ever made. Cary Grant was never selectively sexy.

(flag) He could be bumbling, like in *Bringing Up Baby,* or sinister, like in those Hitchcock flicks, but somehow the image that has seared itself on our brain is that of a man impeccable in his manners, deeply respectful of women—debonair, suave, charming, always ready to light a gal's cigarette or pour her yet another Scotch even though it's 10:00 A.M. A man who holds doors and keeps his promises. A man who buys us presents just because he wants to please, who desires only to be worthy of marrying us. And that accent. Cary, Cary, Cary. Where do you come from? I mean, have you ever heard anyone talk like that in real life? Was that a Connecticut thing, or what? Whence those clipped consonants? From what spring-fed pool of chivalry did Cary Grant emerge, fully formed and dedicated to the service of the female heart? And can somebody please stock that pond? ■

. . . continued

Harrison Ford

BE, RGH, RUM, SIN

Top Drool Pics: *The Fugitive, The Mosquito Coast, Presumed Innocent, Regarding Henry, Sabrina, Star Wars* and its sequels, all of the Indiana Jones movies, *Witness, Working Girl*

Once upon a time, there was a man who smiled. He may not have had the dazzlingly brilliant dental work of others, and the smile may have been just a little crooked as it sheepishly widened across his face, but it revealed a boyishness that made a gal want to wrap her arms around him and nuzzle him as she slow danced to an AM radio hit from the sixties And yet as he zapped bad guys with his lasers and escaped one harrowing scrape after another, his masculinity shone forth like a beacon, promising a package of vulnerability and strength we found irresistible.

And then came the Tom Clancy years. And the Scott Turow years. Suddenly, he was the president. Or the president's advisor. Or a doctor on the lam for a murder he didn't commit. And with these positions of responsibility came a new look, one of grim determination, one of hyperventilation through flared nostrils, one of knitted brow and gritted teeth. And as we waited patiently through explosion after scrape after narrow escape for that reluctant smile, we lamented those long lost days of yore when our favorite everyman took time out for an occasional grin. ■

Words to Live By

Life is like a movie. You just can't pick your genre.

★ Skeet Ulrich as Billy Loomis in *Scream*

And don't overlook these "camp" classics!

■ ***Little Darlings*** *(1980)*
Stars: Kristy McNichol, Tatum O'Neal, Matt Dillon, Armand Assante
Director: Ronald F. Maxwell
Writers: Kimi Peck and Dalene Young

Setting: a girls' summer camp. Premise: Who will lose her virginity first, romantically inclined Tatum O'Neal or tomboy Kristy McNicol? Of course, the hotter question when this came out was which of these two child stars, approaching the troublesome postcuteness adolescent years, would outact the other, thereby establishing herself on the A-list of casting directors throughout the mid-1970s, leaving the other to B films and sitcom wasteland? Hey, we knew much more was at stake than virginity.

Even more fun, the potential deflowerers are the ever naughty Matt Dillon, with whom every thirteen-year-old girl at the time wanted to share ABC gum (already-been-chewed, that is), and the suave older lover, camp counselor Armand Assante. Wild animalistic sex, or dreamy soft-focus sequence? Both scenarios worked just fine in imaginative preteen minds, and that scene with the girls ripping off a condom vending machine was all the more daring in the era when family drugstores with stern pharmacists made even the purchase of that first box of tampons a terrifying experience.

Words to Live By

If you were happy every day of your life you wouldn't be a human being. You'd be a game-show host.

★ Winona Ryder as Veronica Sawyer in *Heathers*

▪ ***The Parent Trap*** *(1961)*
Stars: Hayley Mills, Hayley Mills, Maureen O'Hara, Brian Keith
Director and Writer: David Swift, based on the novel Das doppelte Lottchen *by Erich Kästner*

This one's got all the elements of a camp classic: a peppy little pop title song, warbled by Annette Funicello and Tommy Sands. A darling little title sequence featuring that freakish sixties animation popularized by *Rudolph the Red-nosed Reindeer* and *Davy and Goliath*. An absurd plot featuring identical twins separated at birth (hey, at least they didn't claim to be identical cousins like on *The Patty Duke Show*—now that was *really* surreal). A summer camp setting (and they don't just go to camp all summer, they bring along little pastel party dresses for dances with the boys' camp across the lake). A paid studio dialogue coach who couldn't get Hayley Mills to drop her British accent for more than two words at a crack. Totally happenin' references to popular culture (Ricky Nelson! He's the awesomest!). A groovy jam session featuring Hayley Mills and Hayley Mills doing a beatnik sort of thing in a kinda Liverpudlian accent. Slapstick involving pools and overturned chairs. An appearance by cult fave Nancy Culp (*The Beverly Hillbillies*). Cheesy production values (they use a back projection scene for a stroll-through-the-park sequence—like they couldn't afford to go on location in a damn *park?*). An outrageously implausible plot (identical twins, separated at birth by their divorced parents, meet at summer camp, switch places, and successfully plot to reunite Mom and Dad) with a sugary Disney treatment of divorce that probably single-handedly psychologically screwed up an entire generation of kids who thought a little teen hijinks could reunite their feuding parents and result in a triumphant wedding march as pink-clad junior bridesmaids. Lots of inferior spinoffs, including one with the cult classic title of *The Parent Trap: Hawaiian Honeymoon*. And best of all? An absolutely pointless remake featuring *Dennis Quaid*!

Index

A

B

C

D

E

F

G

H

J

K

L

N

O

P

Q

R

S

T